BUILDING MOTIVATION for CHANGE in SEXUAL OFFENDERS

BUILDING MOTIVATION for CHANGE in SEXUAL OFFENDERS

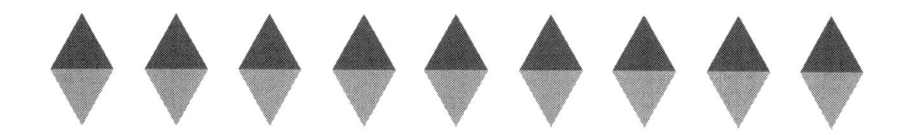

David S. Prescott, LICSW
Editor and Contributor

SAFER SOCIETY PRESS
Brandon, Vermont

Copyright © 2009 by the Safer Society Press, Brandon, Vermont
First Edition
All rights reserved. No part of this book may be reproduced in any form or by any electronic or mechanical means, including information storage and retrieval systems, without permission in writing from the publisher, except by a reviewer who may quote brief passages.

Printed in the United States of America
10 9 8 7 6 5 4

Library of Congress Cataloging-in-Publication Data
Building motivation for change in sexual offenders / David S. Prescott, editor and contributor. -- 1st ed.
   p. cm.
Includes bibliographical references and index.
ISBN 978-1-884444-82-1
1. Sex offenders--Rehabilitation. 2. Sex offenders--Psychology. 3. Sex crimes--Prevention. I. Prescott, David S.
RC560.S47B85 2009
616.85'83--dc22
                      2009031053

The SaferSociety PRESS
P.O. Box 340
Brandon, Vermont 05733
www.safersociety.org
(802) 247-3132

Safer Society Press is a program of the Safer Society Foundation, a 501(c)3 nonprofit dedicated to the prevention and treatment of sexual abuse. For more information, visit our Web site at www.safersociety.org.

Building Motivation for Change in Sexual Offenders
$35.00 plus shipping and handling
Order #WP138

DEDICATION

This book is dedicated to those clients, family members, friends, and colleagues who have inspired me and who keep me motivated: Tony Beech, Steven Bengis, Steven Malcolm Berg-Smith, Maia Christopher, Franca Cortoni, Dennis Doren, Andrew Harris, Jannine Hébert, Tom Lundquist, Ruth Mann, Liam Marshall, Kevin Nunes, Gail Ryan, Joann Schladale, Lloyd Sinclair, Joan Tabachnick, David Thornton, Tony Ward, Robin Wilson, and Pamela Yates.

I am also very grateful to the staff and administrations of Bennington School, the Minnesota Sex Offender Program, the Motivational Interviewing Network of Trainers, NEARI, Rockwood Psychological Services, Safer Society, and Sand Ridge Secure Treatment Center, who all contributed in their own ways.

Finally, this volume would not have been possible without the support at home of my family. Thanks, everyone, for your patience.

CONTENTS

Introduction
    David S. Prescott 1

1. Treatment Readiness and Comprehensive Treatment Programming
    Robin J. Wilson 5

2. Readiness and the Treatment of Sexual Offenders
    Tony Ward, Sharon Casey, and Robyn L. Langlands 29

3. Getting the Context Right for Sex Offender Treatment
    Ruth E. Mann 55

4. Using the Good Lives Model to Motivate Sexual Offenders to Participate in Treatment
    Pamela M. Yates 74

5. A Treatment Approach for Sexual Offenders in Categorical Denial
    Geris A. Serran and Matt D. O'Brien 96

6. The Rockwood Preparatory Program for Sexual Offenders: Goals and the Methods Employed to Achieve Them
    Matt D. O'Brien, Liam E. Marshall, and William L. Marshall 118

7. A Hopeful Approach to Motivating Sexual Offenders for Change
    Heather M. Moulden and William L. Marshall 139

8. Motivational Interviewing in the Treatment of Sexual Abusers
    David S. Prescott 160

9. Using Motivational Interviewing with Sexual
   Abusers in Group Treatment
   David S. Prescott and Marilyn Ross.................. 184
10. Supervising Clinicians Using Motivational Interviewing
    David S. Prescott............................... 206

   Closing Remarks
   David S. Prescott............................... 221

   Appendix: The Violence Treatment
   Readiness Questionnaire 223

   About the Authors 227

   Index 231

BUILDING MOTIVATION for CHANGE in SEXUAL OFFENDERS

INTRODUCTION
David S. Prescott

"There's no such thing as teaching, only learning."
—Monty Roberts, "The Horse Whisperer"

My father was a successful journalist though he had a speech impediment. He always said that it made him a better observer of human behavior. He once observed that, "By stuttering, I learned to shut up and listen. The people I interviewed damned themselves." He was certainly no mental health professional, but my father's observations and reports were better because of his self-discipline about listening rather than talking. Nowadays, educational programs for counselors around the Western world try to teach—with mixed success—the value of not speaking too much in clinical sessions.

While at a residential treatment center in the late 1980s, I introduced myself to a new 17-year-old client named Peter. He promptly swore at me. True to my father's lesson, I tried to remain silent and graceful. Much later, it occurred to me that this young man's profanity was the very best gift he had to offer in that moment. Had he not been interested in dialogue, he would have told me so directly. Instead, he offered immediate resistance, an interpersonal phenomenon. I would later realize that for Peter, swearing at others meant that he was ready, willing, and able to dialogue as long as he could feel safe within the relationship. The adults in his life had abused him badly, and he had adopted their strict code of defiant anti-sociality as a means of keeping himself safe.

Peter had an implicit belief that the world is an unsafe place and that the only way he could survive was to be twice as aggressive as the people in it, including those who had hurt him. This behavior, which many professionals would interpret as hostile resistance, was actually something to respect. Although this relationship may seem obvious, too many professionals lose their perspective with difficult clients every day.

While an extensive body of literature exists regarding difficult clients, the studies are almost silent on the issue of difficult professionals. We need to study ourselves. How is it that good professionals can sometimes go bad when working with people who have sexually abused? Why do so many people resort to punitive practices and policies that are proven to fail? The authors included in this book have provided the following chapters with the hope that the methodologies they utilize when treating challenging clients will be of help to other professionals.

The absence of ground support for professionals working with people who have sexually abused is striking. Many of the first resources available appeared to endorse a harsh and confrontational style of professional interaction. Subsequent research would show such tactics do not work. Alan Jenkins (1990) produced an excellent resource that served as a reference standard for many years. Safer Society Press later published the only book to date (Blanchard 1995) on therapeutic relationships with sexual offenders. This void in available resources is strange to explain, because research clearly shows that provider style influences the success of treatment.

This book seeks to build on the knowledge and wisdom of Jenkins, Blanchard, and like-minded authors who have spoken up but often have not been heard. Where editors often manipulate each chapter into a unified voice, my hope has been to preserve each voice (even including regional differences in spelling), fine-tuning them only enough to broaden each chapter's accessibility to all. The result moves from didactic to practical elements and focuses on problems that many, if not most, professionals have experienced. These include

- helping clients imagine a more fulfilling life;
- working with clients in denial (those who say they have not engaged in sexual aggression);
- understanding how clients become ready to change;
- enhancing motivation in group therapy and with supervisees;

- building the best context where clients can change; and
- awakening internal motivation and preparing clients for change.

However a reader experiences this book, several facts remain. First, no credible evidence exists to prove that punishing people reduces their willingness to cause harm again in the future. Likewise, research has shown that in the long run a harsh, confrontational approach does not work. Unfortunately, it is all too easy for professionals to revert to punishment and harsh confrontation in order to gain some form of compliance. For that reason, my biggest hope is that this collection of writing enhances long-term professional practice. It has been easy enough to assemble chapters that teach. The current state of our knowledge shows that it's time for us to learn.

REFERENCES

Blanchard, Geral T. 1995. *The difficult connection: The therapeutic relationship in sex offender treatment.* Brandon, Vermont: Safer Society Press.

Jenkins, Alan. 1990. *Invitations to Responsibility: The therapeutic engagement of men who are violent and abusive.* Dulwich Centre Publications. (Available through narrativebooks.com.)

Treatment Readiness and Comprehensive Treatment Programming

Robin J. Wilson

The process of personal change can be a frightening thing. When elements of our apple cart are upset, most of us become unnerved even under the best of circumstances. Old habits can be hard to break, particularly when the new ones we are trying to put in their place may not be as fun or interesting. Nonetheless, the process of human growth requires that we engage in a process of continuous quality improvement in which old, less useful ways of doing things are cast aside in favor of greater personal efficacy and efficiency.

Making lasting changes in one's personal life requires some engagement of a problem-solving rubric, whether formally or informally. Most schemes include a rough approximation of the following steps:

- Identify the problem (sometimes, this means simply acknowledging that a problem exists)
- Outline the components of the problem
- Devise and engage alternatives
- Evaluate outcomes
- Make revisions as necessary

It seems pretty simple, at least on paper. However, we know that some processes of the human psyche—like denial and minimization—often serve to thwart this process. Indeed, even the seemingly simple task of acknowledging that we must change some part of our behavior can prove daunting.

So, what if we throw in a wild card, a really big wild card? What if your problem made you one of society's most reviled persons? What if there was some aspect of your makeup (and ultimately your behavior) that rendered you unwelcome in almost every community? Worse still, what if asking for help sometimes made matters worse for you? How quickly would you acknowledge that you had that problem? Yet, as a society, we continue to be angered when sexual offenders deny their offenses, or minimize the harm done to victims. Really, just for a moment, think about the sexual offender's predicament. Acknowledging that you took sexual advantage of a vulnerable person—perhaps, even a child—means that you will receive little positive consideration from anyone, anywhere. However, as a society, this declaration of guilt is what we expect sexual offenders to do. Ultimately, it is what they must do in order to meet society's expectations and have any hope of a life in the community.

One practitioner who trains volunteers to work with high-risk offenders released to the community uses an interesting exercise in the training process. He asks his volunteers to close their eyes and remember the last time they were sexually intimate. Once everyone opens their eyes, he asks to have one person share the particulars of the sexual encounter—in exacting detail. Of course, nobody volunteers. In fact, everyone shudders at the thought that they might be called on to recount such a private and personal event. Although sexuality is at the core of our being, it is something we guard ferociously and are hesitant to share with others—especially in a public forum.

When you think about it, this kind of public revelation of private matters is exactly what society expects sexual offenders to provide. The particularly difficult element of this process is that the sexual acts we demand that offenders share—in minute detail—are repugnant to most people, even to other offenders. Further, we often require that sexual offenders submit to a polygraph check of how truthful they are being, with deceptiveness frequently leading to negative consequences. Other negative consequences can result from being honest about a history of sexual offending. Being a sexual offender in an institutional setting can be dangerous to the offender's health because these offenders are often targets for violence by nonsexual offenders.

The twisted hierarchy normal to prisons puts murderers at the top of the food chain and homosexual child molesters at the bottom. Often, however, sexual offenders even find ways to vaunt themselves above others who have committed even "less acceptable" offenses.

Before I leave readers with the thought that sexual offenders are much maligned unfortunates worthy of our sympathy, let me say clearly that it is not my intention to suggest that we "go softer" on offenders. Rather, it is my intention to suggest that if we truly wish to eliminate sexual abuse of children and other vulnerable people, we need to better understand the dynamics of denial, minimization, and, ultimately, attitudinal and behavioral change. When we put the offenders' perspective and experience in terms described above, it is not so hard to see why so many offenders have a hard time coming clean about their offenses. A lot is at stake: personal reputation, social standing, access to love and support of family and friends, and personal freedom. Another factor is the oft-maligned concept of self-esteem. Generally, the research and treatment literature suggests that we should not focus on self-esteem when working with offenders, including those who commit sexual crimes (Andrews and Bonta 2006; orig. 1994). On the other hand, how could we possibly expect offenders not to have critical deficits in self-esteem that would ultimately impact their chances for successful personal change?

For some sexual offenders, a direct consequence of the hatred expressed by society is a sort of cognitive "shutting down." The once-popular relapse prevention model of treatment for sexual offenders has long been criticized for its negative focus (Yates 2005; 2007). This process of shutting down shares many elements in common with Seligman's (1975) concept of learned helplessness. Learned helplessness is described as a frame of mind in which an individual stops trying to change his/her circumstances because nothing he/she does appears to have any effect on the outcome. For instance, no matter how much insight a sexual offender gains regarding his deviant behavior, and no matter how much effort he puts into learning how to lead an offense-free life, a majority of citizens will still not trust him to be free. For some sexual offenders, this dynamic leads to hopelessness, depression, and a risk for self-harming behavior. The institutionalizing effects of long sentences, coupled with the threat (in some jurisdictions) of possible civil commitment and eventual difficulty establishing stability in the community, give offenders little hope for the future. Ultimately, these processes of poor self-concept and poor self-esteem (shame, in particular) lead to denial and minimization. When combined with other familiar sexual offender tactics, such as victim blaming, projection, and a plethora of faulty thinking known as cognitive distortions, these are collectively known in the business as *ego defense mechanisms*.

In Freudian psychology, ego defense mechanisms are employed by the psyche when a person's self-concept is under threat. In fact, Freud listed a number of processes that we often find employed by persons who have done wrong—including each and every one of us, for things as simple as, "Who left the milk out?" However, for the purposes of this chapter, we are speaking specifically about those persons who have committed monumental wrongs, like sexual offenses. In 21st-century Western culture, it is a reasonably safe bet that most or all persons were raised with the same, basic Judeo-Christian morals, based loosely on the Ten Commandments and associated culture-specific amendments. This cultural influence applies just as much to offenders as to the rest of us. They know right from wrong just as well as we do. Yet, for some reason, offenders are able to either ignore or turn off this awareness of right and wrong to suit nefarious purposes. In 25 years of practice, I estimate that I have seen between eight and ten thousand sexual offenders. Most of these were men or boys, with only a handful being women or girls. I saw the majority of these persons either in assessment or for provision of counseling or other treatment services. Interestingly, excepting those who were particularly psychopathic, I have seen very, very few offenders who were happy with their sexually offensive behavior.

Again, why are we spending so much time outlining the dynamics of openness and honesty in sexual offenders regarding their deviant behavior? Because the process of being frankly able to recount one's wrongdoing, and taking full personal responsibility for the harm done to others, is exactly what we must expect of sexual offenders in treatment, especially if we want them to truly understand why the rest of us are so upset with them. To understand how best to get to the heart of why they do it, and how to stop them from doing it again, we have to accept and understand the particularly difficult task we give offenders when we ask them (or mandate them) to acknowledge their own behavior and to attend treatment.

Effective Interventions

The Andrews and Bonta (2006; orig. 1994) meta-analysis of the principles of effective correctional interventions was a seminal answer to Martinson's (1974; see also Furby, Weinrott, and Blackshaw 1989) damning assertion that "nothing works." Their research showed that, by following a small number of simple rules, treatment programs could dramatically increase correlations between participation and lowered recidivism. Their model has since come to be known as the "risk–need–responsivity" (RNR) model. In simple terms, this model decrees that programs will be more successful in decreasing problematic behavior if they 1) match intensity of intervention to level of assessed risk; 2) specifically target problem areas identified at assessment; and 3) make genuine attempts to respond to client characteristics and issues of motivation. While the majority of Andrews and Bonta's work has focused on offenders in general, Hanson (2006) recently demonstrated that these principles also apply to sexual offenders. In his study, Hanson found that adherence to the RNR principles was associated with reduced sexual recidivism, with the most significant effect found among treatment programs that adhered to all three principles. Accordingly, we have good reason to believe that applying sound social learning in a multidimensional, cognitive–behavioral framework will succeed every bit as much with sexual offenders as with offenders in general.

However, as influential as it has been, the RNR model is not without its critics. For example, proponents of the Good Lives Model (GLM) approach to the treatment of sexual offenders (Ward 2006; Ward and Gannon 2006; Ward, Melser, and Yates 2007) have suggested that the RNR model's focus on criminogenic needs is a necessary but not sufficient condition for effective treatment. Ward (2006) further suggests that it is "necessary to broaden the scope of correctional interventions to take into account the promotion of human goods." In the Good Lives Model, individuals are regarded as active, goal-seeking beings who seek to acquire fundamental, primary human goods—actions, experiences, and activities that are intrinsically beneficial to their individual well-being and that are sought for their own sake (Ward and Gannon 2006; Ward and Stewart 2003). Examples of primary human goods that all of us seek to attain include relatedness/intimacy, agency/autonomy, and emotional equilibrium (Ward 2002; Ward and Stewart 2003). In short, human goods are associated with general well-being, and the sort of balanced, self-determinism argued in the life skills model (Curtiss and Warren 1973).

Although RNR provides a framework for the preparation and evaluation of "effective" programs, critics of the RNR model suggest that it does not necessarily assist clinicians in choosing intervention styles that best engage offenders in therapy. In particular, knowing or asserting that a focus on risk reduction is important does not necessarily ensure that offenders will be motivated to engage in treatment to that end. Given that lack of motivation is an important response factor in treatment (Barrett, Wilson, and Long 2003; Stirpe, Wilson, and Long 2001), and that research clearly indicates that individuals who do not complete treatment re-offend at higher rates than those who complete treatment (Hanson and Bussière 1998), it is obvious that practitioners cannot afford to ignore interventions that are better designed to address offender responsiveness concerns. Furthermore, research in various clinical domains clearly indicates that effective therapist characteristics and behaviors, such as empathy, respect, warmth, and the use of positive reinforcement, are essential to treatment effectiveness, and that they account for significant portions of the variance in outcome (Marshall, Anderson, and Fernandez 1999; Marshall, Fernandez, Serran, Mulloy, Thornton, Mann, and Anderson 2003; Marshall, Marshall, Serran, and Fernandez 2006; Marshall, Serran, Moulden, Mulloy, Fernandez, Mann, and Thornton 2002). Therefore, it is critical for treatment to go beyond the RNR approach, if it is to be maximally effective, because its principal focus on risk management does not provide therapists with sufficient tools to engage and work with offenders in therapy, nor does it provide offenders with sufficient motivation to engage in the treatment process (Mann, Webster, Schofield, and Marshall 2004). In short, we need to teach treatment providers how to "sell" offenders on the process of change, and we need to motivate offenders to "buy" what we are selling.

In a recent paper (Wilson and Yates 2009), Pamela Yates and I argued that the RNR and GLM are ultimately complementary and, when fused, provide a useful framework for the effective treatment of persons who sexually offend. The RNR's focus on ensuring adequate intensity and focus in treatment meshes nicely with the GLM's focus on human goods and the ensuring of sufficient motivation to change. The literature regarding treatment efficacy continues to offer conflicting messages (see Marques, Wiederanders, Day, Nelson, and van Ommeren 2005; Marshall and Marshall 2007; 2008; Seto, Marques, Harris, Chaffin, Lalumière, Miner, Berliner, Rice, Lieb, and Quinsey 2008); however, to paraphrase Abracen and Looman (2005), I believe we have long moved beyond the question of "What works?" and into the realm of "What works best?" We should always be compelled, however, to look for ways to maximize reductions in re-offending. It would seem that an integration of RNR and the GLM might help us to achieve those additional reductions in recidivism by focusing on problem areas and by offering interventions commensurate with risk and need, while ensuring consumer buy-in and attending to the overall well-being and pro-social functioning of offenders.

Comprehensive Treatment Programming for Persons Who Have Sexually Offended

In offering comprehensive treatment programming to persons who have sexually offended, we must take several considerations into account. First, more is at stake with regard to these clients and the risks they pose, in comparison to the risks posed by most other types of offenders. Sexual offenders released to the community are held to a much higher standard. Indeed, most citizens hold that even one sexual recidivist is too many. Consequently, society tends to advocate longer sentences and more stringent controls for sexual offenders. The literature (Hanson and Bussière 1998; Hanson and Morton-Bourgon 2004) is clear that sexual re-offending is the result of a complex interaction of offender-specific and environmental factors that span biological, psychological, and social realms. As such, simply focusing on issues of containment, without attending to offenders as whole beings, will ultimately fail to maximize reduction of risk to the community.

To truly address risk for sexual offending, we must attend to skill deficits and psychological needs in a number of domains. First, intensity of treatment must be in line with the level of risk posed by the offender (in keeping with the risk principle of RNR—see Abracen, Looman, Mailloux, Serin, and

Malcolm 2003; Hanson and Yates 2004; Mailloux, Abracen, Serin, Cousineau, Malcolm, and Looman 2003; Marshall and Yates 2005). Second, consistent with the needs principle, programming must specifically address the various lifestyle areas identified as contributing to risk during both assessment and ongoing intervention. We must remember that sexual offending is a multifaceted problem, with problematic behavior and attitudes existing in a number of domains. Thus, for example, simply focusing on inappropriate acquisition of intimacy is unlikely to truly address risk overall. In this, the concept of "sex-offender-specific" treatment is discarded in favor of a holistic approach inclusive of risk-increasing factors in a multitude of domains.

In keeping with the needs principle of the RNR model, our main concern in treating sexual offenders must continue to be the risk of future sexual offending, as that is the area that puts them most at odds with society. Current literature (Wilson and Yates 2009) strongly suggests that comprehensive approaches are likely to be the most effective in addressing the risks of re-offending. Indeed, the literature is replete with evidence that sexual offense risk is mediated by such concerns as alcohol and substance abuse, poor problem-solving skills, dysregulation of emotion, self-regulation deficits, mental health difficulties, and other treatment-complicating factors. In order to fully address the totality of risk, we must consider all of these areas, and do so in a manner that treats the whole person and aims to increase psychological well-being. In addition to paying attention to the two aspects of the RNR model that are traditionally emphasized—risk and need—it is clear that treatment programming must truly attend to issues of responsivity in attempting to maximize gains and overall reintegration potential. In offering effective interventions, consideration of treatment readiness (Cullen and Wilson 2003) is a necessity, as is attention to approaches that seek to engage clients, rather than ones that simply require that they "do what we want them to" (see Marshall, Thornton, Marshall, Fernandez, and Mann 2001). Further, it is clear that we must do more to engage those we want to change in the process of change, which will require a consistent effort to gauge how offenders are doing in treatment *as whole persons*. It is incumbent on treatment providers to remember that offenders in treatment must have something to work toward, in terms of future planning. As lofty a goal as it may be, treatment providers must assist offenders in recognizing not only their difficulties and problem areas but also their strengths and goals so that they can ultimately achieve well-being and the sort of balanced, self-determined lifestyle promoted by the Good Lives Model.

Problem Identification and Treatment Readiness

Aside from us telling them so, how are offenders to know what their problems are? The current zeitgeist in treatment programming for sexual offenders is the Good Lives Model, as described by Ward and others (Ward and Stewart 2003; Wilson and Yates 2009). What is a "good life"? It has been said (see Thornton 2002, as quoted by Schlank 2008) that many offenders come from backgrounds in which they were provided with very few of the typical aspects of what most successful people would call a "good life." When your developmental history is replete with abuse, poor parenting, poor nutrition, poor role modeling, and a host of other "poor" foundational elements, is it any wonder that many of our offenders are left scratching their heads when we suggest that they need to lead a "good life"? This proposal is a tall order for those without a realistic frame of reference.

In many ways, the recent push to provide treatment readiness programming for sexual offenders derives its origins from efforts to engage deniers in treatment. As a psychologist formerly providing sexual offender assessment and treatment services in the Correctional Service of Canada (CSC), I am mindful of how fortunate I was to work in that environment, arguably one of the most dynamic research and practice networks in the world. In the mid-1990s, sexual offender treatment pioneer Bill Marshall was tasked with finding a way to engage deniers in treatment. The reintegration heyday of CSC took place during the 1990s. In those years, great efforts were made to manage and treat lower-risk offenders in community settings in keeping with the (then) recent findings of Andrews and Bonta (2006; orig. 1994). Many sexual offenders—regardless of risk level—were being held in prison, simply because they refused to admit they had done anything wrong.

Interestingly, Hanson and Bussière (1998; see also Hanson and Morton-Bourgon 2004) published the first of two seminal meta-analyses of the predictors of sexual offender recidivism at about the same time that Marshall was trying to work with deniers. The first meta-analysis was a major landmark in our understanding of the factors most related to risk for future offending but, surprising to most in the field, the researchers' data (later corroborated by the 2004 meta-analysis) strongly suggested that denial and minimization were unrelated to recidivism. The field exclaimed a collective, "How could this be?" Later research (e.g., Nunes, Hanson, Firestone, Moulden, Greenberg, and Bradford 2007) would refine our understanding of the Hanson findings, but it is still unclear whether denial or minimization constitutes a worthwhile factor to consider when attempting to determine who will and who will not reoffend. As with most elements of human behavior, the reasons behind recidivism seem to be more complex than any one single factor. We do know, however, that those who enter treatment and see it through to the end seem to reoffend at lower rates than those who drop out (Marshall, Marshall, Fernandez, Malcolm, and Moulden 2008). We also know that coordinating treatment, throughout the process (see Wilson and Eccles 1998), and beyond, of an offender's reintegration into the community (Wilson 1996), is also likely good clinical and risk-management practice.

To get back to Marshall, his efforts to engage deniers in treatment led to some important findings. Principally, we learned that once we take admission of guilt off the table, many deniers are willing to look at the sort of lifestyle management issues we now know to be important in building the sort of balanced, self-determined lifestyles (Curtiss and Warren 1973) that are incongruent with reoffending. Basically, the approach was like this: "Okay, let's say for the sake of argument that you are completely innocent, and that you did nothing wrong. Look at where you are. You're locked up in a federal penitentiary, facing a long sentence with little chance of early release because the parole board is unimpressed by offenders who fail to take responsibility for their actions. Do you think, just maybe, that there were things going on in your life that you might want to re-examine—maybe even change—so that you don't end up here, locked up unfairly, again?"

Surprisingly, many offenders could see the logic in these assertions and decided to give Dr. Marshall's program a chance. And as some of these men began to explore their lifestyle and interpersonal choices, they also began to share more and more about the poor sexual choices they had made—to the point that many ended up admitting to their offenses and, ultimately, moving into mainstream treatment for sexual offenders. In essence, programming for deniers targeted the sort of precontemplative issues identified by DiClemente and Prochaska (1998) in their transtheoretical stages of change model, roughly equivalent to the "problem identification" step outlined in the beginning of this chapter.

TRY: Treatment Readiness for You

As psychologists working in the Correctional Service of Canada, Murray Cullen and I were acutely aware of the groundbreaking work being done by Marshall and his associates. Dr. Cullen has had great success in helping men with anger and emotion difficulties come to terms with those problems and gain better control of their lives through his popular *Cage Your Rage* workbook series (see Cullen 1992). Together, we recognized that the sorts of issues highlighted by Marshall's efforts were not just applicable to deniers, but applied, as well, to most sexual offenders contemplating treatment. In fact, it occurred to us that any course of change takes some preparation and a certain easing into the process. Consider exercise as a means to lose weight. Do you start slowly and then gradually increase the intensity of your workout, or do you just jump in with both feet and start competing in 10K races?

In the beginning section of this chapter, I outlined reasons why many sexual offenders would have a difficult time agreeing to engage in therapy focusing on their sexually deviant behavior. These barriers to change—also called "treatment interfering factors" by psychologists and other professional sexual offender treatment providers—need to be overcome. In order to make successful lifestyle changes of the sort that will assist offenders in successfully avoiding situations of risk and reoffending, the course of treatment must be intelligently constructed and implemented. This necessary step is the often-overlooked "professional discretion" element of Andrews and Bonta's RNR model, in which well-considered design and in-process reflection are critical to successful behavioral change.

The literature on effective interventions stresses that all successful treatment endeavors must attend to issues of client responsivity. Simply put, all program components must take into account the personal attributes and skill levels of each participant in order to ensure maximum treatment efficacy. Programs also need to ensure that prospective participants understand why they must engage in treatment, and they must believe that such engagement will assist them in making the changes necessary to achieve the sort of balanced, self-determined lifestyle that we promise them will help them to live better lives. Individuals slated for intensive psychotherapy must be ready for that experience. The curriculum in the workbook entitled *TRY—Treatment Readiness for You* (Cullen and Wilson 2003) assists participants who have experienced past behavioral difficulties to identify their own potential stumbling blocks as a natural part of the process of personal change.

TRY is a short-term group intervention aimed at identifying barriers to treatment and increasing motivation to change. As originally conceived, the program was intended to run for eight weeks and was to be offered principally in a group format. Through participation in TRY, clients were told they would

- confront reasons for being in their current life circumstances (i.e., being institutionalized, being required to attend treatment, etc.);
- be introduced to models of change as they apply to behavior;
- learn to deal with cognitive dissonance by confronting ambivalence;
- identify short- and long-term barriers to making pro-social lifestyle changes;
- establish a roadmap for change in future treatment groups; and
- develop hopefulness while decreasing hopelessness and helplessness.

Marshall and his associates (Marshall et al. 2008) published outcomes from the Rockwood Preparatory Program for Sexual Offenders showing clearly that involvement in treatment readiness programming can increase self-efficacy and hope for future success. Although the genesis of their program was related to dealing with deniers, they ultimately found that motivation was the more worthy treatment target, as I did in research completed with two of my graduate students (Barrett, Wilson, and Long 2003; Stirpe et al. 2001). However, of most interest, Marshall et al. (2008) found that offenders who did not complete their preparatory program ultimately received more treatment in higher security settings, had greater difficulty engaging in treatment, and spent more time in prison before release than their peers who completed the preparatory program. That is, offenders who completed treatment readiness programming were better prepared for the process of change, understood the material more quickly, and were more likely to achieve early release.

Comprehensive Treatment Programming that Emphasizes Treatment Readiness in a Civil Commitment Setting

Civil commitment is a somewhat uniquely American approach to long-term sexual offender risk management. Under Kansas's Sexually Violent Predator Act (see *Kansas v. Hendricks* 1997), any person who, due to "mental abnormality" or "personality disorder," is likely to engage in "predatory acts of sexual violence" can be indefinitely confined. In this landmark case, which essentially began the process of sexual offender civil commitment in the United States, Hendricks appealed the finding against him, but the Supreme Court ultimately upheld the decision. In doing so, the Supreme Court defined a "mental abnormality" as a "congenital or acquired condition affecting the emotional or volitional capacity which predisposes the person to commit sexually violent offenses." As such, persons eligible for confinement were limited to those "not able to control" their dangerousness.

In Florida, the Involuntary Civil Commitment for Sexually Violent Predators' Treatment and Care Act became effective on January 1, 1999. Under this act, inmates serving sentences with sexual offense histories (not necessarily for their latest offenses) are reviewed by the Department of Children and Families, prior to release, for possible referral for civil commitment trial. The court then decides who meets criteria for civil commitment as a sexually violent predator (SVP) based, in part, on expert testimony. Those offenders awaiting trial are detained in the same facility as those already civilly committed. Housing and treatment are offered at the Florida Civil Commitment Center (FCCC) in Arcadia, Florida.

The goal of the Florida Civil Commitment Center is to assist all residents in the development of a balanced, self-determined lifestyle. Arguably, the men referred to the FCCC are among the highest risk sexual offenders of all those in Florida who receive determinate sentences for sexual offenses. Consequently, and in keeping with the tenets of the risk principle, the program is long-term and intensive. The FCCC's Comprehensive Treatment Program (CTP) for persons who have sexually offended is a four-phase, multi-modal, holistic approach to identifying and addressing problematic cognitions and behaviors that lead to increased risk for future sexual violence. The program is modeled, with adaptation, on aspects of treatment and risk-management programming designed in part by David Thornton (formerly of Her Majesty's Prison Service in the United Kingdom—see Thornton 2002), Jim Haaven's "New Me Life Planning" model (Haaven, Little, and Petre-Miller 1990), and elements of the Correctional Service of Canada's National Sex Offender Programs model (see Wilson, Cortoni, Picheca, and Nunes 2007).

The traditional model of sexual offender treatment puts principal emphasis on identification of deviant sexual fantasies and high-risk situations, full disclosure of sexual offense histories, and development of new cognitions and behavior—sometimes with little or no attention to treatment readiness and motivation. The FCCC model puts considerable time and effort into the process of preparing treatment participants for change. We believe that this preparation is tantamount to laying the foundation on which all other treatment endeavors will rely for stability. Simply put, it is a lot like painting without priming: without adequate preparation for change many of the concepts we wish participants to incorporate into their new lives will not stick.

Phase I: Preparation for Change

Phase I of the CTP emphasizes identification of the participants' problems, poor methods of problem solving, and treatment-interfering factors (or, barriers to change). All program participants must complete three individual programming components before being advanced to Phase II. Participants begin with participation in Moral Reconation Therapy (MRT—see Little and Robinson, 1988; Little, Robinson, Burnette, and Swan 1999) then move on to Thinking for a Change (T4C—see Glick, Bush, and Taymans 1997). Participation in TRY—Treatment Readiness for You (Cullen and Wilson

2003) commences approximately halfway through T4C. Placement of TRY toward the end of Phase I is intentional, in that this is when CTP participants first begin to speak about lifestyle management issues, specifically as they relate to sexuality. Up to that point, sexual issues may be raised as examples, but they are not the primary focus of intervention.

Moral Reconation Therapy (MRT)
Moral Reconation Therapy is an evidence-based approach to increasing problem-solving and moral decision-making skills. In using exercises and tasks, MRT resembles what is usually described as "cognitive skills" educational programming. However, the skills training with MRT is intended to go beyond usual classroom methods of skills development. Recent literature has shown MRT to be effective in lowering recidivism rates in those who successfully complete the program. The seven parts of MRT are as follows:

1. *Confrontation and Assessment of Self*: Assesses residents' beliefs, attitudes, behaviors, and defense mechanisms
2. *Assessment of Current Relationships:* Includes planning to heal damaged relationships
3. *Reinforcement of Positive Behaviors and Habits:* Residents help others to raise their own awareness of moral responsibility to the community
4. *Positive Identity Formation:* Explores the inner self and the setting of goals
5. *Enhancement of Self-Concept*: Builds self-esteem and positive habits
6. *Increased Impulse Control*: Develops skills to delay gratification and manage their pleasure-seeking behavior
7. *Developing Higher Stages of Moral Reasoning*: Residents are encouraged to demonstrate greater concern for others and for social systems

Thinking for a Change (T4C)
Thinking for a Change consists of exercises that build problem-solving skills. Participants learn how good decisions are made and how to use those good decisions to get along better with their friends, families, and others. The goal

is for participants to quickly identify and appreciate how reevaluating their thinking, belief systems, personal and interpersonal values, and attitudes can help their lives. Participants begin organizing their thoughts using cognitive skills and methods, applying both in an objective and systematic way. T4C has the following goals:

1. Increase awareness of cognitive distortions related to events-thoughts-feelings-actions
2. Identify differences between physical and emotional feelings and examine how they guide behavior
3. Learn to identify high-risk thoughts and feelings
4. Identify unhealthy attitudes and beliefs that lead to unhealthy behaviors
5. Improve problem-solving skills and coping strategies through new thinking
6. Improve communication and listening skills to improve interpersonal relationships

TRY: Treatment Readiness for You

Earlier in this chapter, we discussed that before offenders can go into intensive treatment, they must be ready for that treatment. The Florida Civil Commitment Center is currently piloting the TRY curriculum described above as adapted to a civil commitment population. Because treatment interfering factors in this population are frequently coupled with higher than average degrees of antisociality and a deep anger at the civil commitment process, treatment readiness programming for CTP participants is an even bigger challenge than offering such programming to many sexual offender clients. In the FCCC adaptation, TRY programming helps residents to identify barriers to change as a natural part of the process of personal growth. Increasing motivation to change in this population, however, must also take into consideration entrenched antisocial values and attitudes (some of which can be profound), degrees of institutionalization, comorbid mental health issues, and systemic issues (i.e., civil commitment as a concept, ongoing litigation, and legislative difficulties).

TRY programming at the FCCC is offered in a group setting with two facilitators, ideally one of each gender. Group sizes average 15 participants, who meet weekly for 90 minutes over a 12-week period. The program closely follows the published curriculum; however, some elements (e.g., ambivalence) targeted for one session in the original configuration are extended because of an increased need for focus in this particular population. To date, we have run four cycles with approximately 80 FCCC residents having completed the program prior to advancement to Phase II. At present, no outcome data are available (program evaluation efforts are ongoing). Observations from receiving Phase II facilitators, however, have been that TRY participants appear to have an easier time in the disclosure portion (i.e., giving a complete account of one's sexual offending past).

Phase II: Awareness
In Phase II of the CTP, participants develop an agreed upon and comprehensive identification of the main factors that contributed to past offending. In disclosure, the goal is to completely disclose the entirety of one's history of deviant sexuality and behavior. This process is usually completed with the assistance of polygraph evaluations (although it is important to note that we use polygraph as a tool to assist participants in being honest; we do not use it as a pass/fail tool to aid or inhibit graduation to higher phases of treatment). Once the goals of disclosure are met, participants move into the discovery stage, where the goal is to provide opportunities to demonstrate insight into participants' current expressions of risk factors and to further identify continued barriers to personal balance and self-determinism.

Phase III: Healthy Alternative Behaviors
In Phase III of the CTP, we encourage residents to re-evaluate justifications and attitudes that supported their offending behavior. Ultimately this process leads to increased awareness of deficits in emotional coping and specific problematic emotions, acknowledgment of deviant sexual arousal/interest, reduction of deviant arousal, verbalization of events and behaviors that comprised sexual offenses, and the application of new coping strategies. In the development component of Phase III, the focus of treatment is to help residents reliably control their psychological risk factors. Residents use healthier, more prosocial strategies in situations where risk factors are more common.

This large task is accomplished by addressing the following objectives:

- Develop a representation of "old me"
- Develop a representation of "future me"
- Enact "future me" role plays
- Review a balanced, self-determined lifestyle
- Get to the "future me"

The relationship skills component of Phase III is designed to help residents understand how they relate to others. It helps residents see how they may wish to change patterns of relating. Finally, it enables residents to develop the attitudes and skills that promote healthier ways of relating to others. The development of relationship skills is important. Experiencing problems making and keeping emotionally intimate relationships with adults has a lot to do with reducing risk for sexual reoffending. Persons who commit sexual offenses and have problems with relationships sometimes avoid close relationships, seek but fail to establish close relationships, or enter relationships that are not meaningful.

The empathy and emotional awareness component of Phase III is designed to assist residents as they try to understand and share with others in a more empathic and emotionally healthy manner through

- developing a richer, better-differentiated emotional experience;
- increasing perspective-taking skills in general, and specifically in situations where problems exist in seeing how others might interpret the things we do and say;
- increasing one's ability to share and understand emotions with others in a healthy way;
- reducing unhelpful or unhealthy responses to others' distress (e.g., freezing, self-pity, rescue-ranger); and
- developing and exploring empathy skills in the context of close relationships.

Last, consolidation of treatment gains (i.e., organizing and making them more permanent) comes through ongoing development and supervised practice of self-control over behaviors, thoughts, and emotions. Interventions are defined as contributing to a model of behavior that stresses balance and self-determination. Therefore, consolidation is very helpful in learning how to maintain treatment gains, encourage prosocial behavior, feel better about oneself, make better decisions, and provide support and reinforcement to ensure residents use their newly learned behaviors.

Phase IV: Maintenance and Comprehensive Discharge Planning
Phase IV of the Comprehensive Treatment Program provides additional opportunity to evaluate behavioral change and skill development. Phase IV allows us to gauge to what extent each participant has both acquired and integrated, and is now demonstrating behaviorally the attitudes and skills critical to avoiding future sexual offending behavior. A key component of this last phase of treatment involves volunteering and providing mentoring to persons in earlier phases of treatment. Residents in Phase IV also make preparations for life in the community through structured vocational programming (in which they identify potential sources of employment and engage in practice job interviews); make connections with social supports (including family and friends) and community-based social service agencies (e.g., treatment providers, advocacy organizations, welfare); and identify legal and civic responsibilities (e.g., probation, sexual offender registration, etc.).

Sexual offender assessment, treatment, and risk management is serious business. The potential costs of not doing a good job are huge. The public expects that persons who pose a risk to others will either take whatever treatment is necessary to eliminate that risk or—if they cannot control themselves—will be removed from society, possibly forever. Couple this attitude with the reality that most citizens believe that even one recidivist is too many, and it is easy to see the daunting task facing sexual offender service providers, to say nothing of the tremendous challenges up against the offenders themselves.

In this chapter, I have framed the plight of the offender—who must face both the chilling reality of his own behavioral history and the absolute need to make substantial lifestyle changes, if he ever hopes to be free in the community. My intention was not to seek absolution for offenders, although my mentor (Kurt Freund) was always clear in his acknowledgment of the bitter duality of sexual offenders—inherent dangerousness coupled with a social predicament worthy of compassion. Rather, I hope that readers have been able to acknowledge and identify some of the very real challenges we all face in getting offenders into treatment, having them stay there, and making sure that they actually learn (and incorporate into their core beings) better ways of living—offense free. Addressing barriers to change, treatment-interfering factors, and motivation are key components of any program that has the goal of successfully altering behavior, including the especially lofty objective of the development of a balanced, self-determined lifestyle. The same challenge is true of sexual offender treatment in general. However, traditional programming has done little to consider issues of offender responsivity. In fact, we often mandate sexual offenders to the sort of treatment we think they need, rather than taking the time to find out whether the offender also believes these targets and goals to be important. While I hesitate to suggest that we should leave curriculum development to the clients, there is a certain benefit in at least checking in with clients to see if we are hitting all the necessary targets. Interestingly, we are now seeing more "user satisfaction" data being reported regarding sexual offender treatment endeavors (see Levenson and Prescott 2009; Levenson, Macgowan, Morin, and Cotter 2009). I believe this process of checking in with clients to be a very important element of good clinical intervention.

Treatment readiness programming has been a long time coming in the sexual offender treatment realm. As we refine methods of intervention, we identify areas in need of further exploration. Unfortunately, little research has been published regarding motivation to change in sexual offenders—certainly not nearly as much as we have seen regarding risk assessment and risk management. Ward (2006), in his criticisms of the RNR model, emphasized the need to pay more than mere lip service to the concept of responsivity. Of the components of the RNR model, the one we consistently do most poorly is being responsive to clients' needs in the design and implementation of treatment models. The need to *prepare* and *motivate* clients for participation in treatment is essential. Critical to this foundation is an acknowledgment of how difficult it is to change, especially when we consider the environments in which the changes are to begin (i.e., prison, civil commitment center, etc.) and, second, where they will be implemented (i.e., community). Sanding the surface, keeping it clean, and applying a good coat of primer will help ensure success in any painting endeavor. The same principles apply here.

REFERENCES

Abracen, J., and J. Looman. 2005. Developments in the assessment and treatment of sexual offenders: Looking backward with a view to the future. *Journal of Interpersonal Violence* 20:12–19.

Abracen, J., J. Looman, D. L. Mailloux, R. Serin, and B. Malcolm. 2003. Clarification regarding Marshall and Yates's critique of "Dosage of treatment to sexual offenders: Are we overprescribing?" *International Journal of Offender Therapy and Comparative Criminology* 49:225–30.

Andrews, D. A., and J. Bonta. 1994. *The psychology of criminal conduct.* Cincinnati, OH: Anderson Publishing.

———. 2006. *The psychology of criminal conduct.* 4th Ed. Newark, NJ: Anderson Publishing.

Barrett, M., R. J. Wilson, and C. Long. 2003. Measuring motivation to change in sexual offenders from institutional intake to community treatment. *Sexual Abuse: A Journal of Research and Treatment* 15:269–83.

Cullen, M. C. 1992. *Cage your rage: An inmate's guide to anger control.* Lanham, MD: American Corrections Association.

Cullen, M. C., and R. J. Wilson. 2003. *TRY—Treatment readiness for you: A workbook for sexual offenders.* Lanham, MD: American Corrections Association.

Curtiss, P. R., and P. W. Warren. 1973. *The dynamics of life skills coaching.* Prince Albert, SK: Saskatchewan NewStart Inc. for the Training Research and Development Station, Department of Manpower and Immigration.

DiClemente, C. C., and J. O. Prochaska. 1998. Toward a comprehensive, transtheoretical model of change: Stages of change and addictive behaviors. In *Treating addictive behaviors: Applied clinical psychology,* W. R. Miller and N. Heather (2nd ed., pp. 3–24). New York: Plenum Press.

Furby, L., M. R. Weinrott, and L. Blackshaw. 1989. Sex offender recidivism: A review. *Psychological Bulletin* 105:3–30.

Glick, B., J. Bush, and J. Taymans. 1997. *Thinking for a change.* Washington, DC: National Institute of Corrections.

Haaven, J. L., R. Little, and D. Petre-Miller. 1990. *Treating intellectual disabled sex offenders: A model residential program.* Orwell, VT: Safer Society.

Hanson, R. K. 2006. *What works: The principles of effective interventions with offenders.* Presented at the 25th Annual Convention of the Association for the Treatment of Sexual Abusers, Chicago, IL.

Hanson, R. K., and M. T. Bussière. 1998. Predicting relapse: A meta-analysis of sexual offender recidivism studies. *Journal of Consulting and Clinical Psychology* 66:348–62.

Hanson, R. K., and K. Morton-Bourgon. 2004. *Predictors of sexual recidivism: An updated meta-analysis.* User Report No. 2004–02. Ottawa, ON: Public Safety and Emergency Preparedness Canada.

Hanson, R. K., and P. M. Yates. 2004. Sexual violence: Risk factors and treatment. In Anthology on interventions against violent men, M. Eliasson (ed.), 151–66. *Acta Universitatis Upsaliensis, Uppsalla Women's Studies B: Women in the Humanities 3.* Uppsala, Sweden: Uppsala Universitet.

Kansas v. Hendricks. 1997. 521 U.S. 346.

Levenson, J. S., M. J. Macgowan, J. W. Morin, and L. P. Cotter. 2009. Perceptions of sex offenders about treatment: Satisfaction and engagement in group therapy. *Sexual Abuse: A Journal of Research & Treatment* 21:35–56.

Levenson, J. S., and D. S. Prescott. 2009. Treatment experiences of civilly committed sex offenders: A consumer satisfaction survey. *Sexual Abuse: A Journal of Research & Treatment* 21:6–20.

Little, G. L., and K. D. Robinson. 1988. Moral Reconation Therapy: A systematic step-by-step treatment system for treatment resistant clients. *Psychological Reports* 62:135–51.

Little, G. L., K. D. Robinson, K. D. Burnette, and S. Swan. 1999. Successful ten-year outcome data on MRT®-treated felony offenders: Treated offenders show significantly lower reincarceration in each year. *Cognitive-Behavioral Treatment Review* 5:1–3.

Mailloux, D. L., J. Abracen, R. Serin, C. Cousineau, B. Malcolm, and J. Looman. 2003. Dosage of treatment to sexual offenders: Are we overprescribing? *International Journal of Offender Therapy and Comparative Criminology* 47:171–84.

Mann, R. E., S. D. Webster, C. Schofield, and W. L. Marshall. 2004. Approach versus avoidance goals in relapse prevention with sexual offenders. *Sexual Abuse: A Journal of Research and Treatment* 16:65–75.

Marques, J. K., M. Wiederanders, D. M. Day, C. Nelson, and A. van Ommeren. 2005. Effects of a relapse prevention program on sexual recidivism: Final results from California's sex offender treatment and evaluation project (SOTEP). *Sexual Abuse: A Journal of Research of Research and Treatment* 17:79–107.

Marshall, W. L., D. Anderson, and Y. M. Fernandez. 1999. *Cognitive behavioural treatment of sexual offenders.* Toronto, ON: John Wiley & Sons.

Marshall, W. L., Y. M. Fernandez, G. A. Serran, R. Mulloy, D. Thornton, R. E. Mann, and D. Anderson. 2003. Process variables in the treatment of sexual offenders. *Aggression and Violent Behavior: A Review Journal* 8:205–34.

Marshall, W. L., and L. E. Marshall. 2007. The utility of the random controlled trial for evaluating sexual offender treatment: The gold standard or an inappropriate strategy? *Sexual Abuse: A Journal of Research and Treatment* 19:175–91.

———. 2008. Good clinical practice and the evaluation of treatment: A response to Seto et al. *Sexual Abuse: A Journal of Research and Treatment* 20:256–60.

Marshall, L. E., W. L. Marshall, Y. M. Fernandez, P. B. Malcolm, and H. M. Moulden. 2008. The Rockwood Preparatory Program for Sexual Offenders: Description and preliminary appraisal. *Sexual Abuse: A Journal of Research and Treatment* 20:25–42.

Marshall, W. L., L. E. Marshall, G. A. Serran, and Y. M. Fernandez. 2006. *Treating sexual offenders: An integrated approach.* New York, NY: Routledge.

Marshall, W. L., G. A. Serran, H. Moulden, R. Mulloy, Y. M. Fernandez, R. E. Mann, and D. Thornton. 2002. Therapist features in sexual offender treatment: Their reliable identification and influence on behaviour change. *Clinical Psychology and Psychotherapy* 9:395–405.

Marshall, W. L., D. Thornton, L. E. Marshall, Y. M. Fernandez, and R. Mann. 2001. Treatment of sexual offenders who are in categorical denial: A pilot project. *Sexual Abuse: A Journal of Research and Treatment* 13:205–15.

Marshall, W. L., and P. M. Yates. 2005. Comment on Mailloux et al.'s 2003 study "Dosage of treatment to sexual offenders: Are we overprescribing?" *International Journal of Offender Therapy and Comparative Criminology* 49:221–24.

Martinson, R. 1974. Nothing works: Questions and answers about prison reform. *The Public Interest* 35:22–54.

Nunes, K. L., R. K. Hanson, P. Firestone, H. M. Moulden, D. M. Greenberg, and J. M. Bradford. 2007. Denial predicts recidivism for some sexual offenders. *Sexual Abuse: A Journal of Research and Treatment* 19:91–105.

Schlank, A. 2008. The baby, the bathwater, and pendulum swings: The need to slow down and evaluate research critically. *ATSA Forum* 21:27–37.

Seligman, Martin E. P. 1975. *Helplessness: On depression, development, and death.* New York, NY: W H Freeman/Times Books/ Henry Holt & Co.

Seto, M. C., J. K. Marques, G. T. Harris, M. Chaffin, M. L. Lalumière, M. H. Miner, L. Berliner, M. E. Rice, R. Lieb, and V. L. Quinsey. 2008. Good science and progress in sex offender treatment are intertwined: A response to Marshall and Marshall (2007). *Sexual Abuse: A Journal of Research and Treatment* 20(3):247–55.

Simons, D., B. McCullar, and C. Tyler. 2008. Evaluation of the Good Lives model approach to treatment planning. Presented at the 27th Annual Research and Treatment Conference Association for the Treatment of Sexual Abusers, Atlanta, GA.

Stirpe, T., R. J. Wilson, and C. Long. 2001. Goal attainment scaling with sexual offenders: A measure of clinical impact at post treatment and at community follow-up. *Sexual Abuse: A Journal of Research and Treatment* 13:65–77.

Thornton, D. 2002. Constructing and testing a framework for dynamic risk assessment. *Sexual Abuse: A Journal of Research and Treatment* 14:139–53.

Ward, T. 2002. Good Lives and the rehabilitation of offenders: Promises and problems. *Aggression and Violent Behavior* 7:513–28.

———. 2006. Promoting human goods and reducing risk. *Beyond Retribution* 111–17.

Ward, T., and T. Gannon. 2006. Rehabilitation, etiology, and self-regulation: The Good Lives Model of sexual offender treatment. *Aggression and Violent Behavior* 11:77–94.

Ward, T., J. Melser, and P. M. Yates. 2007. Reconstructing the Risk Need Responsivity Model: A theoretical elaboration and evaluation. *Aggression and Violent Behavior* 12:208–28.

Ward, T., and C. A. Stewart. 2003. The treatment of sexual offenders: Risk management and good lives. *Professional Psychology: Research and Practice* 34:353–60.

Wilson, R. J. 1996. Catch-22: What psychological staff can (and cannot) do for offenders after their sentence expires. *Forum on Corrections Research* 8:27–29.

Wilson, R. J., F. Cortoni, J. E. Picheca, and K. Nunes. 2007. Community-based sexual offender maintenance treatment programming: An evaluation. *Research Report R-188.* Ottawa, ON: Correctional Service of Canada.

Wilson, R. J., and A. Eccles. 1998. Forging a link between institutional and community-based treatment services. *Forum on Corrections Research* 10:39–41.

Wilson, R. J., and P. M. Yates. 2009. Effective interventions and the Good Lives Model: Maximizing treatment gains for sexual offenders. *Aggression & Violent Behavior* 14:157–61.

Yates, P. M. 2005. Pathways to the treatment of sexual offenders: Rethinking intervention. *ATSA Forum* 18:1–9.

———. 2007. Taking the leap: Abandoning relapse prevention and applying the self-regulation model to the treatment of sexual offenders. In D. Prescott (ed.), *Applying knowledge to practice: The treatment and supervision of sexual abusers*, 143–74. Oklahoma City, OK: Wood'n'Barnes.

Readiness and the Treatment of Sexual Offenders

Tony Ward, Sharon Casey, and Robyn L. Langlands

Introduction

Despite the considerable influence of Martinson's (1974) paper, which dismissed offender treatment programmes as ineffective, evidence has slowly accumulated in support of such programmes (see Day and Howells 2002). Innovative work conducted by Canadian, British, and American researchers has led to the refinement of rehabilitation theory and the formulation of explicit practice guidelines (e.g., Andrews and Bonta 1998; Layton-MacKenzie 2000; McGuire 2001). The empirically driven approach adopted by these researchers has come to be known as the "what works" movement. This movement has resulted in the transformation of correctional rehabilitation; evidence-based offender treatments have become an established part of efforts to reduce crime. Prison, probation, and all forensic mental health services now offer such treatments (Day and Howells 2002; McGuire 2001).

In recent years, the "what works" approach, based largely on the research of Andrews and Bonta (2003), has dominated forensic rehabilitation practice despite critiques of the model (notably by Ward and Stewart 2003) and its limited influence in forensic mental health settings (see Howells, Day, and

Thomas-Peter 2004). The model centres on the application of three core principles—risk, need, and responsivity—each of which speaks directly to the type of offender that might be considered to be suitable for rehabilitation. Considering the emphasis of risk management in this approach, it is perhaps unsurprising that significant progress in the development of the Risk–Need–Responsivity (RNR) Model has been in the area of risk assessment. A wide range of tools have been developed and validated to help identify individuals who are most likely to re-offend so that they can be offered the most intensive programmes. This work has been important, given evidence that programmes are most effective when they are offered to those who have at least a moderately high probability of re-offending (Andrews and Bonta 2003). A focus of current research in this area is on the identification and assessment of dynamic risk factors or criminogenic needs (see Webster et al. 2006), as these are particularly important in the determination of treatment targets (most commonly those areas of need that are functionally related to the offending).

Although risk-need assessments can guide decisions regarding the selection of both appropriate candidates and targets for treatment, they offer little guidance on how well any intervention is likely to be received, or the extent to which programmes are able to respond effectively to individual offender needs. The inclusion of the responsivity principle in the RNR model is an acknowledgment that programme suitability is likely to involve more than simply the presence of those characteristics associated with risk. Responsivity refers to the use of a style and mode of intervention that engages the interests of client groups and takes into account their relevant characteristics such as cognitive ability, learning style, and values (Andrews and Bonta 1998). Adhering to the responsivity principle therefore primarily involves adjusting treatment delivery to maximise each individual offender's learning opportunities.

One of the major problems with the formulation of the responsivity principle is its lack of conceptual clarity; as a result, it is difficult to determine how the different processes and structures impacting on responsivity are interrelated, or how they can be reliably assessed. There also has been lack of recognition that the ability to capitalise on therapeutic opportunities involves a dynamic interaction between person, therapy, and contextual factors. In addition to responsivity, motivation to change has been identified in the literature as an important predictor of treatment outcome (McMurran and Ward 2004). Unfortunately, the construct of motivation similarly lacks conceptual depth, and the mechanisms as to how it impacts on treatment preparedness remain unclear. A way forward is to utilise the construct of treatment readiness that has the conceptual resources to take these complex interactions into account.

To support our argument that treatment readiness is a superior construct to responsivity and motivation, we will first outline our conceptualisation of readiness. We will consider how treatment readiness is often confused with the related, but distinct, constructs of responsivity and motivation before describing a recently developed model of readiness. We will then discuss how to assess readiness in offender populations, and reflect on the clinical relevance of such assessments and possible directions for future research. Finally, it is important to note that research on treatment readiness to date has been conducted on general offenders and violent offenders, but no specific studies have been undertaken with sex offenders. In view of the fact that many sex offenders commit other types of offences including violent crimes, however, the research and ideas outlined in the following chapter certainly apply to this group (and arguably also to "specialist" sex offenders).

What Is Treatment Readiness?

Despite the differences between treatment readiness, responsivity, and motivation, there has been little attempt in the literature to distinguish between these three constructs. Responsivity can be divided into internal and external responsivity (Andrews 2001), where attention to internal responsivity factors requires therapists to match the content and pace of sessions to specific client attributes, such as personality and cognitive maturity. In contrast, external responsivity refers to a range of general and specific issues (such as the use of active and participatory methods), and can be further divided into staff and setting characteristics (Kennedy 2001; Serin and Kennedy 1997). Within the broad responsivity principle, there lies an invitation to attend to an offender's motivation to engage in therapy and to commit to change.

Motivation involves assessing whether someone really wants to enter treatment and is therefore willing to change his or her behaviour in some respect (e.g., cease to behave aggressively). Typical clinical criteria for deciding that offenders are motivated to enter treatment include expressions of regret for their offences, a desire to change, and the appearance of enthusiasm about the treatments offered. In an important respect, the judgment that an offender is motivated for therapy is essentially a prediction that he or she will engage in and complete therapy. In current practice, it is widely accepted that offender motivation constitutes an important requirement for selection into rehabilitation programmes, and also that therapists are expected to have the skills to initiate, enhance, and sustain motivation in reluctant individuals. Despite a plethora of literature on motivational interviewing and related interventions, comparatively little attention has been paid to clarifying the relevant underlying mechanisms of motivation, or to considering the relationship between motivational states and other aspects of treatment preparedness. Similarly, no consensus exists regarding what is meant by "offenders' motivation," and no systematic examination has been made of the factors that influence it (McMurran and Ward 2004).

Readiness, on the other hand, is a broader construct than individual motivation and responsivity, given the nature of the client group (i.e., offenders who may not recognise their behaviour as problematic), and given the potentially profound influence of the legal constraints on behaviour and custodial environment in which treatment is offered (see also Casey, Day, and Howells 2005; Day, Tucker, and Howells 2004). The concept of treatment readiness was originally articulated in an offender context by Serin (Serin 1998; Serin and Kennedy 1997), although it has also previously been used in offender substance-use treatment programmes (e.g., DeLeon and Jainchill 1986). Readiness can be broadly defined as the presence of characteristics (states or dispositions) within either the client or the therapeutic situation that are likely to promote engagement in therapy and that, therefore, are likely to enhance therapeutic change (Howells and Day 2003). To be ready for treatment means that the person is motivated (i.e., wants to or has the will to), is able to respond appropriately (i.e., perceives he or she can), finds it relevant and meaningful (i.e., he or she can engage), and has the capacities (i.e., he or she is able) to successfully enter the treatment programme. Treatment readiness therefore incorporates both the constructs of motivation and programme responsivity.

Howells and Day (2003) also emphasise the critical role of the therapeutic alliance in promoting treatment readiness. The term *therapeutic alliance* refers to three different aspects of the relationship between the client and therapist: the collaborative nature of the relationship, the affective bond between client and therapist, and the client's and therapist's abilities to agree on treatment goals and tasks (Bordin 1994; Gaston 1990). Readiness has been shown to be a moderate, but significant and consistent predictor of treatment outcome across a variety of therapeutic modalities and client groups (Bambling and King 2001; Horvath and Symonds 1991), and is likely to be an equally important feature of effective offender rehabilitation programmes. Marshall and colleagues (2003) have recently identified the development of a strong therapeutic alliance as essential to effective sexual offender treatment. Many treatments for personality disorder also emphasise the importance of therapeutic alliance (Benjamin and Karpiak 2001).

The Multifactor Offender Readiness Model
To further develop the concept of treatment readiness delineated by Howells and Day (2003), in 2004, Ward, Day, Howells, and Birgden created the Multifactor Offender Readiness Model (MORM). The major assumption underlying the MORM is that the treatment readiness of offenders is a function of both internal (person) and external (context) factors. Offenders who are ready to enter a specific treatment programme are viewed as possessing a number of core psychological features that enable them to (at least minimally) function in a therapeutic environment and thereby benefit from the interventions provided. These *personal* factors are cognitive (beliefs, cognitive strategies), affective (emotions), volitional (goals, wants, or desires), behavioural (skills and competencies), and personal (sense of self and social context). The *contextual* factors related to these properties are circumstances (mandated vs. voluntary, offender type); location (prison, community); opportunities (availability of therapy and programmes); resources (quality of programme, availability of trained and qualified therapist, appropriate culture); interpersonal supports (availability of individuals who wish offenders well and would like to see them succeed in overcoming their problems); and

programme characteristics (e.g., programme type and timing of treatment). According to the model, these internal and external factors collectively determine the likelihood of an individual offender engaging in, and subsequently benefiting from, treatment. The MORM therefore suggests that an offender will be ready to change offending to the extent that s/he possesses certain cognitive, emotional, volitional, and behaviour properties, and lives in an environment where such changes are possible and supported.

As described in the MORM, readiness is conceived of as a dynamic rather than static phenomenon: an offender is ready *for* something. In the case of treatment, he or she is ready to engage in a process (treatment) that will bring about behavioural change (a non-offending lifestyle). The degree to which engagement in the treatment process is sustained is dependent upon intention. It is conceivable that both internal and external factors may, at any point in the process, serve to weaken or strengthen an offender's intention. Volition is, therefore, more than simply one aspect of intrinsic motivation involved in the formulation of intent; it is the mechanism whereby the impetus for change is maintained. Such a conceptualisation implies that volition extends beyond the required readiness conditions and operates as a mediating variable for the target factors in the model. In other words, volition serves a mediating function between programme engagement and programme performance.

At this point, it is necessary to consider the claim that in some interpretations of responsivity, there are references to obstacles that prevent engagement in treatment (Serin 1998). The addition of this feature increases its utility and makes it conceptually equivalent to the formulation of treatment readiness in the MORM. This contention is flawed for the following reasons. First, readiness refers to the required conditions for engagement in treatment, while the notion of obstacles refers to a lack of these factors. In other words, readiness directs individuals to ask what is required for entry into a programme, while the concept of responsivity obstacles simply focuses attention on what is preventing treatment engagement. It is easier conceptually for those assessing effectiveness to focus on what is required to complete or engage in a task rather than on what is preventing such engagement. Such an approach has greater utility: an offender's engagement in treatment can be diverted or go wrong for hundreds of reasons (i.e., obstacles) while success can result from the discovery of only one path toward solving a problem (i.e., required conditions).

Second, practitioners have not really developed the responsivity concept into a coherent, systematic model; rather, the model tends to be operationalised as a list of factors (see Serin 1998). That is, it is not immediately obvious how the different factors converge, whereas this lineage is clear in the readiness model. Third, the readiness model specifies what the required conditions for treatment engagement are and what can go wrong, whereas the responsivity construct is more ad hoc in nature: the list of obstacles depends on what empirical research discovers, and it therefore may change over time. Finally, the readiness model deals with contextual (e.g., family support, resource availability, relationships) and temporal issues, and is broader in scope. In other words, the readiness model is clearer about the internal and external conditions required to engage in treatment, and it explains how they are interrelated (it is also inclusive of responsivity).

In summary, treatment readiness can be conceptualised as an overarching construct that encompasses both the internal components of responsivity (e.g., offender motivation, problem awareness, emotional capacity to engage with psychological treatment, goals, and personal identity), and external components that may be specific to the custodial environment in which treatment is commonly offered (e.g., availability of programmes, institutional social climates, legal pressure to attend; see Ward et al. 2004). Treatment readiness thus provides a more useful framework within which to assess an offender's likelihood of participating in, and subsequently benefiting from, treatment than either responsivity or motivation because of its greater scope, coherence, testability, and utility (fertility).

Unpacking the MORM

An examination of the academic literature provides a theoretical and empirical basis for the MORM. For example, support for the affective component of the MORM can be found in Proeve and Howells's (2002) argument that the emotions of shame and guilt may be important determinants of treatment readiness for child sex offenders. The authors propose that therapy for child sex offenders involves a movement from shame to guilt. From this perspective, the sex offender is "unready" to work on his or her problems at the beginning of a program because he or she is pre-occupied with the bad self and with the negative evaluations by others. As shame is reduced, constructive guilt slowly predominates and stimulates engagement in treatment and behaviour change. A highly responsive program would, ideally, be capable of varying the type of intervention according to the shame and guilt status of the individual sex offender. Proeve and Howells state, for example, that high shame offenders may be adversely affected, at least initially, by group treatment: "Shame may perhaps be offset by the careful encouragement of support within the group and a focus on the commonality of their inappropriate behaviour rather than on their identity as sex offenders" (page 664).

While the MORM succeeds in providing a conceptual framework that draws together a range of factors that have been hypothesised, or demonstrated, within the literature to be related to treatment engagement, each of the factors identified in the model would benefit from further explication and empirical validation with specific offender populations. In their paper on treatment readiness in violent offenders, Chambers, Eccleston, Day, Ward, and Howells (forthcoming) illustrate how the relationship between cognitive factors and readiness as outlined in the MORM can be usefully applied to violent offenders. The authors suggest that two types of cognitive factors are likely to be particularly important in determining treatment readiness: specific cognitive distortions and general cognitive traits.

An offender may have particular beliefs about his or her offence that make it unlikely that s/he will regard treatment as necessary. Cognitive distortions in offenders have been classified into two broad categories: primary, self-serving, cognitive distortions and secondary, self-serving, cognitive distortions (Gibbs, Potter, and Goldstein 1995). Primary cognitive distortions are described as an attitude that one's own beliefs and needs are paramount and the thoughts of others are inconsequential (Barriga and Gibbs 1996). This type of self-serving attitude is likely to hinder rehabilitation readiness and therapeutic outcomes because primary cognitive distortions encourage the belief that it is one's right to behave in an antisocial way regardless of the consequences of his/her behaviour on others. In turn, self-serving attitudes may cause the offender to be resistant to suggestions of behaviour change in a violence-rehabilitation programme. Someone with a high degree of primary cognitive distortions may therefore not be ready for rehabilitation. In all likelihood, such offenders would be unmotivated to enter therapy, and would be reactant to suggestions of changing their behavior. Perceived coercion in the therapeutic relationship may serve to increase resistance even further. Overall, the effects that primary cognitive distortions have on rehabilitation readiness are potentially severe, and lead to the conclusion that engaging violent offenders in treatment—and overcoming reactance—is a vital treatment target in its own right.

Secondary cognitive distortions, such as blaming others, minimising/mislabeling, and assuming the worst of others, support the primary distortions by enabling the offender to rationalise and justify the offending behavior (Gibbs et al. 1995). Bandura and others have suggested that such strategies serve to protect the offender's self-image following his or her antisocial behaviour (Bandura 1991; Sykes and Matza 1957) by alleviating the negative feelings that would usually be associated with harming someone. If an offender believes s/he has done nothing wrong, then why change? Gibbs et al. offer a detailed description of each of the secondary distortions. Blaming others relates to attributing blame for the behaviour to external sources such as intoxication, or provocation by the victim. Minimising is a distortion that creates the view that violent behaviour is not harmful, and may even be perceived as admirable. Mislabeling may result in a dehumanising label being applied to others, for example, "She's a prostitute and used to getting raped." Finally, assuming the worst means attributing hostile intent to others, thinking that the worst-case scenario in social situations is inevitable, or assuming that improvement in one's own or others' behavior is impossible.

All of these secondary cognitive distortions can specifically impede treatment readiness in their own distinct ways. Blaming others rather than accepting responsibility for committing an offence suggests that a violent offender would be resistant to behavioural modification. In the context of rehabilitation, locus of control (or outcome expectancies) are likely to influence any decision to change behaviour (Bandura 1977). An external locus of control is likely to reduce commitment to behavioural modification, because the offender is less likely to accept responsibility for his/her violence. This decision is detrimental both for violent behavior and engagement in a rehabilitative programme, because if violent offenders believe that they are not responsible for their actions, then treatment programmes are unlikely to be perceived as relevant or meaningful. To enhance treatment readiness, a violent offender's locus of control needs to become internalised.

The minimisation of violent behaviour also may thwart attempts to heighten readiness for rehabilitation if all that the offender has known, both inside and outside of prison, is a subculture of violence. Minimising the actual harm of violence and viewing it instead as a righteous and necessary activity can prove problematic for therapy. If the violent male offender believes that his masculinity is directly related to violence, then he may regard therapy as emasculating. Consequently, such offenders must be provided with alternative avenues to demonstrate and experience their manhood.

The final secondary, cognitive distortion identified by Barriga and Gibbs (1996) is assuming the worst. This cognitive distortion causes attribution of hostile intentions to others, which is particularly detrimental to rehabilitation readiness because it impedes engagement in therapy. If the violent offender is constantly paranoid and attributes hostile intent to the therapist, then it will be difficult to achieve an effective therapeutic relationship.

In addition to primary and secondary cognitive distortions, more general or trait aspects of cognition may influence treatment readiness. Self-efficacy is required for offenders to be able to engage in treatment, change their violent behavior, and then feel confident about maintaining it. If offenders have previous experiences of programmes (or other forms of psychological treatment) that did not lead to mastery, then they may be unlikely to believe that they can benefit from any programme that is being offered.

Howells and Day (2006; 2007) have conducted further work on the concept of treatment readiness, as outlined in the MORM, through an in-depth examination of the relationship between affective factors and treatment readiness, and the application of the MORM principles to high-risk offenders with personality disorders. In their discussion of offenders with personality disorders, the authors emphasise that low treatment readiness may be exacerbated in offenders with mental disorders. In the case of an offender with a personality disorder, the presence of factors that impede readiness, such as deceitfulness, are likely symptoms of the disorder, rather than simply a correlate of his or her offending behaviour (Howells and Day 2007). This association, of course, presents a unique challenge for therapists who are attempting to improve readiness in such offender populations. Therapists need to determine whether treatment programmes are *ready* for groups of offenders with specific needs, such as those with personality disorders. If these programmes are not ready, they should be adapted to ensure that their content and mode of delivery is suitable (Howells and Day 2007).

Measuring Treatment Readiness

Given that one of our central criticisms of the responsivity principle and the construct of motivation is their limited conceptual depth and subsequent lack of testability, it is critical to demonstrate that treatment readiness is, by comparison, a measurable construct. While many of the external readiness factors are not easily assessed or are beyond the control of those delivering programmes (e.g., legal pressure to attend treatment), some practitioners have attempted to measure internal aspects of readiness, including motivation to change. Measures derived from models of motivation, such as the transtheoretical model (Prochaska and DiClemente 1984; 1986), have, however, received only limited support in their application to offender populations (see Casey et al. 2005). It would appear that measures that seek to assess the broader components of readiness have more promise, given the potentially significant influence of extrinsic pressures on people in prison to attend treatment programmes (e.g., DeLeon and Jainchill 1986; Serin 1998; Serin and Kennedy 1997; Ward et al. 2004). These measures include the Attitudes to Correctional Treatment Scale (Baxter, Marion, and Goguen 1995), the Serin Treatment Readiness Interview (Serin and Kennedy 1997), and, more recently, the Personal Concerns Inventory (Offender Adaptation; Sellen, McMurran, Cox, Theodosi, and Klinger 2006). However, none of these measures have been derived from a model of offender readiness, and their psychometric properties, in particular their predictive validity, have yet to be fully established.

The Corrections Victoria Treatment Readiness Questionnaire
In an attempt to address the lack of a robust measure of readiness, Casey, Day, Howells, and Ward (2007) recently developed the Corrections Victoria Treatment Readiness Questionnaire (CVTRQ). The CVTRQ, a measure

of general readiness to enter treatment, was validated on a sample of 166 offenders who were referred to a Cognitive Skills programme that was delivered in community and prison settings in Victoria, Australia.[1]

Factor analysis of the original 40 CVTRQ items produced a 20-item measure, comprised of four components or subscales (labelled "attitudes and motivation," "emotional reactions," "offending beliefs," and "efficacy"). The attitudes and motivation subscale was found to be most strongly related to overall treatment engagement, suggesting this aspect of readiness is likely to be particularly important. That said, the profile of scores across all subscales is likely to reveal those aspects of readiness that are salient for an individual, and that can be used to identify areas for intervention for those low in treatment readiness. The measure showed good psychometric properties: it was internally consistent, had high levels of both discriminant and convergent validity, and strong predictive validity (as measured by treatment engagement; Casey et al. 2007).

The CVTRQ components correspond closely to four of the five individual or personal factors identified in the MORM developed by Ward et al. (2004) and, as such, the data offered empirical support for this model. Although items included in the full scale to assess the volitional or identity factor of readiness did not appear in the final CVTRQ, this deficit does not invalidate either the measure or the model. According to Ward et al. (2004), volition refers to the formation of an intention to pursue a certain goal, and the development and subsequent implementation of a plan to achieve the goal in question. It may be that this type of construct cannot be adequately measured using a simple self-report questionnaire.

The value of any measure of treatment readiness lies in its ability to identify those who will (or will not) go on to benefit from treatment. Casey et

---

1. Cognitive Skills training programmes, which have been widely implemented in correctional settings, are premised on the belief that the cognitive correlates of crime (e.g., impulsivity, deficiencies in problem solving, self-control, anger management, and decision making) can be influenced through intervention (see Gendreau, Little, and Goggin 1996). The utilisation of a cognitive–behavioural approach in these programmes is supported by the results of meta-analytic studies revealing that the greatest reductions in recidivism are associated with this treatment modality (e.g., Andrews, Zinger, Hoge, Bonta, Gendreau, and Cullen 1990; Losel 1995). While initial optimism was high that Cognitive Skills programmes would help reduce recidivism (see Robinson 1995; Robinson, Grossman, and Porporino 1991), more recent evaluations (e.g., McGuire 2001) have led to the conclusion that Cognitive Skills training is perhaps more appropriately viewed as a "foundation" for subsequent programmes.

al. (2007) used therapeutic engagement (as assessed by both facilitators and participants) as the measure of predictive validity, and found that scores on the CVTRQ positively correlated with engagement at the mid-programme point of assessment. This finding is consistent with Ward et al.'s (2004) argument that engagement in treatment is an intermediate goal, and must be reached before change in criminogenic need takes place. Although extensive literature in the field of psychotherapy supports this view, further research is required to explore the relationship between therapeutic engagement, changes in dynamic risk, and behavioural change, for those attending offender-rehabilitation programmes.

While any final decision about referral to treatment should consider the risk-and-needs profile of the individual within the context of the circumstances in which the individual has been assessed, Casey et al. (2007) suggest that offenders who have high scores (at least above 72) on the CVTRQ might be classified as "ready" for treatment. In their sample, a score above 72 equated to approximately 54 percent of those who had been referred to the programme. The authors caution against using a cut-off score as the sole basis for clinical decision making as many more studies with a range of offender groups are required to replicate these findings before the cut-off scores can be considered robust. Nonetheless, the CVTRQ offers a way in which treatment readiness can be easily and quickly assessed by staff with no professional training, for the purpose of informing decisions about programme suitability.

The Violence Treatment Readiness Questionnaire
As noted above, additional research is necessary to establish the utility of the readiness scale for assessment in other offender groups, such as violent or sexual offenders. This appraisal was recently done by Day et al. (forthcoming), who adapted the CVTRQ for the assessment of individuals referred to violent-offender treatment programmes. Assessing treatment readiness in violent offenders is important for a number of reasons. Firstly, the enormous social and economic costs associated with violent offending are such that the development and delivery of programmes to reduce the occurrence of violent crime has become a priority area for many governments. While some evidence suggests that violent crime in some countries may be slowly

decreasing (e.g., Moffatt and Poynton 2006), the number of offenders imprisoned for violent offences has risen steadily over the past few years. Australian statistics, for example, show that nearly half of the sentenced prison population have been convicted of crimes of violence, with nearly one in two (47 percent) having a "most serious offence" that involves violence or the threat of violence, including offences such as acts intended to cause injury (14 percent), robbery/extortion (12 percent), sexual assault and related offences (11 percent), and homicide and related offences (10 percent; Australian Bureau of Statistics 2004). While it is difficult to obtain a true base rate for violent re-offending, the available data indicates that at least 20 percent of convicted offenders will go on to commit further violent offences after release from custody (Dowden and Serin 2001), making the treatment and rehabilitation of known offenders a particularly important area for service development.

Secondly, anger-management and violence-reduction programmes aimed specifically at this population have proliferated in recent years, despite a relatively limited evidence base from which to draw any conclusions about programme effectiveness. In the only published meta-analysis, Polaschek and Collie (2004) identified only nine violent-offender programme evaluations that they considered to be of sufficient methodological rigor to warrant inclusion. Of these, only four studies reported rates of violent recidivism. More recently, Polaschek, Wilson, and Townsend (2005) reported positive outcomes from a New Zealand programme, with 32 percent of the treatment group being reconvicted for a violent offence after release as compared to 63 percent of a matched comparison group (matched on the basis of relevant characteristics such as offence type and sentence). For those treated participants who were re-convicted, survival analysis revealed that the mean number of days to violent re-offence was more than double that for the comparison group.

Finally, a particularly important issue in violent-offender treatment concerns the assessment and selection of appropriate candidates for treatment. While it is generally accepted that programmes should target the higher-risk offenders (Andrews and Bonta 2003), violent offenders are not a particularly homogenous group in terms of their treatment needs (see Davey, Day, and Howells 2005). The need for individualised assessment and case formulation is widely acknowledged before treatment is offered in order to reduce the rates of inappropriate referral to treatment (e.g., Daffern, Howells, and Ogloff 2007; Wong and Gordon 2004). Inappropriate referral can lead to low rates of engagement in treatment and even programme non-completion or drop-out. Rates of attrition from programmes in many correctional programmes appear to be quite high; Dowden and Serin's (2001) findings—that those who dropped out of a Canadian Correctional Service programme for violent offenders had the highest rate of violent re-offending (40 percent), compared with untreated (17 percent) and treated (5 percent) groups—are a cause for much concern (see also McMurran and Theodosi 2004). Their findings do not suggest, however, that high-risk offenders who are assessed as likely to drop out of programmes should not be offered treatment. Instead, those offenders may require additional interventions designed to prepare them to receive the type of intervention delivered in violent-offender treatment (see Day, Bryan, Davey, and Casey 2006).

The Day et al. (forthcoming) study was designed to build on the previous work of Casey et al. (2007) in three ways. First, a brief semi-structured readiness interview was also given to a sub-sample of participants prior to entering the programme. The purpose of this evaluation was to establish whether a face-to-face interview would provide a better predictor of treatment engagement than a self-report measure, given the suggestion that interviews may provide a more reliable method of assessment with offender populations (see Serin and Kennedy 1997). Second, the two clinicians re-administered the measure at the end of the programme to establish whether levels of readiness changed over the course of the programme. If readiness did change over time, then Serin and Kennedy hypothesised that the VTRQ might have the potential to also be used as a measure of change in interventions designed to promote treatment readiness prior to programme participation (see Day et al. 2005). Also, the authors collected data on therapeutic engagement not only at the mid-point of the programme, but also upon completion of the programme. Finally, they collected data regarding participant satisfaction with the programme at the end of the programme, to provide an additional outcome measure and to determine whether participants identified as being higher in treatment readiness would report higher levels of treatment satisfaction. This process allowed for an examination of the extent to which the measure predicted not only engagement, but also treatment performance.

The findings revealed that the offence-specific scale, like the CVTRQ, was a valid and reliable measure in terms of predicting engagement in treatment (in this case, for violent-offender treatment programmes). Although the sample size in Day et al.'s (forthcoming) study is relatively small for scale validation, and the main outcome measure was self-reported engagement with treatment rather than a behavioural measure of change, the VTRQ showed acceptable levels of internal consistency reliability and construct validity. Pre-treatment scores were significantly correlated with treatment engagement. In addition, VTRQ scores were more strongly associated with therapeutic engagement than scores on two other measures that have been used to assess treatment readiness in offenders: the Serin Treatment Readiness Scale (adapted from Serin and Kennedy 1997) and the Readiness to Change Questionnaire (RCQ; Rollnick, Heather, Gold, and Hall 1992). Finally, participants identified as being more treatment ready reported higher levels of treatment satisfaction.

Day et al. (forthcoming) were somewhat surprised to find that scores on the self-report readiness measure were more highly correlated with treatment engagement than scores derived from the semi-structured interview. They suggested that offenders might be more likely to respond in socially desirable ways in face-to-face interviews than when they complete a questionnaire, thus compromising the validity of the interview. The authors acknowledge that it is important to consider issues relating to impression management in any assessment of violent offenders, with the data collected in their study revealing that 6 percent of participants displayed a tendency to "fake bad." It may be, given the possibility of favourable parole decisions being associated with attendance at programmes, that offenders seek to persuade assessors that they are indeed in need of treatment. It should be noted that all measures used in the validation study were self-reported in nature, which can raise questions about the veracity of participant responses. While the authors acknowledge this possibility, the relationship between scores on the readiness interview and two of the convergent validity measures (the RCQ [Rollnick et al. 1992] and Loza-Fanous Self-Efficacy Questionnaire [Loza-Fanous 2004]) were in the same direction as the self-report measure of treatment readiness.

The results of this study also suggest that treatment readiness does increase over the course of participation in programmes. While it is perhaps not surprising that by the end of treatment, participants are able to demonstrate changes in their attitudes and motivation, their emotional reactions to their offences, their offending beliefs, and their efficacy, this data suggests that the VTRQ may have an additional use as a measure of change in interventions designed to increase problem awareness and motivation prior to entry in structured treatment programmes.

Levels of therapeutic engagement also increased between the mid-programme and post-programme points of assessment. This suggests, for violent offenders in the programmes, at least, that the therapeutic alliance continues to develop over the course of the programme, in contrast to other treatments where the alliance may develop relatively early on and then remain stable. This finding illustrates the potential difficulties that violent offenders experience in engaging in therapeutic change, and highlights the need for facilitators to be sensitive to process issues throughout the length of treatment. In addition, Day et al. (forthcoming) noted the strong positive correlation between mid-programme levels of treatment engagement and therapy satisfaction. This finding underscores the importance of establishing the therapeutic alliance early in the treatment process.

Clinical Implications of Treatment Readiness

Now that we have established that treatment readiness can be successfully measured, it is necessary to elucidate how this construct can inform clinical practice with offenders (including sex offenders). First, an awareness of the importance of treatment readiness might promote the development of more sophisticated assessments of individual needs, leading to an improved match between clients and the interventions that are offered in forensic settings. The notion of readiness for treatment can inform these assessments by encouraging practitioners to think beyond notions of self-reported motivation to change, and to consider the clinical impact of what it means for individuals to receive treatment in a forensic context.

Second, and perhaps more importantly, the construct suggests that low readiness can reside either in the individual or the setting, or, indeed, in both. This finding implies that the primary responsibility for modifying low levels of readiness lies with the practitioner and the service in which s/he works. In other words, it becomes the treatment provider's duty to find ways to deliver interventions that meet the individual's needs, and that discourage the tendency to view low levels of motivation or compliance as pathological.

Third, the emphasis on the context in which treatment is offered clearly identifies a need for the development of specialist forensic interventions that acknowledge and respond to these findings. Many programmes that are offered to offenders apply methods and treatments that have been developed in (non-forensic) mental health settings where referrals are often initiated by the (distressed) individual client. It is likely that specialist forensic treatments will prove to be more effective, given that these treatments can draw on criminological theories that seek to explain offending, and can then emphasise the processes by which offenders desist from crime. Offenders can enter treatment with quite low levels of awareness about the problems caused by their offending, and may benefit, at least in the early stages of treatment, from approaches to treatment that seek to address this discrepancy (see Day et al. 2006). The notion of treatment readiness can therefore be used to engage offenders and inform intervention approaches. This approach contrasts with other methodologies that seek to assess and manage offenders. In this respect, the construct is compatible with many of the ideas enshrined in the Good Lives Model of offender rehabilitation (e.g., Ward and Maruna 2007), a model that is both clinically rich and treatment-oriented.

The identification of meaningful engagement as an important intermediate outcome (and perhaps as a necessary condition—for some a sufficient condition—for change to occur in criminogenic need) draws attention to the therapeutic process of programmes, and in particular to the importance of the alliance that is formed between offenders and treatment providers. Effective alliances are those that are perceived by both the client and the therapist as collaborative in nature, and are characterised by a positive emotional bond and an agreement on the goals and tasks of treatment (see Bordin 1994). This type of relationship has been shown to be a moderate, but significant and consistent, predictor of treatment outcome across a variety of therapeutic modalities (e.g., Bambling and King 2001). Expanding evidence reveals that this outcome also applies to sex offender rehabilitation programmes (Beech and Fordham 1997; Beech and Mann 2002). The clinical challenge for facilitators is how to best promote strong and positive alliances with individual offenders within cohesive and supportive treatment groups. It is here that clinical supervision becomes a critical component of effective programme delivery. The focus on engagement in the MORM draws attention to the fact that engagement is a two-way process and that facilitators need appropriate support and resources to be able to work effectively. Often organisational support for treatment providers in forensic settings is limited or ambivalent, and it is important that programme managers and administrators are aware that the provision of meaningful rehabilitation requires the presence of well-skilled, highly trained, and well-supported staff who hold values and attitudes supportive of behaviour change.

Finally, identifying an offender's level of treatment readiness is both therapeutically and financially prudent as it provides therapists with the opportunity to potentially enhance low levels of readiness before treatment commences, potentially leading, in turn, to more successful rehabilitative outcomes. The authors and others have proposed a number of different approaches designed to improve readiness. The approaches range from experiential work and drama-therapy to the use of written narratives (see Day et al. 2006). The most commonly utilised approach to improving readiness, however, is probably motivational interviewing. Motivational interviewing has been shown to be an effective method of improving offenders' motivation to change (e.g., Harper and Hardy 2000; Mendel and Hipkins 2002; Stein and Lebeau-Craven 2002). Inspection of an individual's scores on each of the CVTRQ subscales may reveal particular aspects of readiness that might be addressed within a brief intervention, such as motivational interviewing.

The techniques outlined by motivational interviewing (MI; Miller and Rollnick 2002) are thought to be particularly useful at the beginning of treatment, where they provide the foundation of a level of motivation to engage in therapy and change. This approach is especially pertinent with violent offenders, with whom engagement in therapy is a large hurdle. Cognitive and experiential changes tend to occur in the earlier stages of change, and behavioural processes in the latter stages (Perz, DiClemente, and Carbonari 1996). Thus, considering the cognitive impediments to rehabilitation readiness in violent offenders, the onus is on assisting them in achieving motivation to change, and self-efficacy to change, so that they are more prepared to engage in therapy. Any assessment of treatment readiness should pay particular attention to the possibility of reactance, and emphasise the extent to which the individual has control over what s/he achieves in the programme. Once resistance is reduced, cognitive–behavioral therapy interventions may be introduced to teach offenders problem-solving skills, or to target the thought patterns that actively support their violent behaviour (Ward and Brown 2004).

Despite the efficacy of interventions, such as MI, which are designed to improve treatment readiness, some offenders may continue to show little internal motivation to change their behaviour. In such cases, the therapist may need to place an offender into a treatment programme before s/he is ready in order to benefit from the rehabilitation process. It should be noted that different types of rehabilitation programmes will have different approaches to the management of therapeutic engagement. The treatment of sexual offenders is relevant here, as it is relatively common for sexual offenders to enter treatment maintaining either that their offending did not happen or that it was not problematic. Low levels of problem recognition and motivation would, in some programmes (such as some substance-use programmes), exclude offenders from participation. In sexual offender treatment, however, denial, unless extreme, is rarely grounds for exclusion. In our view, the early stages of these programmes should not be considered as treatment, but more as a preparatory stage of treatment where the task is to increase readiness. It is hoped that internal motivation will develop during the treatment programme, such that the offender accepts responsibility for his/her actions and commits to making changes (Day et al. 2004). Resistant offenders who are coerced into treatment may become less resistant over the course of the programme, which in turn may increase the likelihood that treatment may be beneficial.

Future Directions

The construct of treatment readiness is theoretically rich, encompassing not only individual-difference factors (including cognitive, affective, behavioural, volitional, and identity domains), but also those factors that relate to the external environment in which rehabilitative treatment is offered (Ward et al. 2004). Readiness therefore is broader than other individual-difference factors, which may also clearly impact on treatment engagement (e.g., motivation to change), as may the individual's levels of risk, criminogenic need, and responsivity. While the studies by Casey et al. (2007) and Day et al. (forthcoming) demonstrate that the construct of readiness can be successfully operationalised, further work is required to examine the extent to which treatment readiness relates to these other constructs. An interesting direction for future research would be an exploration of different offender sub-groups to determine whether any one group displays particularly low levels of treatment readiness.

In order to explore these relationships, it is essential to have valid and reliable means of assessing treatment readiness. To this end, one of the most important areas for further research in correctional treatment provision relates to the development of psychometrically robust methods of assessing treatment readiness. Although certain measures, including the CVTRQ and the VTRQ discussed above, are available, few have been validated for use with different offender populations. In addition, existing measures have tended to be designed for specific use in correctional group treatment programmes. Furthermore, to date, these measures do not have published normative data, which makes it difficult to interpret the meaning of a score on an assessment for a particular individual. Larger-scale validation studies are clearly needed to assess readiness across a range of different offender treatment programmes when offered to different populations. While it is apparent that low levels of readiness can be identified using relatively brief, self-report questionnaires (see Casey et al. 2007), validation studies need to be conducted to explore the extent to which readiness is stable over time and to assess whether such measures are reliable indicators of change following interventions, such as motivational interviewing (e.g., Mann, Ginsberg, and Weekes 2002), so that such approaches may be offered to those who are identified as particularly low in readiness.

Another area that warrants further development is the assessment of external readiness factors. While internal readiness factors, such as beliefs about treatment, self-efficacy, and dysphoria, can be relatively easily assessed using self-report measures, external readiness factors are much more difficult to assess, particularly in ways that might inform individual decision making about programme suitability. Ward et al. (2004) have suggested that for readiness to occur, an individual needs to live in an environment where such changes are both possible and likely to be supported by others. A key question here is whether the institution has the psychological, social, cultural, and physical resources to deliver effective treatment to offenders. Measures need to be developed that can reliably assess these factors.

One way to approach this task is to understand these factors in terms of their contribution to what has been termed the "social climate" of the unit in which treatment is offered. This term refers broadly to the extent to which a unit is conducive to therapeutic change. Despite the long history of anecdotal and ethnographic observations relating to the nature of prison cultures and their possible deleterious effects (see Langdon, Cosgrave, and Tranah 2004), the interaction between the therapeutic climate and client outcomes in forensic settings is remarkably under-investigated. One possibility that could be examined empirically is whether treatment readiness mediates the relationship between organisational and cultural factors and clinical outcomes.

Conclusions

Research has consistently shown that rehabilitation programmes for offenders, when they adhere to the general principles of risk, need, and responsivity, do achieve significant reductions in recidivism. Even greater reductions in recidivism can be achieved, however, when readiness is addressed at the level of the individual offender, the programme, and the context. A comprehensive understanding of readiness allows for fuller engagement in treatment, thus increasing the probability of good treatment outcomes. Although the construct of treatment readiness is still being refined and developed, it does offer promise in terms of how we understand, assess, and intervene with offenders for whom rehabilitation has been identified as an important goal. A comprehensive understanding and ability to assess treatment readiness within correctional rehabilitation will enable therapists to enhance treatment outcomes and, ultimately, community safety.

REFERENCES

Andrews, D. A. 2001. Principles of effective correctional programs. In *Compendium 2000: On effective correctional programming: Volume 1*, ed. L. L. Motiuk and R. C. Serin. Canada: Ministry of Supply Services.

Andrews, D. A., and J. Bonta. 1998. *The psychology of criminal conduct*. 2nd ed. Cincinnati, OH: Anderson Publishing.

———. 2003. *The psychology of criminal conduct*. 3rd ed. Cincinnati, OH: Anderson Publishing.

Andrews, D. A., I. Zinger, R. D. Hoge, J. Bonta, P. Gendreau, and F. T. Cullen. 1990. Does correctional treatment work? A psychologically informed meta-analysis. *Criminology* 28:369–404.

Australian Bureau of Statistics. 2004. *Prisoners in Australia*. Canberra, Australia: ABS.

Bambling, M., and R. King. 2001. Therapeutic alliance and clinical practice. *Psychotherapy in Australia* 8(1):38–47.

Bandura, A. 1977. Self-efficacy: Toward a unifying theory of behavioral change. *Psychological Review* 84:191–215.

———. 1991. Social cognitive theory of moral thought and action. In *Handbook of moral behavior and development*, ed. W. M. Kurtines and J. L. Gewirtz, 45–103. Hillsdale, NJ: Erlbaum.

Barriga, A. Q., and J. C. Gibbs. 1996. Measuring cognitive distortion in antisocial youth: Development and preliminary validation of the "How I Think" questionnaire. *Aggressive Behavior* 22:333–43.

Baxter, D. J., A. Marion, and B. Goguen. 1995. Predicting treatment response in correctional settings. *Forum on Corrections Research* 7(3):38–41.

Beech, A. R., and A. S. Fordham. 1997. Therapeutic climate of sexual offender treatment programs. *Sexual Abuse: A Journal of Research and Treatment* 9:219–37.

Beech, A. R., and R. Mann. 2002. Recent developments in the assessment and treatment of sexual offenders. In *Offender rehabilitation and treatment: Effective programmes and policies to reduce re-offending*, ed. J. McGuire, 259–88. Chichester, UK: Wiley.

Benjamin, L .S., and C. P. Karpiak. 2001. Personality disorders. *Psychotherapy* 38:487–91.

Bordin, E. S. 1994. Theory and research on the therapeutic working alliance: New directions. In *The working alliance: Theory, research, and practice*, ed. A. O. Horvath and L. S. Greenberg. New York: Wiley.

Casey, S., A. Day, and K. Howells. 2005. The application of the transtheoretical model to offender populations: Some critical issues. *Legal and Criminological Psychology* 10:1–15.

Casey, S., A. Day, K. Howells, and T. Ward. 2007. Assessing suitability for offender rehabilitation: Development and validation of the treatment readiness questionnaire. *Criminal Justice and Behavior* 34(11):1427–40.

Chambers, J. C., L. Eccleston, A. Day, T. Ward, and K. Howells. Forthcoming. Treatment readiness in violent offenders: The influence of cognitive factors on engagement in violence programs. *Aggression & Violent Behavior*.

Daffern, M., K. Howells, and J. Ogloff. 2007. What's the point? Towards a methodology for assessing the function of psychiatric inpatient aggression. *Behaviour Research and Therapy* 45:101–11.

Davey, L., A. Day, and K. Howells. 2005. Anger, over-control and violent offending. *Aggression and Violent Behavior* 10:624–35.

Day, A., J. Bryan, L. Davey, and S. Casey. 2006. Processes of change in offender rehabilitation. *Psychology, Crime and Law* 12(5):473–89.

Day, A., and K. Howells. 2002. Psychological treatments for rehabilitating offenders: Evidence based practice comes of age. *Australian Psychologist* 37:39–47.

Day, A., K. Howells, S. Casey, T. Ward, J. C. Chambers, and A. Birgden. Forthcoming. Assessing treatment readiness in violent offenders. *Journal of Interpersonal Violence.*

Day, A., K. Tucker, and K. Howells. 2004. Coerced offender rehabilitation—A defensible practice? *Psychology, Crime & Law* 10:259–69.

DeLeon, G., and N. Jainchill. 1986. Circumstance, motivation and readiness, and suitability as correlates of treatment tenure. *Journal of Psychoactive Drugs* 18:203–8.

Dowden, C., and R. Serin. 2001. *Anger management programming for offenders: The impact of programme performance measures.* Ottawa: Correctional Service of Canada Research Report.

Gaston, L. 1990. The concept of the alliance and its role in psychotherapy. *Psychotherapy* 27:143–52.

Gendreau, P., T. Little, and C. Goggin. 1996. A meta-analysis of the predictors of adult offender recidivism: What works! *Criminology* 34:401–33.

Gibbs, J. C., G. B. Potter, and A. P. Goldstein. 1995. *The EQUIP program: Teaching youth to think and act responsibly through a peer-helping approach.* Champaign, IL: Research Press.

Harper, R., and S. Hardy. 2000. An evaluation of motivational interviewing as a method of intervention with clients in a probation setting. *British Journal of Social Work* 30:393–400.

Horvath, A. O., and B. D. Symonds. 1991. Relation between working alliance and outcome in psychotherapy: A meta-analysis. *Journal of Counseling Psychology* 38:139–49.

Howells, K., and A. Day. 2003. Readiness for anger management: Clinical and theoretical issues. *Clinical Psychology Review* 23:319–37.

———. 2006. Affective determinants of treatment engagement in violent offenders. *International Journal of Offender Therapy and Comparative Criminology* 50(2):174–86.

———. 2007. Readiness for treatment in high risk offenders with personality disorders. *Psychology, Crime & Law* 13(1):47–56.

Howells, K., A. Day, and B. Thomas-Peter. 2004. Changing violent behaviour: Criminological and psychiatric models compared. *Journal of Forensic Psychiatry and Psychology* 15:391–406.

Kennedy, S. M. 2001. Treatment responsivity: Reducing recidivism by enhancing treatment effectiveness. In *Compendium 2000: On effective correctional programming: Volume 1,* ed. L. L. Motiuk and R. C. Serin. Canada: Ministry of Supply and Services.

Langdon, P. E., N. Cosgrave, and T. Tranah. 2004. Social climate within an adolescent medium-secure facility. *International Journal of Offender Therapy and Comparative Criminology* 48:504–15.

Layton-MacKenzie, D. 2000. Evidence-based corrections: Identifying what works. *Crime and Delinquency* 46:457–71.

Losel, F. 1995. The efficacy of correctional treatment: A review and synthesis of meta-evaluations. In *What works: Reducing reoffending,* ed. J. McGuire, 79–111. Chichester, UK: John Wiley & Sons.

Loza-Fanous, A. 2004. Motivation, self-efficacy, problem recognition, and locus of control as offender treatment responsivity factors. Dissertation. *Abstracts International: Section B: The Sciences and Engineering* 64(9-B):4679.

Mann, R., J. I. D. Ginsberg, and J. R. Weekes. 2002. Motivational interviewing with offenders. In *Motivating offenders to change: A guide to enhancing engagement in therapy*, ed. M. McMurran, 87–102. Chichester, UK: John Wiley & Sons.

Marshall, W. L., Y. M. Fernandez, G. A. Serran, R. Mulloy, D. Thornton, R. E. Mann, and D. Anderson. 2003. Process variables in the treatment of sexual offenders: A review of the literature. *Aggression and Violent Behaviour* 8:205–34.

Martinson, R. 1974. What works? Questions and answers about prison reform. *The Public Interest* 35:22–54.

Mendel, E., and J. Hipkins. 2002. Motivating learning disabled offenders with alcohol-related problems: A pilot study. *British Journal of Learning Disabilities* 30:153–58.

McGuire, J. 2001. What works in correctional intervention? Evidence and practical implications. In *Offender rehabilitation in practice: Implementing and evaluating effective programmes*, ed. G. A. Bernfield and D. A. Farrington, 25–43. New York: John Wiley & Sons.

McMurran, M., and E. Theodosi. 2004. *Offenders who do not complete treatment: A literature review*. London: Home Office.

McMurran, M., and T. Ward. 2004. Motivating offenders to change in therapy: An organizing framework. *Legal and Criminological Psychology* 9(2):295–311.

Miller, W. R., and S. Rollnick. 2002. *Motivational interviewing: Preparing people for change*. New York: Guilford Press.

Moffatt, S., and S. Poynton. 2006. Long-term trends in property and violent crime in New South Wales: 1990–2004. *Contemporary Issues in Crime and Justice* 90. NSW: Bureau of Crime Statistics and Research.

Perz, C. A., C. C. DiClemente, and J. P. Carbonari. 1996. Doing the right thing at the right time? The interaction of stages and processes of change in successful smoking cessation. *Health Psychology* 15:462–68.

Polaschek, D. L. L., and R. M. Collie. 2004. Rehabilitating serious violent adult offenders: an empirical and theoretical taking stock. *Psychology, Crime, and Law* 10:321–34.

Polaschek, D. L. L., N. J. Wilson, and M. R. Townsend. 2005. Cognitive–behavioural rehabilitation for high-risk violent offenders: An outcome evaluation of the violence prevention unit. *Journal of Interpersonal Violence* 20:1611–27.

Prochaska, J. O., and C. C. DiClemente. 1984. *The transtheoretical approach: Crossing traditional boundaries of therapy*. Homewood, IL: Dow Jones-Irwin.

———. 1986. Toward a comprehensive model of change. In *Treating addictive behaviours: Process of change*, ed. W. R. Miller and N. Heather, 3–27. New York: Plenum Press.

Proeve, M. J., and K. Howells. 2002. Shame and guilt in child sexual offenders. *International Journal of Offender Therapy & Comparative Criminology* 46:657–67.

Robinson, D. 1995. *The impact of cognitive skills training on post-release recidivism among Canadian federal offenders*. Canada: Correctional Service of Canada Research Division.

Robinson, D., M. Grossman, and F. Porporino. 1991. *Effectiveness of the cognitive skills training programme: From pilot to national implementation*. Canada: Correctional Services of Canada Research and Statistics Branch.

Rollnick, S., N. Heather, R. Gold, and W. Hall. 1992. Development of a short "readiness to change" questionnaire for use in brief opportunistic interventions among excessive drinkers. *British Journal of Addiction* 87:743–54.

Sellen, J. L., M. McMurran, W. M. Cox, E. Theodosi, and E. Klinger. 2006. The Personal Concerns Inventory (Offender Adaptation): Measuring and enhancing motivation to change. *International Journal of Offender Therapy and Comparative Criminology* 50:294–305.

Serin, R. 1998. Treatment responsivity, intervention and reintegration: A conceptual model. *Forum on Corrections Research* 10:29–32.

Serin, R., and S. Kennedy. 1997. *Treatment readiness and responsivity: Contributing to effective correctional programming*. Canada: Correctional Services Research Report.

Stein, L., and R. Lebeau-Craven. 2002. Motivational interviewing and relapse prevention for DWI: A pilot study. *Journal of Drug Issues* 32(4):1051–70.

Sykes, G. M., and D. Matza. 1957. Techniques of neutralization: A theory of delinquency. *American Sociological Review* 22:664–70.

Ward, T., and M. Brown. 2004. The Good Lives Model and conceptual issues in offender rehabilitation. *Psychology, Crime & Law* 10:243–57.

Ward, T., A. Day, K. Howells, and A. Birgden. 2004. The multifactor offender readiness model. *Aggression and Violent Behavior* 9:645–73.

Ward, T., and S. Maruna. 2007. *Rehabilitation: Beyond the risk paradigm*. London, UK: Routledge.

Ward, T., and C. Stewart. 2003. Criminogenic needs and human needs: A theoretical model. *Psychology, Crime and Law* 9:125–43.

Webster, S. D., R. E. Mann, A. J. Carter, J. Long, R. J. Milner, M. D. O'Brien, H. C. Wakeling, and N. L. Ray. 2006. Inter-rater reliability of dynamic risk assessment with sexual offenders. *Psychology, Crime & Law* 12:439–52.

Wong, S. C. P., and A. E. Gordon. 2004. A Risk-Readiness Model of post-treatment risk management. *Issues in Forensic Psychology* 5:152–63.

Getting the Context Right for Sex Offender Treatment

Ruth E. Mann

In 2006, Langevin found that within a sample of sexual offenders about half were not interested in receiving treatment. Should we consider this figure to be surprisingly low, or surprisingly high?

In our therapist training programme, one exercise we have used is to ask trainees to recall the worst, most hurtful thing they have done to another person. We then ask them to imagine how it would feel to recount that event to their colleagues on the training course. We suggest that as they recount the event, their colleagues could question them for more details, and could press them to acknowledge the selfishness that lay behind their behaviour. We introduce the idea that they could relive through role-play aspects of the event in front of their colleagues, but take on the role of the person they hurt, in order to fully explore the consequences of their hurtful actions. At some point during this exercise, most trainees start to feel uncomfortable.

Yet, this is mild compared with what we expect from sexual offenders in treatment. Sexual offenders are not fools. They know that society detests them. They know that their lives will be henceforth severely restricted. They know that even among criminals, they are considered the lowest of the low. So why would they ever decide to expose their most shameful acts to others, and permit others to dissect and discuss the dreadfulness of their behaviour, in the name of "treatment"?

The cynical answer would be that sexual offenders participate in treatment because they see this as the only route to restoring some of their freedoms: gaining parole, for example, or reducing their monitoring restrictions. And this is undoubtedly true in some cases. But others seem to have a genuine desire for greater insight into their behaviour. Maslow (e.g., 1968) proposed that humans progress toward "self-actualisation," or "becoming a person" (Rogers 1961); that is, that we are all capable of psychological growth toward higher order motives, where we no longer seek to gratify ourselves in terms of more basic needs, such as sex. It is possible that even the "lowest of the low" are interested in self-actualisation, in understanding and moving away from patterns of behaviour that hurt and harm others.

In this chapter, I will consider some of the obstacles to attending treatment for the convicted sexual offender. The obstacles I will identify are drawn from the findings of a nationwide project commissioned by HM Prison Service in 2002 to understand the reasons why some sexual offenders refuse treatment, and to develop a strategy for increasing treatment uptake. The impetus for this project was the news that a high-profile murder of a child had been committed by a man with a prior history of sexual offences, who had refused to attend a treatment programme during a previous sentence of imprisonment. Understandably and rightly, the prison service wished to minimise the likelihood of such a tragedy occurring again.

Part of this project involved a formal research study into the characteristics of treatment refusers, the main findings of which have been written up separately (Mann, Webster, Wakeling, and Keylock forthcoming). We also investigated the issues through activities such as focus groups with offenders currently in treatment and discussions with prison staff. In this chapter, I will draw on the full range of formal and informal investigations we conducted, in order to identify as many obstacles to treatment as possible. We also asked imprisoned offenders for their ideas about how treatment uptake could be increased, and I will report some of their ideas in the second half of this chapter. Interestingly, the main issues identified, throughout the different phases of the project, shared one notable characteristic: they were to do with the *context* in which treatment took place, and *not* to do with the individual characteristics of the offender. Therefore, this is my key message in this chapter. If we can get the context right for a treatment programme, we offer greater hope of self-actualisation, with a concomitant likelihood of living a satisfying life that does not involve offending, and less danger of stigma and shame being the most likely consequences of entering the programme.

Readers should note that my information is all drawn from prison settings and so this chapter refers entirely to treatment programmes within institutions where liberty is restricted. At least some of the issues are likely to be relevant to treatment programmes in other contexts, but these links are best drawn by those who work in those contexts. It is assumed that for those who deliver community treatment, contextual issues may be different but no less important. For example, Robbers (2008) has described the extent to which the difficulty of surviving in the community as a convicted sex offender stifles the ability of treatment programmes to reach maximum effectiveness.

Obstacles to Entering Treatment

If it is the case that about 50 percent of sexual offenders are uninterested in treatment, it is important to investigate what it is that puts them off. As is often the case, some of the answers may seem like common sense, but to ask offenders directly is always going to prove more instructive than making assumptions. In this section, I shall briefly summarise what we learned from our study of treatment refusers.

Being Uninformed about Treatment/Believing that Treatment Is Ineffective

In our study (Mann et al. 2008), we found that about half of the treatment refusers we interviewed were not informed about the aims of treatment and had drawn conclusions that were cynical. They believed that treatment was provided in order to attract finance into the prison, or to improve the public image of the prison service. In contrast, most treatment accepters believed that the aim of treatment was to prevent future offending. None of the respondents believed that treatment was aimed primarily at enabling self-actualisation.

More than half of those we interviewed said they would be more interested in treatment if they believed it did have self-actualisation as its goal.

Sexual offenders were also uninformed about what treatment involved, and about its effectiveness. In particular, we were repeatedly told "prison myths" such as "this programme came from Canada/USA where it has now been stopped because it does not work." Our findings are not unique: in a U.S. study, Shearer (1999) found that many prisoners believed that prison treatment is a waste of taxpayers' money. We also found that prisoners' views were influenced by prison staff, and that some prison staff had been heard or reputed to say that treatment was not effective.

Competing Priorities

As correctional professionals, we may believe strongly that the treatment programmes we offer are the most important activity that an offender can engage in. However, offenders do not necessarily share this belief. Both Ward (2002) and Jones (2002) have commented that offenders often refuse treatment because they have more pressing concerns to attend to, such as starting, maintaining, or grieving relationships (Jones 2002). Jones also cites a study by Erez (1987) who surveyed North American offenders' views about their most pressing needs. Two-thirds of those surveyed indicated that they felt that their main needs were in the areas of education or work. (In our study, investigation of this issue was corrupted by the deniers' stance that "proving my innocence" was their most pressing concern.) As Jones commented, "The tendency of some offenders to go to work rather than attend group may be a reflection of this . . . priority; to interpret this as laziness or avoidance may be unjustified" (Jones 2002). It is also important to remind ourselves that education and work are important protective factors that can help offenders desist from offending (e.g., Maruna 2001). We do not yet have sophisticated enough treatment outcome data to be confident that attending a treatment programme will be more beneficial, in terms of risk reduction, than gaining a work skill or maintaining a relationship.

Concern about Side Effects

Just as many patients with a medical condition may worry about the side effects of any medication they are prescribed, so sex offenders worry that treatment may leave them feeling bad about themselves, or that pharmacological treatments will leave them demasculinised (Langevin et al. 1979). In our study, treatment refusers reported more often than treatment accepters that they had observed others in treatment suffering negative side effects, such as low mood. It may be that treatment refusers look at others through a pre-attentive filter, so that they attend to negative signs in others but fail to notice signs of positive adjustment. We have observed that those who do attend treatment seem to experience drops in self-esteem at points within treatment, although uniformly report higher self-esteem by the end of treatment. Perhaps treatment refusers draw their conclusions from observations of those who are currently engaged in treatment, rather than from those who have completed treatment, who are a less identifiable group.

Concerns about Poor Individual Responsivity of the Programme
Individual responsivity refers to the ability of a programme to recognise and respond to the individual needs and differences of all those taking part. In particular relation to sex offender programmes, gay offenders, for example, may be concerned that programmes will have a heterosexist orientation (with some reason, given the heterosexual assumption of many psychometric measures designed for sexual offenders). Offenders from black or minority ethnic cultures may be concerned that programmes are based on white, Eurocentric values and practices, particularly if treatment staff are primarily white. Offenders who are intellectually disabled may fear that treatment will be like school, and that they will not be able to understand what they will be taught. Furthermore, offenders may suspect (with good reason, given the individualist stance of much correctional work) that sex offender treatment will fail to acknowledge the complicated external circumstances in which they offended, but will focus entirely on internal, stable explanations (see Maruna and Mann 2006). For reasons such as these, many sexual offenders may decide that treatment is unlikely to adequately recognise the situational determinants of their crimes, but will try to "place them into boxes" or force upon them an explanation for their offending which they do not feel takes account of the full picture.

Distrust of Key Professionals
It is well established in the medical literature that patients often refuse medical treatment because they do not trust their doctors. Patients can perceive their

doctors to lack interest or concern in their experiences, to provide inadequate explanations for their recommendations, to disbelieve or disregard some of their symptoms, to fail to provide a range of options for treatment, and to put pressure on patients to adopt a particular medical solution (Spirings and Miree 1993). It is easy to see the potential parallel with sex offenders. In fact, it is all the more likely that sex offenders will meet with professionals who fail to show much concern for their experiences, who wish to focus on the consequences of their actions rather than being interested in the offender's own history, and who put pressure on the offender to attend treatment.

One additional important concern for offenders that we have observed is a fear of the role their treatment professional may play in assessing their risk. This is an ethical and clinical dilemma for many treatment providers. Treatment providers know a great deal about offenders and are well placed to identify the presence of risk factors and the presence of continuing offence-paralleling behaviours. When treatment is provided under the auspices of a correctional system, the system may require reports on offenders from all those who engage with them, including treatment providers, in order to assist correctional decisions such as awarding privileges, moving to lower-security settings, and of course release on parole. Furthermore, research into the nature of sexual offence risk factors suggests that information about attitudes revealed in a treatment setting is a better predictor of recidivism than information revealed in a more adversarial setting. There are therefore strong pressures on treatment providers to use the knowledge they have about offenders to produce risk assessment reports.

On the other hand, it is regarded as professionally unethical for treatment providers to also comment on risk. In our jurisdiction, we try to manage these competing pressures by assigning different professionals to risk assessment and treatment, but by providing the written information (homework, treatment providers' logs, and so forth) to the risk assessor. This meets the ethical obligation but it may not entirely solve the problem of distrust. Offenders perceive the process of risk assessment to be one of the greatest burdens of imprisonment, and this process is inextricably associated with psychologists, who are also the professional group most heavily involved in treatment provision. This association, if present in any system, is likely to be a key factor in maintaining distrust of treatment professionals.

In support of this argument, Mann et al. (2008) found that the majority of sex offenders felt that psychologists should deliver treatment programmes. At the same time, more than half of the treatment refusers we interviewed said they did not trust psychologists.

Expectation of Hostile Responses from Others
Sexual offenders typically are reviled in prison, just as they are in the wider community. They face danger of physical and verbal assault because of the nature of their conviction. Robbers (2008) described how sex offenders living in the community experienced similar hostilities with their lives being restricted by their fear of violence or humiliation. Such experiences led to a general distrust of others, including the correctional system and the people living and working within it. What makes more sense is the finding that sex offenders in prison survive by "learning to pass" as non–sex offenders (Schwaebe 2005). Similarly, Robbers reported that some sex offenders in her community sample had concluded that lying about their past was the only way to survive.

In our sample (Mann et al. 2008), about two-thirds of the sex offenders we interviewed described having had bad experiences in prison, which they perceived to be a result of their sex offender status. They described verbal abuse, being belittled and made to feel stupid, bullying, intimidation, and physical violence.

Pressure from Friends or Family
Social and family factors are often overlooked in attempts to understand an offender's views on treatment. However, the stance of significant others has proved to be an important influence on decisions about disclosure of offending and treatment engagement. Lord and Willmot (2004) found that the majority of offenders in denial had family members who believed they were innocent. Sixty-seven percent of their sample of ex-deniers cited the fear of losing the support of family and friends as the chief reason for maintaining their denial. In our study, we found compelling figures to support this dynamic further. Most of our sample of deniers "knew or believed" that their family members believed they were innocent. Most of the admitters knew or believed that their family thought they were guilty. To add to the strength of the influence, most deniers reported that if they had a personal problem, they would first turn to

their family and friends. A higher proportion of treatment accepters reported that they would first consult professionals for help. However, the influence of family seems related to denial rather than treatment refusal. Those who admitted their offence but refused treatment were not so influenced by their families as those who denied their offence.

Fear of Stigma

Engaging in a treatment regimen, whether it be medical or psychological, raises the risk of the client feeling stigmatised by his illness or condition. Where "lurid cultural stereotypes" (Nations and Monte 1996) are associated with a condition, people are particularly likely to distance themselves from anything that makes their situation identifiable. I am sure it is not necessary to persuade readers that lurid stereotypes persist about sexual offending, and that few people would wish to be publically identified as a sexual offender. As one focus group member put it, "It's a stigma that the people who attend the group are . . . scabs, the bottom of the barrel."

To investigate this issue, we asked prisoners about their perceived status in prison. We hypothesised that those who felt they had high status would be more worried about losing that status if they were more publically identified as sexual offenders. As expected, we found that men who accepted the offer of treatment were most likely to perceive their status among other prisoners as average. Men who refused treatment were most likely to perceive their status among other prisoners as good. A greater proportion of men who refused treatment also believed that it would be harder for them to survive in prison if they entered a treatment programme, compared to men who accepted treatment.

Conclusions

It is abundantly clear that sexual offenders in prison are heavily influenced by the attitudes of those around them about the efficacy of treatment. They are influenced by non-treatment staff, by other prisoners, and by their families and friends. They care about maintaining their close relationships, maintaining their status, maintaining their emotional equilibrium, and maintaining their physical and emotional safety. They juggle these priorities against pressure to undertake treatment in a context where the aims of treatment may be poorly communicated, and where the efficacy of treatment may be inconsistently presented. If we wish to increase the uptake of treatment among imprisoned sexual offenders, then we need to sympathetically understand these tensions and seek to alleviate them through carefully planned responses. The next section of this chapter introduces some ideas about how this could be done.

Improving the Context of Treatment

Efforts to improve the context of treatment need to address offenders' perceptions of their environment as being adversarial (or indeed, address aspects of their environment that clearly are adversarial). It may not be a surprise that many of the suggestions below are rather congruent with motivational interviewing (MI) principles (listening, empathising, and offering choice). It is not practical to expect that an agency can train its entire staff, including non-treatment staff, to a high level of MI skill. However, an agency can decide to endorse some of the principles of MI, and leaders in an organisation can effect considerable change through modelling the principles that they wish all staff to follow. Some simple strategies are listed below.

Listen

One of the lessons we learned from interviewing treatment refusers was how often they can fade out of sight. Repeatedly our interviewees told us that they had been offered treatment, turned it down, were not asked to explain their concerns, and then were never approached again. They carried on with prison life, but once listed in official records as a "refuser" they were not subjected to any further discussions about treatment. In fact, they had plenty to say about why they had not wanted to do treatment, and the experience simply of venting their concerns to a non-judgemental listener (as is required in a research role) often left them suddenly less negative about treatment. Our role was to do no more than listen, and with the pressure to try and persuade removed from the interaction, we found that a number of our previously resistant interviewees spontaneously requested to talk to the treatment staff at the end of the research interview. We are aware that some of these men subsequently entered treatment and found it beneficial.

Recognise the Offender's Perspective and Experiences
Expressing empathy is the first principle of motivational interviewing (Miller and Rollnick 2002). As Miller and Rollnick stated, it is vital to understand the client's situation as "one of being 'stuck' through understandable psychological principles." Sex offenders who resist treatment and/or deny their offending are often assumed to be expressing their general failure to take responsibility for their actions. In fact, our data (Mann et al. 2008) supported Rogers and Dickey's (1991) "adaptational model of denial" whereby the offender appraises the costs and gains of disclosing his offending in an adversarial and possibly physically unsafe immediate setting, located within a wider societal context that loudly expresses revulsion toward sexual offenders. This may not be a failure to take responsibility for one's actions, but an understandable conclusion given the offender's perception of his situation. The first response to refusers and deniers should be to listen to their perceptions about their context and strive to understand their anxieties about being identified, being labelled, and being punished. Through this process of being heard, individual offenders may start to overcome their fears of opening up to others about their offending and its causes.

Enhancing Personal Relationships Between Staff and Offenders
Clearly, listening and expressing empathy are vital skills to enhance the quality of staff–offender relationships. However, there are many other efforts that staff can make to overcome resistance to treatment. The literature on reducing resistance to medical treatment lists many suggestions for building trusting, collaborative, respectful, and informative rapport with resistant clients. Some of the options may seem initially hard to achieve in systems where the demands on staff are already considerable. But perhaps we should look afresh at our prisons and institutions in case we can do more of the following: follow up appointments when patients miss them (with a caring rather than disciplinary emphasis); allow patients to choose between several therapists; be prepared to discuss at length the benefits and costs of a particular treatment regimen; make an effort to take the perspective of

the patient at all times, rather than focusing on what you believe to be good for him; and finally, take every step possible to afford the client a sense of dignity (Bebbington 1995). If these kinds of arrangements improve treatment take-up in non-forensic environments, the principles are worth looking at, where possible, in the custodial setting.

Identify and Counter Myths

It seems that many treatment refusers have heard and believed myths associated with the origins and purposes of sex offender treatment. We could infer, therefore, that better information about treatment should assist in overcoming resistance. Research suggests that verbal communication works better than written communication (e.g., Munetz and Roth 1985) and that such communication is better delivered informally rather than in a psycho-educational style, preferably in the context of a relationship that has already been developed.

Communicate Strength-Based Treatment Aims

Ward (e.g., Ward 2002; Ward, Mann, and Gannon 2007) has written extensively about the benefits of augmenting a risk–needs treatment model with an emphasis on the development of strengths and the goal of a good life for the offender. He has also placed this approach in the context of a broader recognition that offenders continue to possess human rights, even though they may have violated the human rights of others. Given our findings that prisoners tend to believe treatment does not have their best interests at heart, and that they would feel more positively about treatment if they thought the aims were different, it seems important to review our treatment programmes in terms of their aims and content. It is possible to maintain a focus on building strengths while at the same time addressing criminogenic needs—the two goals are not mutually exclusive (see Ward and Mann 2004). This allows the aims of treatment to be openly and clearly communicated. Unfortunately, given the strongly negative public opinion on sexual offending, any correctional system that publically declares that it has an aim to assist sexual offenders achieve "a good life" may attract public criticism for not prioritising the protection of the public, even though the two aims are not necessarily contradictory. It requires effort to articulate descriptions of a treatment programme using language that simultaneously meets the needs of both offenders themselves and the public who have legitimate expectations about its benefits to their safety.

Make Referrals Quickly, with Sensitivity and Respect

The first person to mention the option of treatment to a sex offender is not usually a treatment professional. It may be a judge, a social worker, a custodial officer, or a probation officer. The danger is therefore present that treatment may be suggested in a way that is unhelpful. Offenders in our focus groups felt that the idea of treatment should be raised by someone who understands and values treatment. As the idea can initially be anxiety-provoking, the focus group members suggested the best format was to raise awareness of the idea of treatment, provide some helpful written material that gives more detail, and then arrange a meeting to discuss the offender's reaction. The most desirable types of information were testimonials from treatment graduates, descriptions of the programme, and information on effectiveness.

Offer Clear and Transparent Information about Treatment Methods and Outcomes

Since conducting this investigation, in HM Prison Service we have produced a magazine-style information leaflet, a DVD showing testimonials from treatment participants (including their comments on what is hard about treatment), and a lengthier guide to treatment that is issued to those who express an interest before they are formally asked to give consent. All of these materials are designed to stand alone as sources of information, but it is clearly far more desirable to ensure that face-to-face communication supplements and enhances any written communications. Anecdotal evidence about the impact of these materials suggests they have improved uptake, but even more notably have enabled participants to settle much more quickly into their treatment groups.

Ensure Risk Assessments Take Account of Progress in Treatment

Risk assessment for sexual offenders should follow structured frameworks or schemes, as this approach is more accurate than relying on unstructured clinical judgement. Unfortunately, however, the state of current knowledge is not sufficient to permit quantitative reductions of a risk assessment outcome because someone has attended a treatment programme. The extent to which treatment may have reduced an individual's risk is still left to professional judgement and consequently, such judgements may be inconsistent or unreliable. Some professionals may argue that the literature on treatment effectiveness remains equivocal and therefore there are no grounds for reducing risk levels for those who have engaged in treatment. Others may simply practise in an over-cautious manner, perhaps fearing the consequences should they suggest risk has been reduced and the offender subsequently offends. Leaving a risk assessment at its pre-treatment level, however, is clearly demotivating for the offender. As one member of a focus group put it, "It seems it doesn't matter how well you do, you're still high risk." In fact, it is reasonable to suppose that offenders who do fairly well in a modern cognitive–behavioural programme that targeted most of their criminogenic needs are less likely to reoffend. Adopting this principle more consistently in risk assessment reports may help to communicate to treatment participants that their efforts are worthwhile.

Educate Non-Treatment Staff
Non-treatment staff clearly have a key role to play, both in supporting treatment and in being able to discuss it in an informed way. Any correctional system will contain a range of views about the efficacy of psychological treatment, and doubtless there will always be staff who loudly espouse much more punitive practices for sexual offenders. Non-treatment staff deserve to be properly educated about the process and outcome of the treatment programmes we would like them to support, and their doubts and questions need to be heard and discussed, just as I am arguing we should do with offenders themselves. In HM Prison Service, when we initially began treatment in 1991, we did not recognise the negative impact that non-treatment staff could have on their colleagues who worked on treatment programmes. Instigating a programme of staff awareness training proved to be an important way of tackling the perceived differences of opinion between the different staff groups. Without educative input, non-treatment staff will likely hear and believe the same myths about treatment as offenders hear.

Clear Leadership to Promote Pro-Social Modelling and Supportive Environment

As noted above, and as so richly described by Schwaebe (2005), sex offenders in prison live in a hostile environment and often fear for their physical safety. Bullying and intimidation, related to the nature of their convictions, are common. In such a climate, it is hard to be the person who speaks up about the importance of treating sex offenders decently. However, if we are to encourage the offenders in our care to lead decent, respectful lives that do not violate the rights of others, our correctional systems must demonstrate those values first. It is the role of the leader of any correctional or secure institution to set this standard.

Work with Families and Support Networks

In many therapeutic fields, the benefits of involving family members with the identified patient have been emphasised. Bebbington (1995) recommends "the best way to use relatives is to extend the sense of collaboration to cover clinicians, carers, and patients." In studies with substance abusers (e.g., Siddall and Conway 1988), family support for those in treatment has been shown to reinforce retention and reduce the probability of relapse. In the light of our data, such an approach may be particularly helpful with those offenders who admit guilt but refuse treatment, because this group initially reported that their family members knew they were guilty.

Use Intrinsic Motivators and Avoid Extrinsic Motivators

Extrinsic rewards are rewards that are contingent on someone engaging in certain behaviour, such as paying them money or giving gifts. Intrinsic rewards are positive internal states (affective or cognitive) that result from engaging in behaviour that one values. The balance produced, for any activity (e.g., employment) in terms of intrinsic reward (e.g., satisfaction) vs. extrinsic reward (e.g., salary) can vary from one person to the next, but also can vary for an individual over time. Social psychological theory and research indicates that intrinsic motivation is more powerful than extrinsic motivation in encouraging behaviour change. Those who participate in new behaviours or activities because they expect some extrinsic reward see the behaviour as purely a means to an end. In some contexts, giving someone an extrinsic reward for a behaviour that previously would have produced intrinsic reward can actually lead to deterioration in motivation. External reward systems, such as privilege systems (Liebling, Muir, Rose, and Bottoms 1999), which do of course serve many useful purposes in secure settings, may not always be an effective way to encourage participation in correctional treatment. In our focus groups, treatment participants acknowledged that they enjoyed the privileges they had earned by taking part in treatment. But they also tended to miss the point of an incentive system, believing that the system they had experienced threatened them with loss of privileges if they failed to comply, rather than offering them privileges for compliance. Because of this view, some prisoners reported that they felt more suspicious about treatment if they were threatened with removing privileges for refusing. As they saw it, "Treatment can't be that good if you have to force someone into doing it." They suggested that incentive schemes cloud the decision about whether to enter treatment because "you feel backed into a corner." Another group felt that incentives should not be linked to treatment because this practice rejects the ethos of treatment, which teaches people to make their own choices about how they behave. It seems clear that any incentive scheme that is linked to treatment participation should operate consistently so that the scheme rewards compliance, rather than punishing non-compliance.

Intrinsic motivation can be enhanced by assisting people to explore their intrinsic values and drawing links between the activities of a treatment programme and the benefits that are intrinsically desired. Again, Ward's Good Lives Model of treatment provides an excellent demonstration of this principle.

Utilise Treatment Graduates
Our focus groups yielded very strong consensus about the valuable role that treatment graduates can play in motivating and informing others about what to expect from treatment. As noted above, the focus groups suggested that a DVD of treatment participants talking about their experiences in treatment would have a greater impact on those contemplating treatment than any amount of urging or persuading by staff. Treatment graduates can also be used as mentors to those earlier in treatment. As Fernandez and Marshall (2000) noted, such a role provides sexual offenders who have had a positive

treatment experience with the opportunity to use their new found interpersonal and empathy skills to provide support and nurturance to others.

Provide Choice
One of the founding principles of motivational interviewing is that the client is responsible for choosing and carrying out personal change (Miller and Rollnick 1991). To apply this principle to sex offender treatment means that ideally treatment would be voluntary. Paradoxically, the potential clients of our programmes may be more likely to enter treatment if they feel they are free to refuse treatment. However, in many settings sex offender treatment is compulsory, and in this situation, it is important that the treatment process itself explicitly seeks to offer choices *within* treatment where possible.

Explore and Monitor the Motivations of Treatment Staff
In this chapter, I have made certain assumptions about the values of sex offender treatment programmes. I have assumed, for instance, that such programmes do respect the human rights of offenders, and are interested in offenders' self-actualisation as a concomitant goal with reduced reoffending. However, of course treatment staff are drawn from a wider population where the norm is to abhor sexual offenders. Western culture, in the main, does not draw much of a line between the offender as a human being and the offending that he perpetrates. In effect, offenders are seen as no more than their offending (which I have succumbed to myself, in fact, by referring to them as "offenders" throughout this chapter). Because treatment staff live, work, and relate to others in this culture of offender vilification, they may not be able to resist its influences at all times. This is a unique aspect of sex offender treatment, compared to almost any other therapeutic line of work. Treatment staff can get compassion fatigue, they may find they dislike some of their clients, they may get upset by some of the details that they hear about, and they may disagree strongly with some of their clients' beliefs. They also have personal lives that can go wrong and a significant proportion of them, it can be assumed, have been the victims of sexual abuse or know someone who has been. In this climate, treatment staff can have "good" periods, where they fully demonstrate the values of treatment and fully recognise the human rights of their clients. They will

also have bad periods where they feel distressed, angry, or punitive. Pithers (1997) has documented what can happen in a sex offender treatment programme when the goals of treatment start to slip. If we want to increase the uptake of treatment, we need to ensure that the treatment we provide is as it should be. This requires treatment, and treatment staff, to be monitored closely.

Conclusions

In this chapter, I have deliberately avoided straying too far into commentary on the content or design of treatment. I have focused instead on the less well-documented issue of the external context in which a treatment programme is provided. It is clear that treatment context provides a significant proportion of the explanation for treatment refusal. It is also clear that addressing contextual issues requires the involvement of those who manage the wider system in which treatment is located, as treatment providers alone are not able to overcome all these obstacles. Despite the considerable barriers facing those who have been convicted of a sexual offence, the fact that so many do seek treatment and report it to have been beneficial (Wakeling, Webster, and Mann 2005; Robbers 2008) is extremely encouraging.

Acknowledgments

The author gratefully acknowledges the following contributors to the projects described in this chapter: Steve Webster, Helen Wakeling, Helen Keylock, Dave Atkinson, Caroline Schofield, Lindsay Leigh, Alan Flynn, Julia Long, and Rebecca Milner. I would also like to thank Jo Shingler and Lori Chilton for their helpful comments on an earlier draft of this chapter.

REFERENCES

Bebbington, P. E. 1995. The content and context of compliance. *International Clinical Psychopharmacology* 9:41–50.

Erez, E. 1987. Rehabilitation in justice: The prisoner's perspective. *Journal of Offender Counselling, Services and Rehabilitation* 11(22):5–19.

Fernandez, Y. M., and W. L. Marshall. 2000. Contextual issues in relapse prevention treatment. In *Remaking relapse prevention with sex offenders*, ed. D. R. Laws, S. M. Hudson, and T. Ward, 225–35. Thousand Oaks, CA: Sage Publications.

Jones, L. 2002. An individual case formulation approach to the assessment of motivation. In *Motivating offenders to change*, ed. M. McMurran, 31–54. New York: John Wiley.

Langevin, R. 2006. Acceptance and completion of treatment among sex offenders. *International Journal of Offender Treatment and Comparative Criminology* 50:402–17.

Langevin, R., D. Paitich, S. Hucker, S. Newman, G. Ramsay, S. Pope, G. Geller, and C. Anderson. 1979. The effects of assertiveness training, provera and sex of therapist in the treatment of genital exhibitionism. *Journal of Behavior Therapy and Experimental Psychiatry* 10:275–82.

Liebling, A., G. Muir, G. Rose, and A. E. Bottoms. 1999. Incentives and earned privileges for prisoners: An evaluation. *Home Office Research Findings* 87. London: Home Office.

Lord, A., and P. Willmot. 2004. The process of overcoming denial in sex offenders. *Journal of Sexual Aggression* 10:51–61.

Mann, R. E., S. D. Webster, H. C. Wakeling, and H. Keylock. Forthcoming. *Why do sex offenders refuse treatment?*

Maruna, S. 2001. *Making good: How ex-convicts reform and rebuild their lives.* Washington, DC: American Psychological Association.

Maruna, S., and R. E. Mann. 2006. A fundamental attribution error? Rethinking cognitive distortions. *Legal and Criminological Psychology* 11:155–77.

Maslow, A. 1968. *Toward a psychology of being.* New York: Van Nostrand.

Miller, W. R., and S. Rollnick. 2002. *Motivational interviewing: Preparing people to change addictive behaviour.* New York: Guilford Press.

Munetz, M. R., and L. H. Roth. 1985. Informing patients about tardive dyskinesia. *Archives of General Psychiatry* 42:866–71.

Nations, M. K., and C. M. G. Monte. 1996. "I'm not dog, no!": Cries of resistance against cholera control campaigns. *Social Science & Medicine* 43:1007–24.

Pithers, W. D. 1997. Maintaining treatment integrity with sexual abusers. *Criminal Justice and Behavior* 24:24–51.

Robbers, M. L. P. 2009. Lifers on the outside: Sex offenders and disintegrative shaming. *International Journal of Offender Therapy and Comparative Criminology* 53:5–28.

Rogers, C. 1961. *On becoming a person: A therapist's view of psychotherapy.* Boston: Houghton Mifflin.

Rogers, R., and R. Dickey. 1991. Denial and minimisation among sex offenders: A review of competing models of deception. *Annals of Sex Research* 4:49–63.

Schwaebe, C. 2005. Learning to pass: Sex offenders' strategies for establishing a viable identity in the prison general population. *International Journal of Offender Therapy and Comparative Criminology* 49:614–25.

Shearer, R. A. 1999. Resistance to counselling by offenders who abuse substances. *Annals of the American Psychology Association* 2:7.

Siddall, J. W., and G. L. Conway. 1988. Interactional variables associated with retention and success in residential drug treatment. *International Journal of the Addictions* 23:1241–54.

Spirings, E. L. H., and L. F. Miree. 1993. Non-compliance with follow-up and improvement after treatment at a headache centre. *Headache* 33:205–9.

Wakeling, H. C., S. D. Webster, and R. E. Mann. 2005. Sexual offenders' treatment experience: A qualitative and quantitative investigation. *Journal of Sexual Aggression* 11:171–86.

Ward, T. 2002. Good Lives and the rehabilitation of sex offenders. In *Sexual deviance: Issues and controversies*, ed. T. Ward and S. Hudson. Thousands Oaks, CA: Sage Publications.

Ward, T., and R. E. Mann. 2004. Good Lives and the rehabilitation of sex offenders: A positive approach to treatment. In *Positive psychology in practice*, ed. A. L. Linley and S. Joseph. Hoboken, NJ: Wiley.

Ward, T., R. E. Mann, and T. A. Gannon. 2007. The Good Lives model of offender rehabilitation: Clinical implications. *Aggression and Violent Behavior* 12:87–107.

Using the Good Lives Model to Motivate Sexual Offenders to Participate in Treatment

Pamela M. Yates

It is essential in the rehabilitation of sexual offenders to offer treatment that has the potential to alter behavior so as to reduce the likelihood of future offending. Currently, available research suggests that treatment that is most likely to be effective is cognitive–behavioral in its approach (Hanson et al. 2002; Lösel and Schmucker 2005) and is matched to offenders' levels of risk, criminogenic needs, and personal characteristics (i.e., the Risk–Need–Responsivity (RNR) model; Andrews and Bonta 2006; Hanson 2006). Treatment that meets these two conditions has been shown to be more effective in reducing recidivism than treatment that does not.

Cognitive–behavioral treatment involves sexual offender specific interventions to alter cognition, beliefs, affect, and behavior, and to develop targeted skills such that the likelihood of resolving problems associated with offending is reduced (see Marshall, Anderson, and Fernandez 1999; Yates 2002; Yates et al. 2000). Current effective treatment of sexual offenders focuses on changing known risk factors associated with re-offending—such as antisocial attitudes, intimacy deficits, and sexual deviance—and varies in intensity to match individual static and dynamic risk levels and factors, and is responsive to individual offenders' personal and interpersonal circumstances, abilities, learning styles, and characteristics (see Hanson 2006; Hanson and Yates 2004; Yates et al. 2000). In addition, treatment that is delivered by skilled, pro-social therapists who demonstrate such characteristics as warmth, empathy, and directiveness, and who are positively reinforcing and use supportive but non-confrontational challenging, is also associated with improved progress in treatment (Hanson 2006; Marshall 2005; Marshall et al. 2003). Lastly, as discussed throughout this book, the use of specific strategies designed to increase motivation to participate in treatment is also essential to working with sexual offenders. As such, it is evident that there are multiple and various characteristics associated both with treatment and with its delivery that increases the likelihood of engaging offenders in treatment and reducing recidivism.

Within this context, it is important that treatment is tailored to individual responsivity characteristics. Responsivity is defined by personal characteristics, such as specific competencies, learning styles, and personalities, which individuals present prior to treatment (Andrews and Bonta 2006). Although responsivity in many treatment programs is often narrowly defined as a focus predominantly on motivation, other responsivity factors are important to address, and treatment styles and modes of delivery must be matched to these factors in order to be effective. For example, specific treatment methods, such as individual versus group intervention or insight oriented treatment versus more concrete approaches, should be varied in order to respond effectively to offenders' personal characteristics so as to increase the likelihood of maximal benefit from treatment.

Although several possible offender responsivity characteristics should be addressed in treatment, it is essential for treatment providers to motivate offenders to engage and participate in treatment, particularly since sexual offenders may not possess internal motivation to engage with the treatment process, at least initially (Prescott 2007, 2008; Thornton 1997; Yates forthcoming), and may not therefore be willing to undertake the complex and difficult process of change. Importantly, research indicates that individuals who do not complete sexual offender treatment re-offend at higher rates than individuals who complete treatment (Hanson and Bussière 1998; Hanson et al. 2002), a finding that emphasizes the need on the part of therapists to inculcate and enhance motivation among sexual offenders to participate in, and to complete, treatment. As can be seen throughout this collection of writings, numerous approaches and methods are available to therapists to enhance motivation. The present chapter provides an overview of a relatively recent treatment approach, the Good Lives Model (GLM; Ward and Gannon 2006; Ward and Stewart 2003), and the potential of this model to enhance the motivation of offenders to participate in sexual offender treatment and to increase responsivity of treatment to offender needs.

The Good Lives Model

As a full review of the Good Lives Model (GLM) is beyond the scope of this chapter, the reader is referred to Ward and Stewart (2003) and Ward and Gannon (2006). The GLM was developed in response to analysis of current treatment approaches and the identification of potential shortcomings to these approaches. Specifically, analysis of the RNR model suggested that its focus on risk reduction, while necessary to treatment, is unlikely to be sufficient to fully engage and motivate offenders and to inculcate long-lasting change (Mann, Webster, Schofield, and Marshall 2004; Ward and Brown 2004; Ward and Gannon 2006; Ward, Melser, and Yates 2007; Ward and Stewart 2003). It is argued that this approach is unable to provide clinicians with sufficient tools to engage and to work with offenders in therapy as a result of a focus primarily on avoidance goals and risk reduction (e.g., Mann et al. 2004; Ward and Brown 2004; Ward, Mann, and Gannon 2007; Ward, Melser, et al. 2007), and because it ignores the importance of personal identity, agency, and self-directedness in the change process (e.g., Maruna 2001; Ward and Maruna 2007). Current treatment models also pay insufficient attention to the therapeutic alliance. The quality of the therapeutic alliance has been shown, in both general clinical practice and with sexual offenders, to be essential to treatment. The variety of treatment models applied accounts for the significant variance in treatment outcome (Marshall et al. 2003; Wong, Witte, and Nicholaichuk 2002; Yates 2003). When treatment models fail to work, it is usually because they fail to acknowledge that human beings naturally seek and require certain goods in order to live fulfilling and personally satisfying lives (Ward and Stewart 2003; Ward, Yates, and Long 2006).

Lastly, various treatment models are often translated in practice into a "one size fits all" manner that fails to take individual needs into account, thus failing to adhere to the responsivity principle. These problems are exacerbated by the application of a traditional relapse prevention (RP) approach to treatment, which focuses predominantly on the identification and avoidance of situations that may place individuals at risk to re-offend (Laws 2003; Laws and Ward 2006; Yates 2003, 2005, 2007; Yates and Kingston 2005; Yates and Ward 2007).

To augment current models and to achieve greater impact, an integrated approach using both the GLM and the Self-Regulation Model (Ward and Hudson 1998) has been proposed (Ward et al. 2006; Yates and Ward 2008) within an RNR framework and using cognitive–behavioral methods. In this integrated model risk and skills-development are addressed in treatment, but the scope of treatment is expanded to assist offenders in achieving productive and satisfying lives in addition to managing re-offending risks. Consistent with current effective practice, this model utilizes a cognitive–behavioral, risk–needs–responsivity approach that is skills based. It targets those risk factors that are demonstrated—both empirically and in an individual case—to be associated with risk to re-offend, and it emphasizes a collaborative approach that involves establishing a strong therapeutic alliance and using effective clinical approaches and methods (Andrews and Bonta 2006; Beech and Fordham 1997; Hanson 2006; Hanson et al. 2002; Hanson and Yates 2004; Lösel and Schmucker 2005; Marshall et al. 1999; Shingler and Mann 2006; Ward, Mann, et al. 2007; Yates 2003; Yates et al. 2000).

The Good Lives Model is a strengths-based, positive psychological approach to rehabilitation, in which the aim of treatment is to enhance individuals' capacity to live meaningful, constructive, and satisfying lives, once equipped with the necessary resources to achieve well-being in socially acceptable and personally satisfying ways (Aspinwall and Staudinger 2003; Ward and Gannon 2006; Ward and Stewart 2003). The GLM proposes that all individuals, including sexual offenders, are active, goal-oriented beings who seek to achieve specific goals in life. These goals (termed *primary human goods* in the model) are actions, states, or experiences that are inherently beneficial and that are sought for their own sake rather than as the means to some other ends (Arnhart 1998; Deci and Ryan 2000; Emmons 1999; Schmuck and

Sheldon 2001). Examples of primary human goods include relatedness, mastery, happiness, and autonomy (Emmons 1999; Nussbaum 2000; Ward and Stewart 2003). Instrumental, secondary goods represent the concrete means or strategies used to pursue and achieve primary human goods. For example, an individual may seek employment in a specific area of interest to him in order to meet a need for mastery in work through the process of acquiring the goods of knowledge and autonomy. In pursuing the primary good of relatedness, individuals may seek to establish a variety of personal relationships, such as friendships or intimate/sexual relationships. Within the GLM, sexual offending is regarded as reflecting socially unacceptable attempts to pursue such primary human goods (goals), the shape of which activities results from the individual's developmental history and specific problems in acquiring goods (Ward and Brown 2004; Ward and Gannon 2006; Ward and Stewart 2003; Yates and Ward 2008).

A central notion, therefore, in the application of the GLM to the treatment of sexual offenders is that treatment aims to enhance individuals' well-being and capacity to attain a satisfying life, in tandem with risk management (Ward, Melser, et al. 2007; Ward et al. 2006; Yates and Ward 2008). Fundamental to treatment within the GLM framework is the notion of a *Good Lives plan* or *Good Lives conception*—an individual's (typically implicit) plan for living, which incorporates important and valued goods that they, as active psychological agents, seek to achieve and that lead to meaningful, satisfactory, and worthwhile lives that are not conducive to offending (Ward and Gannon 2006; Ward and Stewart 2003; Ward et al. 2006). The Good Lives plan or conception represents a type of "blueprint" that includes broad ideas of both the individual's personal identity and those goals and activities that are important in achieving the type of life the individual would like to attain. Failure to acquire certain goods and to effectively implement the Good Lives plan results from specific problems inherent in the Good Lives conception or its implementation and in the manner by which individuals seek to attain human goods. That is, within the GLM, problems encountered are not the goods or goals in and of themselves, but rest with actions and capacity to attain goods and achieve goals.

The GLM proposes specific flaws in individuals' Good Lives plans that reflect problems in the manner by which individuals pursue primary human goods and seek to meet their needs. In the case of individuals who offend sexually, it is hypothesized that problems acquiring primary goods and implementing the Good Lives conception reside in four major types of difficulties. The first type of problem reflects the means used to secure primary human goods (i.e., secondary or instrumental goods and associated actions). Specifically, this problem reflects either an individual's deficits in ability or capacity to attain goods and/or the specific behavior in which the individual engages in order to achieve goods. For example, an individual may highly value intimacy (the primary human good of relatedness), which, as a result of developmental history or deficits in the capacity to establish adult relationships, the individual achieves via establishing intimate relationships with children. The second type of flaw represents a problem with the scope or the variety of primary goods the individual seeks. In these cases, important goods are not highly valued by the individual and are not included in the individual's Good Lives plan, resulting in a narrow plan and chronic dissatisfaction or lack of a sense of fulfillment. Thus, the individual shapes an unbalanced life with crucial goods not included in his lifestyle. For example, the individual may not consider interpersonal relationships to be important and, therefore, does not pursue such relationships. That decision results in social isolation or in a lack of intimacy or positive social contacts in his life. In addition, such individuals may place too great a value on a particular good, such as sexual activity, with little or no emphasis on acquiring other goods, an imbalance that causes him dissatisfaction. The third type of problem (coherence) represents conflict among goods sought. It occurs when individuals simultaneously attempt to attain goods in ways that are incompatible, a process that inhibits the attainment of one or more goods and results in psychological distress. For example, individuals who highly value both intimate relationships as well as autonomy with respect to sexual freedom or even autonomy with respect to a relationship itself are likely, as a result, to experience conflict in a relationship and perhaps its ultimate demise and subsequent feelings of loneliness or loss of intimacy. The last problem represents a lack of skills or capacity to attain valued goods as a result of the absence of psychological, social, or other resources. Lack of capacity can be *internal* (e.g., specific skill deficits or problematic attitudes) or *external* (e.g., poor social support or lack of educational and work opportunities). Examples of lack of capacity include impulsivity or deficits in general or sexual self-regulation (internal capacity), a social network that includes negative influences or antisocial peers (external capacity), or an inability to adapt and adjust to changes in life circumstances as these arise. As indicated above, these flaws negatively affect individuals' abilities to acquire primary human goods and/or lead individuals to attempt to attain goods in harmful and socially unacceptable ways. In addition, these flaws may manifest specific risk factors for sexual offending that require intervention in treatment. Thus, the GLM proposes that sexual offending results from failed attempts to attain valued goods and suggests that there is a relationship between these failed attempts and dynamic risk factors for offending. For example, the dynamic risk factor of poor general self-regulation may reflect flawed means used to attain autonomy (e.g., via aggression) or a lack of internal capacity to regulate behavior or emotional responses (e.g., impulsivity or poor problem solving). From the perspective of the GLM, dynamic risk factors represent the distortion or absence of the internal and external conditions required to secure certain human goods. Impulsivity therefore suggests that an individual lacks self-regulation skills and is, therefore, unable to function autonomously, resulting in problems reflecting on one's situation, developing a plan to secure the goods that will meet needs, putting a plan into action in a specific environment, and/or evaluating the adequacy of the plan and revising it, if necessary. Thus, the good of autonomy remains unmet, and the individual continues to attempt to attain autonomy via flawed means, manifesting as the dynamic risk factor of poor self-regulation.

Typically in sexual offender treatment, dynamic risk factors are assessed prior to treatment, are targeted for change in treatment, and are monitored for stability in supervision and ongoing evaluation of risk and its manageability. Within the GLM, dynamic risk factors are conceptualized as internal or external obstacles that frustrate or block the achievement of primary human goods and that are markers of some form of impairment or problem in the Good Lives conception or plan. The presence of risk factors, therefore, functions as "red flags" and alerts clinicians to problems in the way offenders seek to achieve primary human goods and to construct meaningful and purposeful lives. So, although the activity is harmful, the good sought is regarded as a common, acceptable human pursuit that individuals are unable to attain via non-offending means. Within the GLM, it is therefore suggested that strengthening individuals' capacity to attain primary human goods will reduce the influence of dynamic risk factors and, as a result, help them to desist from further offending (Ward and Gannon 2006; Ward and Maruna 2007; Ward, Polaschek, and Beech 2006).

Viewed in this way, the link between primary human goods and dynamic risk factors becomes evident, and the need to address both human needs and risk management in the treatment of sexual offending is evident. Within the GLM approach, it is essential that therapists construct, in collaboration with clients, a positive, strengths-based treatment plan (i.e., one that builds capabilities and internal and external resources) that motivates offenders to achieve valued goods and goals in ways that are socially acceptable and personally meaningful. Treatment, therefore, focuses on planning across the multiple domains of a person's life rather than solely on the elimination or management of individual risk factors. It is suggested that proceeding in this manner will be more effective in assisting offenders to live better lives, will result in lowered risk, and will be more effective in motivating offenders to participate in treatment than traditional cognitive–behavioral or relapse prevention programs (Ward and Maruna 2007; Ward et al. 2006; Yates and Ward 2007).

The Good Lives Model and Treatment

Treatment using the integrated Good Lives/Self-Regulation approach (Ward et al. 2006; Yates and Ward 2008) involves five broad steps. First, the offender must learn to think of himself as someone who can attain important primary human goods in socially acceptable and personally satisfying ways. That is, he must come to believe that change is both possible and worthwhile. Second, the offender learns about the ways in which he has pursued primary goods in the past, and the influence of his goals, strategies, behaviors, and self-regulation capacity on achieving those goals. Third, treatment helps offenders to develop the scope, strategies, coherence, and abilities necessary to construct and implement a Good Lives plan (i.e., addressing the four flaws in the Good Lives plan that lead to lack of goal fulfillment and the related dynamic risk factors). In doing so, individuals' offending is understood within in the context of a problematic or unhealthy Good Lives conception when offending occurred and/or throughout the individual's life, and treatment goals include activities designed to help the offender to construct and attain a healthy Good Lives plan (i.e., to resolve flaws in the Good Lives plan and learn to meet valued goals). Fourth, the offender must explicitly understand patterns of behavior, risk factors, self-regulation style and capacity, and the relationship of these to both offending and attempts to attain primary goods. Lastly, treatment assists the individual to develop strategies and skills to achieve pro-social and personally meaningful goals and to manage risk while working toward the implementation of a healthy Good Lives plan.

Treatment within the integrated GLM begins with comprehensive pre-treatment assessment that results in a provisional case conceptualization or formulation (Ward et al. 2006; Yates and Ward 2008). While conducting this assessment, treatment is framed as an activity that will help individuals live better lives. Primary and secondary goods are explicitly assessed and individuals are informed that treatment will assist them to achieve these goals. Framed in this way, it is expected that treatment using the GLM will be more motivating to offenders than predominantly risk-based treatment, since it is explicitly presented to offenders as a means to improve their lives and achieve their goals. In addition to evaluating traditional concerns such as dynamic risk and other psychological factors, pre-treatment evaluation also includes assessment of individuals' goals, the importance of various primary human goods in their lives, the manner in which they achieve these goods (i.e., secondary goods), problems or flaws acquiring goods, and the relationship between primary goods and offending (Yates, Kingston, and Ward 2009).

Following assessment, a case conceptualization or formulation is constructed that examines Good Lives goals, treatment targets, and treatment strategies that are differentially developed and implemented in accordance with the individual's self-regulation capacities and responsivity factors (Ward et al. 2006; Yates et al. 2009). The aim of this case formulation is to provide a comprehensive understanding of individual offenders' Good Lives plans, goals with respect to this plan, goals with respect to offending, risk factors, internal and external capabilities and constraints, and the inter-relationships between these factors. The individual's Good Lives plan will direct and shape the intervention conducted. The case conceptualization includes both risk management and Good Lives goals that will form the targets of treatment. The treatment plan resulting from the case conceptualization is shaped to individuals' interests, and treatment activities, such as homework assignments, are tailored to individual needs as well as risk factors. This approach is consistent with the responsivity principle generally (Andrews and Bonta 2006), and is expected to increase the salience of treatment and its personal meaning to the individual, thus serving to enhance motivation and engagement (Yates et al. 2000).

Building on this assessment and case conceptualization, treatment then proceeds to implement common components, such as analysis of offense dynamics (e.g., offence cycle or progression), self-regulation, intimacy and relationships, sexuality, cognition, and so forth (Yates 2003; Yates et al. 2000; Marshall et al. 1999), in a manner that is structured and directive but also tailored to the individual. Treatment within the GLM framework thus includes components designed to target risk factors, and it utilizes cognitive–behavioral methods and approaches such as assisting offenders to understand their offense patterns and developing strategies to deal with problematic areas and to prevent reoffending. What is different within the GLM framework is that treatment is not exclusively focused on problems, but also incorporates the various primary goods that the individual has identified as important in his life, and works explicitly to assist him to develop strategies to actively attain these goals. In addition, treatment focuses on helping offenders resolve flaws in their Good Lives plans and to develop the internal and external capacity and conditions conducive to achieving these goods, taking into account their lives and environmental contexts. Individuals' existing strengths and abilities are explicitly recognized and built upon in treatment. Therapists reinforce these existing skills and strengths so that they become entrenched in the individual's repertoire as methods to manage risk and achieve goals. Lastly, treatment helps offenders to develop a more adaptive personal identity that allows for a sense of meaning and fulfillment (Maruna 2001). Such a focus on developing a "success identity" or establishing a concept of their "ideal self" (Haaven and Coleman 2000) will assist in fulfilling basic needs and increasing self-efficacy such that the individual is better able to adjust his behavior to achieve success (Carver and Scheier 1990; Haaven and Coleman 2000) as well as to enhance functioning. Thus, treatment is viewed as an activity that adds to an offender's repertoire, rather than being focused on removing, avoiding, or managing problems (Ward, Mann, et al. 2007). The aim is to return the individual to as normal a level of functioning as possible, and to only place restrictions on activities that are linked to offending and problematic behavior (Ward, Mann, et al. 2007).

Implicit in the GLM is the notion of establishing approach goals through treatment. As noted above, treatment within the traditional RNR and RP models focuses on risk management via the identification and management (particularly avoidance) of problems. Although this is an appropriate and necessary focus of treatment in implementing the GLM approach, treatment also deliberately focuses on developing approach goals to assist offenders in attaining their goals and living as fulfilling a life as possible, a life in which risk management is employed only when necessary. While avoidance goals are developed as required for risk management, treatment concentrates on prosocial approach goals, which are more readily achieved than avoidance goals (Emmons 1999; Mann 2000; Mann et al. 2004), and on the reinforcement of existing strengths, skills, and capabilities. It is argued that this approach is more likely to create intrinsic motivation for change and reduce the likelihood of motivation for change being solely or predominantly extrinsically driven (e.g., to avoid trouble with the law or to gain release to the community). The reality is that most offenders are much more focused on their own problems and quality of life than on the harm they have caused to the victims of their offenses. Hence, incorporating offenders' goals as well as society's goals into treatment is more likely to tap into offenders' intrinsic motivation for change. Finally, while achieving the goal of reduced recidivism and victim harm, reducing the risk of sexual re-offending is achieved by assisting sexual offenders to develop the skills and capabilities necessary to achieve the full range of primary human goods.

Thus, in the GLM, specific approach goals are developed that assist in the achievement of important goods without offending rather than only the management and avoidance of problems resulting from attempts to achieve such goals. In treatment, this is a particularly important distinction, as avoidance goals (i.e., goals that are defined in terms of preventing a negative or undesirable outcome) are rarely attained and do not result in a sense of satisfaction (Livesley 2003). Such avoidance goals are not reflections of an individual's sense of self or personal identity, and also focus attention on information that signals failure rather than success (Cochran and Tesser 1996). By contrast, approach-oriented goals focus the individual on success and on the realization of desired outcomes, thereby focusing attention on information that signals success and enhancing cognition that is focused on success (Cochran and Tesser 1996). As such, the focus in the GLM on approach goals is more likely to result in increased self-management of risk and active efforts to be successful in managing risk in order to achieve a desired goal (i.e., a particular primary good).

In keeping with this approach, treatment components and activities are framed such that approach goals are integrated fully and opportunities to attain these are available (Ward, Mann, et al. 2007). Thus, for example, the establishment of group norms and rules at the start of treatment is conducted such that the primary goods of community, agency/autonomy, and relatedness are important elements of treatment, with group norms and conduct including the means to attain these (i.e., expected conduct of group members) included. For example, to establish the good of agency, group members themselves develop the rules, norms, and expected conduct, and are responsible for the management of these in the group. Work on deviant sexual arousal and fantasy includes explicit discussion of positive skills development to attain satisfying sexual activity (personalized to individual offenders) in addition to development and rehearsal of strategies to manage deviant arousal or fantasy when this occurs. Components that traditionally focus on deficits—such as intimacy, social competency, and empathy—go beyond identifying deficits and problems and work to develop strategies to overcome these issues. Such treatment also includes discussion, reinforcement, and refinement of strengths and the addition of skills to actively work toward establishing positive, pro-social, approach goals in these areas. Thus—as with current practices—offenders who receive treatment that utilizes the GLM develop a plan that includes strategies to manage behavior that is based on an understanding of offense dynamics and skills developed (typically referred to as a relapse prevention plan). However, this plan is framed as a *Good Lives plan* or *plan for living* that is based on individuals' valued goods and that includes approach goals and strategies to attain these goods in addition to more traditional risk-based skills. Clinicians utilizing this approach suggest that, in addition to monitoring risk and potential relapse during post-treatment maintenance and community supervision, monitoring of the successful implementation of the Good Lives plan also be conducted to ensure the individual is actively working toward attaining psychological well-being and a satisfying life (Yates and Ward 2008).

Consider the example of a child molester who has offended against children, with pre-treatment assessment determining that the main dynamic risk factors are intimacy deficits and lack of social support. Relatedness, including both intimate and non-intimate relationships, is very important to the individual, but he does not place a strong value or weight on the good of community connections more generally. Autonomy and independence are also very important to him, as is mastery in work. Within a strict risk management paradigm (such as RP within the RNR approach), this individual would be taught to recognize high-risk situations (e.g., access to children, feelings of loneliness) and would learn strategies to avoid or escape such situations and to deal more effectively with loneliness. For example, he may be taught to differentiate between loneliness and being alone, learn the benefits associated with being alone, learn cognitive self-talk to counter feelings of loneliness when these emerge, and learn to "enjoy" or be comfortable being alone. With respect to intimacy deficits, the individual would learn to identify these and to avoid and counter thoughts of intimate relationships and sexual activity with children via cognitive restructuring. In some extreme cases, the individual might be prohibited from establishing any intimate relationships in an effort to reduce potential risks. The risk management focus associated with such interventions is obvious. Within the GLM, however, the treatment plan and Good Lives plan that results from treatment, while also identifying and developing strategies to cope with risk, would include explicit approach goals to assist this offender to actively seek both intimate and non-intimate relationships (i.e., secondary goods to attain the primary good of relatedness). Because the individual also strongly values autonomy, the specific activities and strategies learned are those that allow him to develop and gain a sense of independence, both in such relationships and more generally. In addition to identifying flaws with respect to attaining relationships (i.e., intimacy deficits), treatment would assist in developing the internal capacity and external opportunities to attain intimacy, such as inculcating skills and strategies to acquire healthy relationships and activities that would increase the probability of encountering adult partners. Furthermore, because the individual does not strongly value community connections in general, the strategies developed would be focused on acquiring individual relationships rather than on such activities as joining larger social groups. Only in extreme cases of very high risk would avoidance of adult partners be promoted, and then only as a temporary measure while risk management and positive strategies are developed. Lastly, because this offender highly values mastery in work, treatment would assist to develop those required skills and, where possible, help him to attain meaningful employment. The job then can assist in meeting the offender's goals and can increase his sense of autonomy and independence, and potentially help in the formation of positive, pro-social relationships.

As is clear in this example, the individual's goals of attaining intimacy and/or sexual satisfaction and autonomy are not regarded as problematic within the GLM approach, but the problems are located in the means the offender has chosen to attain these goals and in his capacity to pursue them. Because these goals are important to the individual, treatment has to develop active strategies to allow the offender to meet these needs, rather than to solely avoid and manage situations that may pose a risk (e.g., avoiding children or intimate activity). Common treatment targets such as intimacy deficits are reframed to more positive approach-oriented objectives of attaining healthy relationships. The offender is regarded as an autonomous individual who is an active participant in developing treatment goals and strategies to achieve valued goods. While this method is generally true within the GLM approach, it is particularly important in the example described, as the individual highly values autonomy and independence. It is evident, then, how the aim of treatment within the GLM is to add to an individual's repertoire, rather than having treatment focused on removing, avoiding, or managing problems. The end goal is to return the individual to as normal a level of functioning as possible, placing restrictions only on activities that are linked to problematic behavior (Ward, Mann, et al. 2007). Such an approach will not only assist individuals to develop a healthy lifestyle and psychological well-being, but also serve to reduce the risk posed because the need can be met appropriately and without offending. As indicated above, it is proposed that using this approach will increase motivation and also result in a lowered need for offending because individuals can lead more fulfilling lives when they are able to meet important needs in their lives.

The Good Lives Model and Motivation

Motivational enhancement has become an important part of intervention in various domains, most notably in the treatment of substance abuse (Miller and Rollnick 1991), although in recent years it has been applied more broadly to other therapies. Motivational interviewing (MI; Miller and Rollnick 2002) and the transtheoretical model of change (Prochaska and Norcross 2004) acknowledge that individuals approach change with differing degrees of readiness and ambivalence, and that this varies both between individuals and within an individual at given moments in time (Arkowitz and Miller 2008). Such ambivalence, fluctuations in motivation, and resistance are regarded as normal aspects of the change process and are expected to occur within treatment. When considering change, individuals weigh the pros and cons and, when the positive aspects of change outweigh the negative, motivation to change increases. In treatment using MI, resistance encountered is regarded as ambivalence, clients' reasons for and against change are regarded as equally valid, and the aim of treatment is to enhance motivation to change by resolving ambivalence and shifting the balance in favor of change (Arkowitz and Miller 2008). Although treatment is directive, it is also a collaborative partnership between the client and the therapist. Treatment aims to create an atmosphere in which clients are viewed as autonomous and in which emphasis is placed on understanding individuals' concerns and their frame of reference (Arkowitz, Miller, Westra, and Rollnick 2008). The therapist creates an atmosphere in which the client, rather than the therapist, is viewed as the agent of change, including when ambivalence and resistance to change emerge (Arkowitz and Miller 2008). Specific techniques are employed to resolve ambivalence, such as the therapist expression of empathy, developing discrepancy between the client's goals or values and his actions—viewing ambivalence and resistance as normal rather than as obstacles to change—and supporting the client's self-efficacy (Miller and Rollnick 2002). In MI there are various specific strategies that are used, depending upon the client's readiness or stage of change. They can include the provision of information and incentives and the use of decisional balance techniques with individuals who have begun to contemplate change (Arkowitz and Miller 2008; DiClemente 1991; Miller and Rollnick 2002).

Motivational interviewing has been found to be effective across a number of problem areas in initiating and invoking behavior change over time (Arkowitz and Miller 2008). Although the approach has been relatively infrequently applied to cognitive–behavioral therapy, motivational interviewing can be combined with this approach (Arkowitz et al. 2008; Leahy 2002) with such groups as sexual offenders and other correctional clients. For example, motivational interviewing can be used as a pretreatment component of cognitive–behavioral intervention as well as throughout treatment when ambivalence and/or resistance to change is encountered. Furthermore, cognitive–behavioral intervention can be delivered in the collaborative clinical style of motivational interviewing (Arkowitz et al. 2008).

This very brief overview of motivational interviewing makes obvious the relationship between motivational enhancement and the GLM and the manner in which these approaches are complementary in treatment. It illustrates the possibility that the application of the GLM to the treatment of sexual offenders holds potential for increasing motivation and engagement. In fact, one basis of the development of the GLM was to enhance motivation to a greater extent than risk/avoidance-based approaches (Ward and Stewart 2003). As indicated previously, and consistent with motivational enhancement approaches, a fundamental principle of the GLM is that individuals are autonomous, goal-seeking beings, and treatment using this approach is explicitly conducted on the assumption that offenders can, and should, be active decision makers in their lives. Similarly, the focus of motivational interviewing interventions on understanding the benefits of change and regarding the client as the agent of change is consistent with the GLM treatment focus as a way for individuals to achieve a good life. In applying the GLM, treatment begins with, and later builds on, assessment of individuals' own goals and valued goods, and treatment planning explicitly includes helping the individual to attain these. Framing treatment in terms of meeting one's goals in life will increase levels of intrinsic motivation, reduce resistance that occurs during treatment, facilitate cost/benefit analysis of change, and permit the resolution of ambivalence toward change. As assessment of primary goods is also linked to offending behavior (Yates et al. 2009), establishing the relationship of primary and secondary goods and dynamic risk factors is also enabled. Individuals come to understand risk in terms of flawed attempts to attain goods, and they learn new strategies and skills to attain goods in non-offending ways as well as to manage risk. Furthermore, the case conceptualization approach described above enables clinicians to understand offending in the context of individuals' lives, and how best to assist them to manage risk and attain goals without offending. Such individual tailoring of treatment thus takes both a directive and client-centered approach, consistent with motivational interviewing, and is also consistent with the responsivity principle generally. This approach is also more likely to increase motivation than a solely risk-based approach by focusing on the benefits of treatment and of change to offenders (i.e., what is "in it" for them), and facilitating shifting the balance in favor of change. Consistent with the principles of motivational interviewing, throughout the course of treatment using the GLM, ambivalence is acknowledged as a normal part of the change process and resistance to the therapist or to therapeutic interventions is regarded as simply a sign of this ambivalence. Using motivational interviewing techniques, the therapist works to shift the direction of ambivalence in favor of change, and the specific technique of developing discrepancy can be linked to change in narrative identity with respect to how individuals see themselves and who they want to be. As such, the underlying principles of the GLM are clearly consistent with the theory and principles of motivational enhancement as well as with its spirit of collaboration and the importance placed on an effective therapeutic relationship with the client in treatment (Shingler and Mann 2006; Ward, Mann, et al. 2007).

In practice, to increase initial engagement and likelihood of treatment participation, pre-treatment and/or introductory GLM/motivational sessions can focus on cognitive–behavioral treatment as a way to assist clients to achieve important goals in their lives, as described previously. Furthermore, in applying the construct of narrative identity (Haaven 2006; Haaven and Coleman 2000; Maruna 2001), treatment can be framed in terms of who the individual is, who he would like to be, and how treatment can assist him to attain this. In these models, the individual is *not* informed that he needs to develop an entirely new personal identity or "new me," but that aspects of his personal identity or "old me" are important and that treatment will build on these. Understanding that he does not need to start over entirely, that he is not a "bad person," that treatment will build on strengths and on what is important to him—and with efforts placed on reinforcing and validating these concepts—the offender's motivation generally will increase and his resistance decrease. Consistent with motivational-enhancement approaches, the individual can then weigh the costs and benefits with respect to change in terms of attaining a good life and a new personal identity, and his ambivalence toward change can be resolved in favor of committing to and actually attempting change. Motivating offenders will be easier if they are reassured in treatment that the goods they seek are acceptable, and that the problem resides in how the goods are sought, rather than in the goals themselves or in their personal identity.

Thus, the Good Lives Model and motivational interviewing are consistent in that both regard the client as active, autonomous, and self-directed and both view the therapist as a collaborator or helper rather than as an expert on the individual offender's life and behavior. Also consistent with motivational interviewing, within the GLM, the language used is reframed to be future-oriented, optimistic, and approach goal oriented (Ward, Mann, et al. 2007). For example, a relapse prevention component of treatment may be termed self-management (Yates et al. 2000) or life change, intimacy deficits reframed as intimacy building (Ward, Mann, et al. 2007), and deviant sexual arousal reconceptualized as healthy sexual functioning. In addition to being consistent with the spirit of motivational enhancement, such language is active and promotes positive thinking with respect to the future as well as to skills development.

In addition to the above, the strong focus in the GLM on establishing approach goals and developing and reinforcing active strategies to attain these is further consistent with motivational enhancement approaches and is expected to increase motivation and engagement with treatment. In addition, as described previously, approach goals are more likely than avoidance goals to increase cognition and behavior that are associated with success, to promote psychological stability when stressful situations are encountered, and, therefore, to increase clients' self-efficacy, a fundamental objective of motivational approaches.

Conclusions

Motivating sexual offenders to participate in and complete treatment is an important and challenging task for clinicians. Intervention that enhances motivation is particularly important since research demonstrates that sexual offenders who do not complete treatment re-offend at higher rates than those who successfully complete treatment, and because shortcomings have been identified in current approaches with respect to motivating offenders to participate in treatment. This chapter provides an overview of the Good Lives Model of sexual offender treatment, which, it is suggested, is an approach that can increase motivation, particularly in comparison to current models focused on risk mitigation and risk avoidance. The GLM is consistent with well-established principles associated with motivational enhancement approaches and it is proposed that this positive psychological model, with its directive yet client-centered focus, which regards offenders as active decision makers and as agents of change in attaining psychological well-being and satisfying lives, will enhance outcome of treatment among this population.

REFERENCES

Andrews, D. A., and J. Bonta. 2006. *The psychology of criminal conduct*. 4th edition. Cincinnati, OH: Anderson.

Arkowitz, H., and W. R. Miller. 2008. Learning, applying, and extending motivational interviewing. In *Motivational interviewing in the treatment of psychological problems*, eds. Arkowitz, Miller, Westra, and Rollnick, 1–25. New York, NY: Guilford.

Arkowitz, H., W. R. Miller, H. A. Westra, and S. Rollnick. 2008. Motivational interviewing in the treatment of psychological problems: Conclusions and future directions. In *Motivational interviewing in the treatment of psychological problems*, eds. Arkowitz, Miller, Westra, and Rollnick, 324–42. New York, NY: Guilford.

Arnhart, L. 1998. *Darwinian natural right: The biological ethics of human nature*. Albany, NY: State University of New York Press.

Aspinwall, L. G., and U. M. Staudinger, eds. 2003. *A psychology of human strengths: Fundamental questions and future directions for a positive psychology*. Washington, DC: American Psychological Association.

Beech, A., and A. S. Fordham. 1997. Therapeutic climate of sexual offender treatment programs. *Sexual Abuse: A Journal of Research and Treatment* 9:219–37.

Carver, C. S., and M. F. Scheier. 1990. Principles of self-regulation: Action and emotion. In *Handbook of motivation and social behavior*, eds. E. T. Higgins and R. M. Sorrentino, 3–52. New York, NY: Guilford.

Cochran, W., and A. Tesser. 1996. The "What the hell" effect: Some effects of goal proximity and goal framing on performance. In *Striving and feeling: Interactions among goals, affect, and self-regulation*, eds. L. L. Martin and A. Tesser, 99–120. New York, NY: Lawrence Erlbaum.

Deci, E. L., and R. M. Ryan. 2000. The "what" and "why" of goal pursuits: Human needs and the self-determination of behavior. *Psychological Inquiry* 11:227–68.

DiClemente, C. C. 1991. Motivational interviewing and stages of change. In *Motivational interviewing: Preparing people to change addictive behaviour*, eds. W. R. Miller and S. Rollnick, 191–202. New York, NY: Guilford Press.

Emmons, R. A. 1999. *The psychology of ultimate concerns*. New York: Guilford.

Haaven, J. 2006. Evolution of old/new me model. In *Practical treatment strategies for forensic clients with severe and sexual behavior problems among persons with developmental disabilities*, ed. G. Blasingame. Oklahoma City, OK: Wood 'N' Barnes Publishing.

Haaven, J., and E. M. Coleman. 2000. Treatment of the Intellectually Disabled Sex Offender. In *Remaking relapse prevention with sex offenders: A sourcebook*, eds. Ward, Hudson, and Laws, 369–88. Thousand Oaks, CA: Sage Press.

Hanson, R. K. 2006. *What works: The principles of effective interventions with offenders*. Presented at the 25th Annual Convention of the Association for the Treatment of Sexual Abusers. Chicago, IL.

Hanson, R. K., and M. Bussière. 1998. Predicting relapse: A meta-analysis of sexual offender recidivism studies. *Journal of Consulting and Clinical Psychology* 66:348–62.

Hanson, R. K., A. Gordon, A. J. R. Harris, J. K. Marques, W. Murphy, V. L. Quinsey, and M. C. Seto. 2002. First report of the collaborative outcome data project on the effectiveness of psychological treatment for sex offenders. *Sexual Abuse: A Journal of Research and Treatment* 14:169–94.

Hanson, R. K., and P. M. Yates. 2004. Sexual violence. Risk factors and treatment. In *Anthology on interventions against violent men*, ed. M. Eliasson. Uppsala, Sweden: Department of Industrial Relations.

Laws, D. R. 2003. The rise and fall of relapse prevention. *Australian Psychologist* 38:22–30.

Laws, D. R., and T. Ward. 2006. When one size doesn't fit all: The reformulation of relapse prevention. In *Sexual offender treatment: Controversial issues*, eds. W. L. Marshall, Y. M. Fernandez, L. E. Marshall, and G. A. Serran, 241–54. Hoboken, NJ: John Wiley & Sons.

Leahy, R. L. 2002. *Overcoming resistance in cognitive therapy*. New York, NY: Guilford.

Livesley, J. W. 2003. *Practical management of personality disorder*. New York, NY: Guilford.

Lösel, F., and M. Schmucker. 2005. The effectiveness of treatment for sexual offenders: A comprehensive meta-analysis. *Journal of Experimental Criminology* 1:117–46.

Mann, R. E. 2000. Managing resistance and rebellion in relapse prevention intervention. In *Remaking relapse prevention with sex offenders: A sourcebook*, eds. D. R. Laws, S. M. Hudson, and T. Ward, 197–200. Thousand Oaks, CA: Sage Press.

Mann, R. E., S. D. Webster, C. Schofield, and W. L. Marshall. 2004. Approach versus avoidance goals in relapse prevention with sexual offenders. *Sexual Abuse: A Journal of Research and Treatment* 16:65–75.

Marshall, W. L. 2005. Therapist style in sexual offender treatment: Influences on indices of change. *Sexual Abuse: A Journal of Research and Treatment* 17:109–16.

Marshall, W. L., D. Anderson, and Y. M. Fernandez. 1999. *Cognitive behavioral treatment of sexual offenders*. Chichester, UK: Wiley.

Marshall, W. L., Y. M. Fernandez, G. Serran, R. Mulloy, D. Thornton, R. E. Mann, and D. Anderson. 2003. Process variables in the treatment of sexual offenders: A review of the relevant literature. *Aggression and Violent Behavior* 8:205–34.

Maruna, S. 2001. *Making good: How ex-convicts reform and rebuild their lives*. Washington, DC: American Psychological Association Books.

Miller, W. R., and S. Rollnick. 1991. *Motivational interviewing: Preparing people to change addictive behavior*. New York, NY: Guilford.

———. 2002. *Motivational interviewing: Preparing people for change*. 2nd edition. New York, NY: Guilford.

Nussbaum, M. C. 2000. *Women and human development: The capabilities approach*. New York, NY: Cambridge University Press.

Prescott, D. S. 2007. Getting back on track: Addressing treatment-interfering factors in a group setting. In *Applying knowledge to practice: The treatment and supervision of sexual abusers*, ed. D. Prescott, 201–21. Oklahoma City, OK: Wood and Barnes.

———. 2008. A group for integrating treatment lessons into daily life. *Forum* XX (Fall). Beaverton, OR: Association for the Treatment of Sexual Abusers.

Prochaska, J., and J. Norcross. 2004. *Systems of psychotherapy: A transtheoretical analysis*. 5th edition. New York, NY: Wadsworth.

Schmuck, P., and K. M. Sheldon. 2001. *Life goals and well-being*. Toronto, ON: Hogrefe & Huber Publishers.

Shingler, J., and R. E. Mann. 2006. Collaboration in clinical work with sexual offenders: Treatment and risk assessment. In *Sexual offender treatment: Controversial issues*, eds. W. L. Marshall, Y. M. Fernandez, L. E. Marshall, and G. A. Serran, 225–39. Hoboken, NJ: Wiley.

Thornton, D. 1997. *Is relapse prevention really necessary?* Paper presented at the meeting of the Association for Sexual Abusers. Arlington, VA.

Ward, T., and M. Brown. 2004. The Good Lives model and conceptual issues in offender rehabilitation. *Psychology, Crime, & Law* 10:243–57.

Ward, T., and T. Gannon. 2006. Rehabilitation, etiology, and self-regulation: The Good Lives Model of sexual offender treatment. *Aggression and Violent Behavior* 11:77–94.

Ward, T., and S. M. Hudson. 1998. The construction and development of theory in the sexual offending area: A metatheoretical framework. *Sexual Abuse: A Journal of Research and Treatment* 10:47–63.

Ward, T., Mann, R., and T. Gannon. 2007. The Good Lives Model of offender rehabilitation: Clinical implications. *Aggression and Violent Behavior* 12:87–107.

Ward, T., and S. Maruna. 2007. Rehabilitation: Beyond the risk-paradigm. *Key ideas in criminology series,* series editor, Tim Newburn. London: Routledge.

Ward, T., J. Melser, and P. M. Yates. 2007. Reconstructing the risk need responsivity model: A theoretical elaboration and evaluation. *Aggression and Violent Behavior* 12:208–28.

Ward, T., D. L. L. Polaschek, and A. R. Beech. 2006. *Theories of sexual offending.* Hoboken, NJ: John Wiley & Sons.

Ward, T., and C. A. Stewart. 2003. The treatment of sex offenders: Risk management and Good Lives. *Professional Psychology: Research and Practice* 34:353–60.

Ward, T., P. M. Yates, and C. A. Long. 2006. *The self-regulation model of the offence and relapse process. Volume II: Treatment.* Victoria, BC: Pacific Psychological Assessment Corporation. Available at www.pacific-psych.com.

Wong, S., T. Witte, and T. P. Nicholaichuk. 2002. *Working alliance: Utility in forensic treatment programs.* Ottawa, ON: National Health Services Conference.

Yates, P. M. 2002. What works: Effective intervention with sex offenders. In *What works: Risk reduction: Interventions for special needs offenders,* ed. H. E. Allen, 115–63. Lanham, MD: American Correctional Association.

———. 2003. Treatment of adult sexual offenders: A therapeutic cognitive-behavioral model of intervention. *Journal of Child Sexual Abuse* 12:195–232.

———. 2005. Pathways to the treatment of sexual offenders: Rethinking intervention. *Forum* (Summer):1–9. Beaverton, OR: Association for the Treatment of Sexual Abusers.

———. 2007. Taking the leap: Abandoning relapse prevention and applying the self-regulation model to the treatment of sexual offenders. In *Applying knowledge to practice: The treatment and supervision of sexual abusers,* ed. D. Prescott, 143–174. Oklahoma City, OK: Wood 'n' Barnes.

———. Forthcoming. Is sexual offender denial related to sex offence risk and recidivism? A review and treatment implications. *Psychology Crime and Law Special Issue: Cognition and Emotion.*

Yates, P. M., B. C. Goguen, T. P. Nicholaichuk, S. M. Williams, C. A. Long, E. Jeglic, and G. Martin. 2000. *National sex offender programs (moderate, low, and maintenance intensity levels).* Ottawa: Correctional Service of Canada.

Yates, P. M., and D. Kingston. 2005. Pathways to sexual offending. In *The sex offender. Volume 5,* eds. B. K. Schwartz and H. R. Cellini, 3:1–15. Kingston, NJ: Civic Research Institute.

Yates, P. M., D. A. Kingston, and T. Ward. 2009. *The self-regulation model of the offence and re-offence process. Volume III: A guide to assessment and treatment planning using the integrated Good Lives/self-regulation model of sexual offending.* Victoria, BC: Pacific Psychological Assessment Corporation. Available at www.pacific-psych.com.

Yates, P. M., and T. Ward. 2007. Treatment of sexual offenders: Relapse prevention and beyond. In *Therapists' guide to evidence-based relapse prevention,* eds. K. Witkiewitz and G. A. Marlatt, 215–34. Burlington, MA: Elsevier Press.

———. 2008. Good Lives, self-regulation, and risk management: An integrated model of sexual offender assessment and treatment. *Sexual Abuse in Australia and New Zealand: An Interdisciplinary Journal* 1:3–20.

A Treatment Approach for Sexual Offenders in Categorical Denial

Geris A. Serran and Matt D. O'Brien

Introduction

In this chapter, the authors review approaches that have typically been used in sexual offender treatment and compare them to approaches successfully utilized on offenders who categorically deny their sexual offending.

We then critique this treatment approach and provide a discussion of how Marshall, Thornton, Marshall, Fernandez, and Mann (2001) came to develop their innovative approach to treating these clients. We outline our own program's form with reference to Marshall, Marshall, Serran, and Fernandez's (2006) description of their treatment program for admitting sexual offenders. We provide promising early results from this treatment approach. The chapter concludes with a case study that demonstrates treatment gains that clinicians can attain using this approach.

Approaches to Treating Denial

Over time, many therapists in the sexual offender treatment field have come to see denial of offending as a significant barrier to effective treatment. Consequently, many treatment providers have typically excluded deniers from their treatment programs (Happel and Auffrey 1995; Schwartz 1995).

However, as Cohen (1995) argues, this exclusion is neither therapeutically sensible nor legally appropriate. The authors share Cohen's view that every effort should be made to involve all offenders in treatment, since they all pose future threats to others. As Maletzky (1996) states, "To deny a crime is natural; to deny treatment to those who deny is a crime itself."

A number of published studies have considered treatment interventions designed to move convicted and incarcerated sexual offenders from levels of categorical denial to acceptance of responsibility for their sexual offending, so they can then enter programs designed for those who admit to their offences. As Schneider and Wright (2004) summarise, the assumption of most of these approaches is that admitting to the offence is a necessary pre-requisite for successful treatment progress; this position has certainly been offered by Lombardo and DiGiorgio-Miller (1988), Barbaree and Cortoni (1993), and Winn (1996).

One of the earliest reports of treatment of deniers was the intervention described by O'Donohue and Letourneau (1993). This seven-session program included cognitive restructuring and educational components. The authors reported a 65 percent change from denier to admitter status at post-treatment, although the numbers of participants was small (n=17).

Marshall (1994) reported on a 12-week rolling program that focused on acceptance of the client but not the offence. Central to this approach was having a mix of admitters and deniers in the same program. The senior members of the program were seen as pivotal in helping the client to give a disclosure in which he increasingly admitted to further details. Using this approach, the 25 group members who entered the program as deniers were reduced to just two upon completion of the program.

Schlank and Shaw (1996) presented an account of the procedure they employed, which involved 16 sessions focusing on why people deny and providing face-saving ways in which people could change their position. The sessions included a focus on victim empathy and relapse prevention components. In the authors' study, five of the ten clients admitted to their offences, post-intervention.

Brake and Shannon (1997) reported a similar reduction using their pre-treatment program for categorical deniers. The goal of this program was to "lessen denial about the instant offence . . . once this has been accomplished the offender is referred to an offence-specific treatment program." The program consisted of 21 sessions conducted on an individual basis. Brake and Shannon were able to demonstrate that this procedure produced a significant reduction in denial in 54 percent of their participants. The components of this program included: face-saving, motivation about change, explanations of the purpose of denial, reframing, and victim empathy.

Other programs referred to in the literature, but not accompanied by research data, include Jenkins (1990) whose "invitations to responsibility" approach involved three years of individual and group psychotherapy, and Winn (1996), whose approach involved "metaconfrontation," described as "a strategic process of challenging the offender to challenge himself." Other strategies have focused on individual motivational interviewing (Mann, Ginsburg, and Weekes 2002), and individual assessment feedback procedures, including the results of phallometry (Bradford and Greenberg 1998).

The approaches outlined above appeared to have some limited degree of success, as measured by a reduction in denial, but were mostly seen to be lengthy, in some cases somewhat challenging and confrontational, and in hindsight quite possibly unnecessary, given that their goal was clearly founded on an assumption that moving an offender from denial to acceptance is a necessary condition for successful treatment. No evidence is available to confirm that this is the case, and in fact, some evidence actually indicates—perhaps counter intuitively—that this supposition is wrong. Early research suggests that continued denial is predictive of poor treatment outcome (Marshall and Barbaree 1988; Simkins, Ward, Bowman, and Rinck 1989; Barbaree 1991). In contradiction of these early findings, however, Maletzky (1993) found no differences in the long-term outcome of treated deniers versus treated admitters. Kennedy and Grubin (1992) and Beckett, Beech, Fisher, and Fordham (1994) found that reducing denial and minimization did not necessarily equate with changes in other treatment targets. A number of authors have reported that denial of a sexual offence in adolescents actually means that they are less likely to reoffend sexually (Kahn and Chambers 1991; Langstrom and Grann 2000). In their meta-analyses of sexual-offender recidivism studies of primarily adult males, Hanson and Bussiere (1998) and Hanson and Morton-Bourgon (2004) found no relation between denial of the sexual offence and sexual-assault recidivism in both treated and untreated offenders.

A possible reason for these surprising findings was offered by Hanson (2003) who provided some evidence that demonstrates that attitudes tolerant of sexual offending are related to recidivism (Hanson and Harris 2000; Hudson, Wales, Bakker, and Ward 2002). Consequently he reasoned that "excusing one's own behaviour is less problematic than believing that it is okay for others to do the same thing." Some researchers have also argued that equating denial with risk has been a logical fallacy, citing evidence that many high-risk offenders can be quite open about their offending in contrast to some low-risk offenders who have higher levels of denial (Beech and Fisher 2002; Fisher, Beech, and Browne 1998; Simourd and Malcolm 1998).

The evidence negating the need to work to overcome denial, coupled with the need to provide these offenders with effective treatment, led Marshall et al. (2001) to conceive of an alternative approach for treating sexual offenders in categorical denial. The approach was developed in direct response to the fact that other efforts to have them admit responsibility had not proved wholly successful. Thus attempts to get deniers to admit their guilt were abandoned, while the focus remained on therapists addressing pertinent and problematic issues. The support for focusing on the latter was provided by the work of Andrews, Zinger, Hoge, Bonta, Gendreau, and Cullen (1990) in the general offender literature, and by the work of Hanson et al. (2002), Marshall and McGuire (2003), and Losel and Schmucker (2005) in the specific literature on effective approaches with sexual offenders. In other words, the exact same relevant criminogenic needs that would normally be addressed in the treatment of sexual offenders who admit to their offending are also addressed, separately, with the deniers. As outlined below, this approach is predicated on the premise that offenders are not asked to discuss their offence, and their denial is not challenged. By adopting this approach, offenders are not released untreated and at higher risk to reoffend. Laws (2002) suggests that this method of treatment is an extremely clever approach to denial: "By making a simple promise and keeping to it, the therapists engage the clients in a program they say they do not need, for a problem they say they do not have, to prevent another offence that they say they did not commit in the first place."

The "Rockwood" Approach

At Rockwood Psychological Services, the general approach to treating men who have sexually offended is grounded in positive psychology and the Good Lives Model (Ward and Stewart 2003). The foundation of our treatment model is based on group process and emphasizes the importance of therapist characteristics. We encourage group cohesion and a positive group climate. Our approach is flexible and individualized to each client, as opposed to the typical psychoeducational, manualized approach. We emphasize the development of a trusting client–therapist relationship. Our research on therapeutic process in sexual offender treatment demonstrated that positive therapist characteristics were directly related to treatment outcome. Specifically, therapists who displayed warmth, empathy, rewardingness, and directiveness achieved positive treatment change (Marshall, Serran, et al. 2002, 2003).

It is with this foundation that we have developed and implemented our treatment program for deniers.

Deniers' Program Outcome

Our Deniers' Program commenced in 1998 at Bath Institution, a moderate-security institution in Kingston, Ontario, Canada. We had noticed a number of clients refusing treatment because they were categorically denying their offences. Their attitude created a problem, because these clients were therefore "stuck" at Bath. They took up space that could have been used for other potential program candidates, and they were eventually released with no treatment. Often, these men were seen as resistant and treated as such. Some of them stated that they would be willing to participate in programming, but they would not agree to enter a program where they would be forced to admit to their offences.

From 1998 to mid-2005, we had 56 men who completed the Deniers' Program and were released into the community. We run approximately one program each year, consisting of eight participants. Of these, approximately 68 percent were convicted of sexual assault, while the rest had been convicted of some other sexual offence (e.g., indecent exposure), incest, or murder.

Of these 40 percent had adult victims, 37.5 percent had pubescent victims, and 22.5 percent had prepubescent victims. Over half (52.5 percent) were released on their warrant expiry, 40 percent on their statutory release date, and 7.5 percent achieved a day parole. In our follow-up analyses, 87.5 percent did not reoffend sexually, 10 percent breached their conditions, and 2.5 percent reoffended sexually. These results, while preliminary, are extremely promising. We are in the process of expanding our recidivism study.

Our Approach to Treating Denial

In designing our program, we essentially decided to model after our regular program, with one exception: We assured the group members that we would not challenge their denial regarding their sexual offence. Our goal in treatment is to help participants identify problems in their lives that put them in a position to be accused of sexual offending or that generated sufficient animosity in others that someone accused them of an offence they claim they did not commit. This stated goal motivates these men to fully participate in treatment. Consistent with our admitters' program, we address all dynamic factors relevant to sexual offending. In the following pages, we highlight an overview of our program components.

Preparatory Sessions
Initially, the deniers present as suspicious and distrustful of our program. Generally they are quite focused on re-trying their cases. They might appear disinterested (e.g., falling asleep or sitting slumped over) or they might engage in problematic group behaviour (e.g., whispering, giggling, making inappropriate comments). Others fail to engage meaningfully in session discussions. Due to the clinical value of our general preparatory program for readying offenders for treatment, we begin providing several preparatory sessions for the deniers.

These sessions are motivational in nature and provide information about the behaviour that will best contribute to them achieving their goals (e.g., early release). Group rules (confidentiality, participation, attendance, respect) are discussed and group members are encouraged to contribute to building group rules. We also provide group members with information about their treatment, final reports, and risk assessments. We generally follow up with an all-inclusive group exercise, usually on the topic of self-esteem. Although self-esteem is not an explicit dynamic risk factor, per se, it is relevant for other factors, such as relationships and lifestyle. Low self-esteem across various domains also characterizes sexual offenders (Fernandez, Anderson, and Marshall 1999; Marshall, Anderson, and Champagne 1996). Enhancing self-esteem is highly motivational and facilitates other aspects of treatment (Marshall, Anderson, and Fernandez 2000). The domains where self-esteem deficits are evident include relationship functioning, physical appearance, academic and occupational performance, and social functioning. Clients are required to identify several strengths in each area of functioning, and to share those strengths with the group during discussion. This exercise allows the therapist to develop insight into each client's view of himself. Group members are encouraged to identify strategies to improve their confidence, usually through engaging in activities such as sports, creativity, etc. All of these opportunities are available in the institution, and group members are encouraged to pursue them.

Disclosure

Group members begin by providing their versions of the accusations against them. Our purpose is not to challenge their versions. This exercise gives us a good opportunity to demonstrate to the clients that we are not trying to force them to admit to the offence. Doing so would compromise the integrity of the program and damage efforts to engage these difficult clients in treatment. Instead, we focus on themes and key issues, encouraging the clients to explore their decision-making skills and to identify potential poor decisions (e.g., consuming excessive amounts of alcohol, spending time with negative peer groups).

Life Story

Group members are asked to complete an autobiography, which in turn is presented to the group. Men are encouraged to include in their stories both the problems and the successes in their lives. The problem areas they identify help us to determine the specific issues to concentrate on during treatment.

Their strengths are often aspects we can utilize to encourage positive change. One issue we have noticed is the occasional group member who presents with the "perfect" life. This group member is one of the most challenging to work with as he is not willing to acknowledge any responsibility for his life, in general. In this type of case, we would provide direct feedback to each client, telling him that it is important that he understand and identify problem areas in his life. We use strategies of reinforcing successive approximations, so that initially we reinforce any semblance of the behaviour we want, followed by reinforcing more complex behaviours. If our client continues to insist that he has no problems, we explain the consequences of continuing to present as such. Our overall goal is to identify key themes and to use these during the remainder of the program exercises.

Intimacy and Relationships
This aspect of treatment involves a discussion of adult attachment, including a presentation of Bartholomew's four adult styles of attachment (secure, preoccupied, fearful, and dismissive) (Bartholomew and Horowitz 1991). We assist clients in identifying their attachment style and its costs and benefits, and we help them to develop a more secure approach to relationships. We discuss characteristics of a healthy relationship, including trust, communication, the value of equitability, and healthy sexual behaviours. We also address such issues as coping with rejection, loneliness, and jealousy. Group members discuss their previous relationships and are especially encouraged to consider any unhealthy patterns (e.g., numerous casual interactions, tendency to avoid conflict, failure to communicate). Group members identify and practice positive relationship skills, including communication and feedback, compromise, developing trust, and choosing an appropriate partner. Healthy sexuality is discussed in the context of a healthy intimate relationship. Group members are taught that communication and strong intimacy are factors related to increased sexual satisfaction.

Coping Strategies and Emotion Management
Research has demonstrated that sexual offenders have dysfunctional coping strategies (Cortoni and Marshall 1995, 1996; Marshall, Serran, and Cortoni 2000). Inadequate coping creates increased stress and distress, which increases

the likelihood of coping through sex and fantasy (Looman 1999; McKibben, Proulx, and Lusignan 1994). Group members are required to identify problems from their past and describe how they dealt with those problems. The discussion centres on various alternative strategies, and the benefits and costs of those strategies. We discuss the different coping styles (emotion-focused, task-focused, and avoidance-focused) (Endler and Parker 1990). Group members are encouraged to identify strategies they have used that were not especially effective and to learn to develop more effective strategies. Skill building (e.g., assertiveness) and practice are encouraged. Additionally, we encourage clients to identify and appropriately express their emotions in order to develop better emotional regulation.

Victim Harm

We discuss the consequences of victimization in general as opposed to dealing with any specific person. Each client is required to identify the effects of sexual abuse on victims both in the short and long term. The participants are then informed that by understanding those effects, they will be more sensitive to the signs of sexual abuse. This approach will help them to avoid or withdraw from situations where abuse might be occurring so that no one can accuse them of offending. We generally wait until later in the program to address this area—until we have established the trust among our clients that we are not trying to trick them into admitting to the offence.

Problem Analysis

This aspect of treatment is essential, akin to our Understanding of the Offence exercise or the offence analysis. Clients are required to examine the circumstances and their actions around the time of the offence. The goal is to help them identify background problems and action choices made at the time of the offence (e.g., anger, intoxication, perceived failures, problems in relationships). These are in effect the dynamic factors that we want to modify during treatment. Group members are asked to consider lifestyle factors, poor problem solving, poor emotion-management, relationship patterns, and childhood experiences that are relevant.

Group members are then asked to consider factors that would place them at risk of being accused in the future (a risk-factors and awareness exercise).

These factors will differ for each group member although some similarities might be present, as well. The factors could include, for example, having casual sexual relationships, particularly when alcohol is involved; using a computer in an isolated area; having unsupervised contact with minors; feeling depressed, lonely, isolated, or rejected.

Self-Management and Release Planning
Following the problem analysis, group members construct a self-management plan in which they design strategies and learn the behaviours necessary to allow positive approaches. We focus on helping them to build a positive and satisfying lifestyle, noting that this approach will decrease the likelihood of their being falsely accused. Group members are required to set realistic and positive goals for themselves in several domains (knowledge, work, spirituality, relationships, and creativity). Group members are also asked to develop a support network consisting of family, friends, organizations (e.g., John Howard Society, Salvation Army), and professionals (e.g., counsellors). We encourage the development of approach rather than avoidance goals, as these are more motivating and easier to achieve.

Our approach to self-management is centred in Ward and Stewart's (2003) Good Lives Model. By emphasizing the development of skills, attitudes, and beliefs that are supportive of a positive and prosocial lifestyle, group members will be less likely to offend. In a collaborative and constructive manner, we work with each client to help him identify an individualized set of goals consistent with his interests and abilities. Next, we help the client to identify, develop, and practice the skills required to achieve his goals.

Case Study

The following case study describes the application of the approach outlined above for treating a sexual offender who categorically denies committing his offences. The focus is on the problems in the offender's life which led him to being in a position where he could be accused of an offence. By being required to take responsibility for these problematic behaviours, the client achieves the same goal as in our conventional treatment program. The case study illustrates how offenders can be engaged with this approach and confirms how successful treatment can be.

Offending History

Juan (not his real name) was a 39-year-old Hispanic man serving a sentence of four years for sexual interference, sexual assault, and sexual touching. He pled not guilty but was found guilty at jury trial. Juan advised that he was not appealing his conviction or sentence "for purely financial reasons." According to official documentation the victim reported that she met Juan through a chat program on the computer and that she told him that she was age 13. During their conversation he lied and informed her that he was 18 years old. The victim reported that she spoke to him on the computer about once or twice a week for about six months. Eventually they agreed to meet and Juan picked the victim up a short distance from her house. He then took her to his mother's house where he resided. Once at the house they went into his bedroom. Juan met with the victim in this way on about 10 occasions. The sexual offending began with him touching her and quickly progressed to sexual intercourse. The victim disclosed the sexual relationship to a friend who told officials at her school. She explained to the police that she would not have consented to the sexual intercourse had she known his true age. The police found that Juan had been accessing teenage sex sites when they looked at his computer, and additionally found records of sexually suggestive chats he had had with minors.

Presentation

Juan, a teacher, admitted to inviting the victim to his mother's house but stated he did so because he was providing her with private computing tutoring. He said that he had met her after she had answered an internet advertisement for a tutor. According to him, after a few email messages with regard to session dates and payment options, he agreed to pick the victim up, because she told him that she did not have a ride. He admitted that his computer was in his bedroom, in the house he shared with his mother. He stated that this was where all tutoring sessions took place. Juan claimed that after the fourth session he wrote a note to the girl's parents advising them of the amount that they owed for the tutoring. Juan stated that after the girl showed up on the fifth session without payment, he informed her that he was ceasing tuition until payment was received. According to Juan, the police showed up unexpectedly a week later and charged him with sexual offences. Juan stated in interview that he felt that the victim "got herself into a situation," since she had probably told her friends that she was having a relationship with an older male in order to make herself appear popular and attractive. He suggested that she probably then felt unable to retract this "false information" as it would have caused her great embarrassment in front of her family and friends. He adamantly denied any wrongdoing. Of note, his mother firmly believes that her son is innocent. Juan responded well to the two preparatory sessions held before the program proper commenced. By the end of those sessions, it was clear that all remaining suspiciousness about the approach had gone, and he was expressing an interest at developing a better future for himself.

Problem Analysis ("Disclosure")
Juan was asked to discuss what had happened on the days when the alleged offences took place with a view to understanding how he could have placed himself where he could be falsely accused of a sexual offence. Juan's actual disclosure in group was almost verbatim that which he had provided in both his initial assessment and his pre-program interview. When asked afterward if the accusation had taught him anything, he initially stated that he was "stupid" to have his computer in his bedroom as he had come to realise that it did not look good to others that he was taking a girl into his bedroom. "Tutoring young girls in my bedroom was a dumb idea," he said. He stressed his plan to move his computer to a public location so as to avoid the chance of further accusation, which he agreed would be even harder to argue against and would make him look guilty of the first set of offences. He expressed frustration at this situation but appeared to accept it as the way things now would need to be for him. Similarly he discussed how he had come to terms with not being able to teach anymore. He said that this depressed him as he loved to impart knowledge to others. Following a really important group discussion on this, and following a group member's suggestion, Juan became enthused that he could still teach adults and that this could be at least as rewarding. Juan, sensing that perhaps some other group members might question his

version of events, voluntarily stressed that he did not condone sexual activity with young people. He did not initially explain why, however, and so the treatment team invited him to do so. Importantly, Juan then outlined the reasons, saying that to do so would be both morally and legally unacceptable. Juan was then asked, as are all group members in this program, whether there was anything else that he might have done, or ways in which he might have presented, that could have made him more vulnerable to accusation. Juan focused on his passivity, explaining that he has always been a people pleaser, a characteristic of which others have sometimes taken advantage. He elaborated, outlining his tendency toward internalising his problems and withholding them from others. He talked of experiencing some problems with self-esteem, loneliness, and taking on too much work "which leads to stress, which I have difficulty coping with." These problems were treatment targets that were later worked through with Juan.

Life Story (Identification of Relevant Factors)
Juan was invited to share with the group problems he had encountered in his life within the context of providing an autobiography. The treatment team looks out for problems that are long standing and indirectly relevant, or *stable dynamic risk factors*, and those that are immediate precursors to the alleged offence, or *acute dynamic risk factors*. Juan outlined a difficult early childhood in South America prior to moving to Canada with his family when he was eight years old. He talked of experiencing some difficulties in adapting to life in North America, particularly the racism he experienced and the resulting feelings of loneliness and of being an outsider. Juan stated that he had always lived with his mother and confirmed that he planned to return to the family residence after his release from prison. At this stage of the program, he adamantly denied that this goal got in the way of his developing independence or intimacy with others. He recounted that his father was an alcoholic who verbally abused his mother at times and explained that his father's behaviour might relate to Juan's feelings of protectiveness over his mother. To his credit, Juan indicated that he has an ongoing tendency to focus on helping others to the exclusion of ensuring that his own needs were appropriately met. "Ninety-nine percent of the time, if there is a conflict, I am the one to give in. I hate conflict of any kind." He acknowledged that this tendency

had created problems for him and that, as a result, he probably would have a greater need to appropriately assert himself in the future. He also stated again that he has a tendency to internalize problems and consequently withhold them from others. He appeared willing to try to involve others in his problems, and offered to express his emotions to others to a greater degree in the future. Juan was asked to report back to the group on his efforts at having deeper, more open engagement with others on an ongoing basis during the remainder of the program. He clearly found it quite a challenge initially, but over time, he was able to share positive experiences with the group, for which they reinforced him. In summary, although Juan categorically denied responsibility for the offences, he acknowledged responsibility for certain attitudes, emotions, and behaviours that placed him at risk of being accused.

Intimacy and Relationships
During the component of the program that specifically addressed intimacy and relationships, Juan informed the group that he had had three serious intimate relationships in his lifetime. He informed the group that the first of these ended because he was not prepared to commit at that point. The second relationship had apparently ended because his partner chose to return to her native country. Juan described the third relationship as "great" but it was broken off due to her family's concern about inter-racial relationships. He cited this last relationship as an example of a time when he should have been more assertive, and the group agreed. Similarly he said that he was coming to see that in the first two cases he had remained with his partners too long after the relationship had really run its course. Juan clearly grasped the impact of his own loneliness and jealousy on his third relationship, though he gave no indication that either conditions had been a particular problem for him in the past. Juan listed a number of qualities in a future partner that he would consider to be desirable and also added the qualities that he believed he would be able to bring to a relationship himself. He outlined the ways in which he believed he could meet future partners. Other group members took this opportunity to raise the fact with him that he was approaching his 40s and still lived with his mother. Juan, though still clearly resistant to this point, agreed to think it through in more detail before coming to a decision. In another session where attachment styles were the main focus, Juan,

not unlike many other group members, stated that his attachment style was secure, citing evidence that he has never been one to go straight from relationship to relationship. The treatment team sensitively addressed with Juan his aforementioned "people-pleasing" tendencies and preference to "focus on the other person." He acknowledged that he might also have a tendency toward a more preoccupied style, at times, which was a positive outcome, especially since self-esteem issues were to be the next focus on the program.

Self-Esteem

Juan produced an excellent self-esteem assignment in which he outlined a range of positive qualities he possessed, without qualification, across a wide range of dimensions. He also presented with a fairly consistently good level of self-esteem during the program. He did acknowledge, however, with some prompting, that his lack of assertiveness and apparent desire to generally shield his problems and deficiencies from others meant that he did not always feel that he was being attended to himself. Juan updated the group again on his efforts at improving his level of assertiveness. He reported that the efforts were going well and that he felt better about himself—more effective and validated—by what he was doing.

Coping Strategies and Emotion Management

Juan was particularly open to learning and thinking about this element of the program. He said that over the course of the program, he had been coming to recognize that he might be helped by adopting a more communicative coping style at times of stress whereby letting others around him know of his problems in general, or of his problems with them, more specifically. He also said that he could now see that utilizing humour to diffuse situations, while sometimes appropriate, had the capacity to mask the solution to the problem or conflict. He indicated to the group that he was capable of employing good and analytical problem solving much of the time. He appeared to recognize, however, that problems could occur when he spent too much time in analysis before moving into action. He indicated that physical exercise helped him to relieve stress and that his hobbies, while in some ways helping him to avoid thinking about his problems, also gave him some time to further reflect upon them.

Victim Harm
Juan was able to provide a lengthy list of the harmful effects experienced by victims of sexual abuse. His list included the following: nightmares, distrust, intimacy problems, self-loathing, isolation, fear of men, shame, feelings of being out of control, and decreased self-esteem. He took a prominent role in the ensuing discussion and added a number of other likely consequences that he had not previously considered. Juan approached this exercise in a very mature and appropriately serious manner.

Self-Management Plan and Release Planning
Juan came up with what was considered to be a constructive and positive self-management plan. He accepted that a number of key changes needed to be made to his lifestyle so as to minimise the chance of further accusations. For example, he accepted that he would no longer be able to tutor children, should not be around children without other suitable adults being present, should limit his alcohol intake at parties, and should move his computer to a more communal area in the house and avoid chat rooms. In addition to these more avoidance-focused strategies Juan set out a number of more approach-goal and appropriate future-oriented strategies aimed at ensuring that he would lead a more positive and fulfilling life from that point on. He talked of improved dialogue and assertion with those around, and he discussed his plans to set himself up in a new business venture about which he was excited. Juan also talked of teaching adults on a voluntary basis so as to maintain the same rewards he felt he had previously gotten from teaching children. Importantly, he outlined his plan to have a much busier leisure life than he ever had before, with a better "work–life balance." Finally, and critically, Juan outlined his plans to work toward taking more control in his relationships with others.

Juan produced a good release plan. He produced a good list of supports, outlining the ways in which each would help. He mentioned living with his mother, but also listed the action necessary to find a place of his own should he come to this decision eventually. He outlined the steps he was taking to secure a place in a halfway house and on a pre-release program. This was all taken as evidence of Juan's commitment to work toward self-improvement in the future. Juan accepted that further treatment might be deemed necessary and stated that he would be happy to attend as long as it didn't require him to "admit to something that I didn't do."

Summary

Juan was considered to have done well on the program. He identified a number of key areas in which he had experienced problems in the past, and he worked on strategies to address them. He appeared keen to consider alternate viewpoints and to work toward self-improvement. He also indicated that he would continue to consider the validity of points with which he did not immediately agree. He was able to set helpful goals, both approach and avoidance goals, for the future. He planned to develop better relationships with others, to improve his self-esteem, to continue to work on asserting himself, and to focus on enjoying life again and not putting himself under so much stress. Juan had previously been assessed as being a low-moderate risk of sexual recidivism. Following his participation in this program he was considered to have reduced his risk level to low.

Professional Concerns and Questions

We have experienced a wide range of reactions from professionals after describing our treatment approach to dealing with denial. While some people respond positively to the approach, many others are quite sceptical about its likely value. In fact, we ourselves initially found it unusual and personally challenging to conduct a treatment program without challenging denial or encouraging the man to admit to his offence(s). In most instances, in fact, we do encourage admission at the pre-treatment interview. If there is any potential for the man to acknowledge his offence or even very minimal portions of it, and he is receptive to treatment, we treat him in our regular program. The reason we do this is because in general, professionals working with him (e.g., parole officers, community treatment providers) will be more receptive if he is admitting to his offences.

We also know, however, that forcing someone to admit or being confrontational is neither effective nor helpful for him. Therefore, if after motivational discussions it is evident that a client is maintaining a position of denial, we feel, at least given our limited data, that it is better to do something than nothing. The treatment approach we described above is designed to reduce risk by addressing dynamic risk factors, and it does so in a positive and constructive manner. While some may argue that denial might in fact be a risk factor for recidivism, we would argue that by addressing the strongest risk factors, we reduce the likelihood of recidivism.

Attempting to force admission through confrontation or through the use of a polygraph may feel as though it is producing results in the short term. But what is our long-term goal? If we want individuals to engage and to actually be motivated to address their dynamic risks, what *is* best practice?

One specific area of caution should be noted. We have not treated high-risk sexual offenders in our deniers' program and therefore we cannot at this time recommend this treatment for those who are high risk. This is not to say that a treatment model for high-risk sexual offenders who deny could not be developed; however, it would need to be based around high-intensity as opposed to moderate-intensity treatment.

Recommendation to Clinicians

The approach taken in this program is strongly recommended for use with clients who present in categorical denial, but who express some interest in working toward a more favourable parole outcome and/or who express some interest in dealing more productively with general problems that they may have encountered in their lives. Such individuals can be motivated to engage in effective treatment aimed at helping them to identify problems that potentially put them in a position in which they could be accused of sexual offending.

Conclusions

Working with categorical deniers has posed a problem for treatment providers. Often these men have refused treatment or have upset the group climate and been suspended from treatment. We have presented an effective and motivational approach that addresses the key issues resulting in the offending behaviour without directly dealing with the issue of their denial. This approach serves to get clients "on side" (buying into the program) and treated while simultaneously addressing issues relevant to risk.

REFERENCES

Andrews, D. A., I. Zinger, R. D. Hoge, J. Bonta, P. Gendreau, and F. T. Cullen. 1990. Does correctional treatment work? A clinically relevant and psychologically informed meta-analysis. *Criminology* 28:369–404.

Barbaree, H. E. 1991. Denial and minimization among sex offenders: Assessment and treatment outcome. *Forum on Corrections Research* 3:30–33.

Barbaree, H. E., and F. A. Cortoni. 1993. Treatment of the juvenile sexual offender within the criminal justice and mental health systems. In *The juvenile sex offender*, H. E. Barbaree, 57–76. New York: Guilford Press.

Bartholomew, K., and L. M. Horowitz. 1991. Attachment styles among young adults: A test of a four-category model. *Journal of Personality and Social Psychology* 61:226–44.

Beckett, R., A. Beech, D. Fisher, and A. S. Fordham. 1994. *Community-based treatment of sex offenders: An evaluation of seven treatment programmes.* Home Office Occasional paper. London: Home Office.

Beech, A. R., and D. D. Fisher. 2002. The rehabilitation of child sex offenders. *Australian Psychologist* 37:206–14.

Bradford, J. M., and D. M. Greenberg. 1998. Treatment of adult male sexual offenders in a psychiatric setting. In *Sourcebook of treatment programs for sexual offenders*, ed W. L. Marshall, 247–56. New York: Plenum Press.

Brake, S. C., and D. Shannon. 1997. Using pre-treatment to increase admission in sex offenders. In *The sex offender: New insights, treatment innovations and legal developments*, ed. B. D. Schwartz and H. Cellini. Kingston, NJ: Civic Research Institute.

Cohen, F. 1995. Right to treatment. In *The sexual offender: Corrections, treatment, and legal practice*, ed. B. K. Schwartz and H. R. Cellini, 24.1–24.18. Kingston, NJ: Civic Research Institute.

Cortoni, F. A., and W. L. Marshall. 1995. *Childhood attachments, juvenile sexual history and adult coping skills in sex offenders.* Paper presented at the 14th Annual Research and Treatment Conference of the Association for the Treatment of Sexual Abusers, New Orleans.

———. 1996. *Juvenile sexual history, sex and coping strategies: A comparison of sexual and violent offenders.* Paper presented at the International Congress of Psychology, Montreal.

Endler, N. S., and J. D. Parker. 1990. Multidimensional assessment of coping: A critical evaluation. *Journal of Personality and Social Development* 58:844–54.

Fernandez, Y. M., D. A. Anderson, and W. L. Marshall. 1999. The relationship among empathy, cognitive distortions, and self-esteem in sexual offenders. In *The sex offender:*

Theoretical advances, treating special populations and legal developments, Vol. 111, ed. B. K. Schwartz, 4.1–4.18). Kingston, NJ: Civic Research Institute.

Fisher, D., A. R. Beech, and K. Browne. 1998. Locus of control and its relationship to treatment change and abuse history in child sexual abusers. *Legal and Criminological Psychology* 3:1–12.

Hanson, R. K. 2003. Empathy deficits of sexual offenders: A conceptual model. *Journal of Sexual Aggression* 9:13–23.

Hanson, R. K., and M. T. Bussiere. 1998. Predicting relapse: A meta-analysis of sexual offender recidivism studies. *Journal of Consulting and Clinical Psychology* 66:348–62.

Hanson, R. K., A. Gordon, A. J. R. Harris, J. K. Marques, W. D. Murphy, V. L. Quinsey, and M. C. Seto. 2002. First report of the Collaborative Outcome Data Project on the Effectiveness of Psychological Treatment of Sex Offenders. *Sexual Abuse: A Journal of Research and Treatment* 14:169–95.

Hanson, R. K., and A. J. R. Harris. 2000. Where should we intervene? Dynamic predictors of sex reoffense recidivism. *Criminal Justice and Behavior* 27:6–35.

Hanson, R. K., and K. Morton-Bourgon. 2004. *Predictors of sexual recidivism: An updated meta-analysis.* (Cat. No. P53-1/2004-2E-PDF) Ottawa: Public Works and Government Services Canada.

Happel, R. M., and J. J. Auffrey. 1995. Sex offender assessment: Interrupting the dance of denial. *American Journal of Forensic Psychology* 13:5–22.

Hudson, S. M., D. S. Wales, L. W. Bakker, and T. Ward. 2002. Dynamic risk factors: The Kia Marama evaluation. *Sexual Abuse: A Journal of Research and Treatment* 14:103–19.

Jenkins, A. J. 1990. *Invitations to responsibility.* Adelaide, South Australia: Dulwich Centre Publications.

Kahn, T. J., and H. J. Chambers. 1991. Assessing reoffense risk with juvenile sex offenders. *Child Welfare* 70:333–45.

Kennedy, H. G., and D. H. Grubin. 1992. Patterns of denial in sex offenders. *Psychological Medicine* 22:191–96.

Langstrom, N., and M. Grann. 2000. Risk for criminal recidivism among young sex offenders. *Journal of Interpersonal Violence* 15:855–71.

Laws, D. R. 2002. Owning your own data: The management of denial. In *Motivating offenders to change: A guide to enhancing engagement in therapy,* ed. M. McMurran, 173–92. New York: John Wiley & Sons, Ltd.

Lombardo, R., and J. DiGiorgio-Miller. 1988. Concepts and techniques in working with juvenile sex offenders. *Journal of Offender Counseling, Services and Rehabilitation* 13:39–53.

Looman, J. 1999. Mood, conflict and deviant sexual fantasies. In *The sex offender: Theoretical advances, treating special populations and legal developments,* Vol. III, ed. B.K. Schwartz, 3.1–3.11. Kingston, NJ: Civic Research Institute.

Losel, F., and M. Schmucker. 2005. The effectiveness of treatment for sexual offenders: A comprehensive meta-analysis. *Journal of Experimental Criminology* 1:117–46.

Maletzky, B. M. 1993. Factors associated with success and failure in the behavior and cognitive treatment of sexual offenders. *Annals of Sex Research* 6:241–58.

———. 1996. Editorial: Denial of treatment or treatment of denial? *Sexual Abuse: A Journal of Research and Treatment* 8(1):1–5.

Mann, R. E., J. I. D. Ginsburg, and J. R. Weekes. 2002. Motivational interviewing with offenders. In *Motivating offenders to change*, ed. M. McMurran. Chichester: Wiley.

Marshall, W. L. 1994. Treatment effects on denial and minimization in incarcerated sex offenders. *Behavior Research and Therapy* 32:559–64.

Marshall, W. L., D. A. Anderson, and F. Champagne. 1996. Self-esteem and its relationship to sexual offending. *Psychology, Crime & Law* 3:81–106.

Marshall, W. L., D. A. Anderson, and Y. M. Fernandez. 2000. *Cognitive behavioural treatment of sexual offenders*. London: John Wiley & Sons.

Marshall, W. L., and H. E. Barbaree. 1988. The long-term evaluation of a behavioral treatment program for child molesters. *Behavior Research and Therapy* 26:499–511.

Marshall, W. L., L. E. Marshall, G. A. Serran, and Y. M. Fernandez. 2006. *Treating sexual offenders: An integrated approach*. New York: Taylor & Francis Group.

Marshall, W. L., and J. McGuire. 2003. Effect sizes in treatment of sexual offenders. *International Journal of Offender Therapy and Comparative Criminology* 46:653–63.

Marshall, W. L., G. A. Serran, and F. A. Cortoni. 2000. Childhood attachments, sexual abuse, and their relationship to adult coping in child molesters. *Sexual Abuse: A Journal of Research and Treatment* 12:17–26.

Marshall, W. L., G. A. Serran, Y. M. Fernandez, R. Mulloy, R. E. Mann, and D. Thornton. 2003. Therapist characteristics in the treatment of sexual offenders: Tentative data on their relationship with indices of behaviour change. *Journal of Sexual Aggression* 9:25–30.

Marshall, W. L., G. A. Serran, H. Moulden, Y. M. Fernandez, R. E. Mann, and D. Thornton. 2002. Therapist features in sexual offender treatment: Their reliable identification and influence on behaviour change. *Clinical Psychology and Psychotherapy* 9:395–405.

Marshall, W. L., D. Thornton, L. E. Marshall, Y. M. Fernandez, and R. E. Mann. 2001. Treatment of sex offenders who are in categorical denial: A pilot project. *Sexual Abuse: A Journal of Research and Treatment* 14:205–15.

McKibben, A., J. Proulx, and R. Lusignan. 1994. Relationships between conflict, affect, and deviant sexual behaviours in rapists and pedophiles. *Behaviour Research and Therapy* 32:571–75.

O'Donohue, W., and E. Letourneau. 1993. A brief group treatment for the modification of denial in child sexual abusers: Outcome and follow-up. *Child Abuse and Neglect* 17:299–304.

Schlank, A. M., and T. Shaw. 1996. Treating sexual offenders who deny their guilt: A pilot study. *Sexual Abuse: A Journal of Research and Treatment* 8(1):17–23.

Schneider, S. L., and R. C. Wright. 2004. Understanding denial in sexual offenders: A review of cognitive and motivational processes to avoid responsibility. *Trauma, Violence and Abuse* 5:3–20.

Schwartz, B. K. 1995. Group therapy. In *The sexual offender: Corrections, treatment, and legal practice*, ed. B. K. Schwartz and H. R. Cellini. Kingston, NJ: Civic Research Institute.

Simkins, L., W. Ward, S. Bowman, and C. M. Rinck. 1989. The multiphasic sex inventory: Diagnosis and prediction of treatment response in child sexual abusers. *Annals of Sex Research* 2:205–26.

Simourd, D. J., and P. B. Malcolm. 1998. Reliability and validity of the level of service inventory-revised among federally incarcerated sex offenders. *Journal of Interpersonal Violence* 13:261–74.

Ward, T., and C. A. Stewart. 2003. The treatment of sex offenders: Risk management and Good Lives. *Professional Psychology Research & Practice* 34:353–60.

Winn, M. E. 1996. The strategic and systemic management of denial in the cognitive–behavioral treatment of sexual offenders. *Sexual Abuse: A Journal of Research and Treatment* 8(1):25–36.

The Rockwood Preparatory Program for Sexual Offenders: Goals and the Methods Employed to Achieve Them

*Matt D. O'Brien, Liam E. Marshall,
and William L. Marshall*

This chapter outlines the research supporting the development of a treatment preparatory program for sexual offenders. The chapter focuses on the specific goals of the program and the rationale behind each, and provides a detailed explanation of the methods employed to achieve those goals.

Background

Research has shown that programs designed to introduce and prepare participants for treatment for various psychological problems increase the effectiveness of future group treatment for those participants (Mayerson 1984). Other studies have demonstrated that pre-treatment interventions produce positive effects on increased motivation (Curran 1978; Strupp and Bloxom 1973), self-disclosure (Garrison 1978; Whalen 1969), self-exploratory verbalizations (Annis and Perry 1977, 1978; Garrison 1978; Heitler 1973), perceived personal value, and investment and participation (Conyne and Silver 1980; Corder, Haizlip, Whiteside, and Vogel 1980). We propose that such positive effects should be transferable to sexual offenders, in order to enhance their participation in subsequent core treatment programs. Thus, a program was designed to enhance treatment motivation by addressing issues that research has connected with resistance to treatment. We use five primary approaches: (1) inform clients about the components and processes of treatment, (2) present the outcome data currently available, (3) outline the benefits to clients of participating in treatment, (4) demonstrate that treatment can be a positive experience, and (5) ensure that the focus of treatment is not exclusively on the participants' offending. The program's designers reasoned that the implementation of any program that utilizes these techniques, when delivered in a positive therapeutic manner, ought to enhance motivation for, and participation in, subsequent core treatment programs. Marques, Nelson, Alarcon, and Day (2000), in their review of the Californian SOTEP program, found that offenders who failed at treatment were well versed in the skills and strategies needed to avoid re-offending, but were insufficiently motivated to change their ways. This finding suggests that in treatment, it is necessary to help group members create new appealing life goals that inspire them to live their lives without offending by increasing the cognitive dissonance between their preferred self-image and their offending behavior.

In the Ontario region of the Correctional Service of Canada, sexual offenders are first placed in an induction centre where they receive a thorough behavioral assessment over a period of approximately four months. Despite this rigorous and extensive assessment, the prisoners still spend a significant amount of unstructured time in their cells. All that excess time in their day-to-day lives presented us with an opportunity to implement and try out a preparatory program. In the structure currently underway, six to eight offenders at a time attend the program in a rolling format, sometimes referred to as an open, group format. The treatment involves two 2.5-hour sessions per week. Treatment is available to any sexual offender willing to participate, provided space is available. For a more comprehensive overview of the Preparatory Program, see Marshall and Moulden (2006).

One of our main intentions in the way we designed the program was to address the findings of the research of Mann and Webster (2002), which indicate that the most common oppositions offenders have about entering treatment are lack of trust in key professionals, bad experiences with the system, lack of awareness of treatment effectiveness, concern over possible side effects, belief that therapy would focus solely on offence-related details, disinterested professionals who lack concern for them, lack of validation of their anxieties, and concern that broader life goals would not be taken into account during treatment.

The manner in which we have addressed these and other pertinent issues is outlined below. The goals are listed in an order that is commonly followed; however, given the flexibility of the approach, the needs of each individual client, and the nature of the open-ended program (meaning that clients in the group are frequently at different stages of the treatment process from their peers), it is not uncommon for therapists to focus on the goals in a different order, or indeed focus on several goals simultaneously.

1. Goal: To Describe Treatment Efficacy

Rationale
By giving clients a summary of basic current and relevant recidivism data, particularly as it pertains to the institution to which an inmate may eventually be transferred, therapists help to motivate clients to recognize that change will be beneficial to them. Therapists cannot initially assume that clients will be aware of this, particularly given the common negative rumors that circulate throughout institutions about sexual offender programs. This information also helps clients to realize that treatment can be beneficial, but only if they apply themselves to their programming.

Method
Using a flipchart, the therapist writes up the recidivism rates for cognitive–behavioral treatment of sexual offenders, as reported by Hanson et al. (2002) from their meta-analysis. This presentation shows clients that treatment has a large impact on recidivism (ES=.28), higher than the effect of many commonly used medical treatments (e.g., ES=.08 chemotherapy for breast cancer; see Marshall and McGuire 2003 for comparisons of effects' sizes from medicine, psychotherapy, and offender interventions). Clients also hear information relating to the recidivism rate of treated vs. non-treated

sexual offenders at each of the four Ontario regional institutions that operate sexual offender programs. For example, we inform clients of a study conducted by Looman, Abracen, and Nicholaichuk (2000), who reported a recidivism rate of 24 percent, for high-risk sexual offenders who completed the high-risk sexual offender program, against a 52 percent recidivism rate for a matched untreated group of high-risk sexual offenders. An overview study of moderate-risk sexual offenders, conducted by Marshall, Marshall, Serran, and Fernandez (2006), found that only 3.2 percent of treated sexual offenders recidivated compared to an expected rate of 16.8 pecent.

2. Goal: To Provide Treatment-Related Information

Rationale
Without knowing the information described above, clients nonetheless become preoccupied with concerns over possible side effects of treatment (Mann and Webster 2002). Clients also are prone to become overly and unhelpfully anxious about what is likely to be asked of them, both in the Preparatory Program and during the core programs that follow.

Method
During a client's first session, the therapist outlines the components and practicalities of the Preparatory Program and describes subsequent assessment procedures and treatment programs that the client will attend. An increased understanding of risk-assessment procedures significantly reduces clients' resistance to the procedures. To increase clients' comfort and to reduce any sense they might have that treatment is overly complex, the therapist also discusses links between individual treatment topics. The therapist is explicit about the aims, goals, and content of therapeutic exercises in order to promote the clients' understanding and openness. The therapist stresses that treatment does not focus solely on offence-related details, but makes sure that clients are aware that broader life goals are a central focus of the work. Therapists encourage group members to mention any myths or rumors that they may have heard about treatment so that the therapist can have an opportunity to address those issues. The therapist explains group rules and stresses

the least obvious points. In this way, group members are not patronized, and therapists send out a clear message that they believe they are working with adults who can accept responsibility for their own behavior.

Therapists lead discussions on how clients can get the most out of treatment and how they can be as successful as possible in their futures. Therapists help clients to understand the link between changes brought about by treatment and their subsequent functioning in the world. It is useful for each therapist to ask the group to discuss the nature and value of participation. This conversation can help to set up and foster a culture of participation for new group members from the outset. Therapists also inform group members of the possible results of successfully completing treatment, such as being able to move to a lower-security facility or being able to earn an earlier parole.

3. Goal: To Overcome Resistance

Rationale

Resistant clients or those in denial are among those who enter the Preparatory Program. Their presence in these programs is required, consistent with Correctional Service of Canada guidelines. Therapists do what they can to accommodate such clients.

Method

When a client in the program presents as resistant, therapists are careful not to do anything to promote further resistance, such as pressing them early on to make contributions to the group. Instead, the program allows for those clients' resistance and encourages rewards for any contributions that they do make. Therapists focus on engaging resistant clients in a patient and gradual manner. Although such clients should not initially be pressured to produce assignments, it is helpful when therapists remind the clients that they will be required to complete similar exercises in their next program and that to be as successful as possible later on, they are likely to benefit from practice while in the Preparatory Program.

For those rare clients who present in the Preparatory Program as being in "categorical" denial (i.e., "I did not commit an offence"), the focus should be on those areas of their life that they do consider to have been problematic in some way. We often suggest to them that there must have been some problems in their lives that led them to be "falsely accused," and that if they address these issues, they will be less likely in the future to find themselves in similar situations where they can again be falsely accused.

4. Goal: To Enhance Motivation for Change

Rationale
The overarching goal of the program is to motivate sexual offenders at an early stage in treatment to believe that change is needed and that it will be beneficial to them. That approach is likely to enhance the effects of subsequent treatment, thereby increasing the clients' commitment to leading more positive and productive lives.

Method
Helping clients to set goals for the future and to make self-motivational statements (also referred to as "change talk"; see chapter 8 of this book) is one way therapists can help clients to strengthen their commitment to change. This approach is, of course, in keeping with the central tenets of motivational interviewing, as developed by Miller and Rollnick (1991, 2002). Through this approach, therapists in the program ensure that they respect the clients' freedom to make choices about their own treatment, as this is an essential component in establishing a commitment to change (Linehan 1993; Miller and Rollnick 1991). As such, clients frequently have the option as to which assignment to complete next. They are also encouraged to complete assignments in the manner that is most helpful and that makes most sense to them. They are not given total autonomy, however. Some more explicit direction is often necessary. This process helps clients develop an understanding that they have control over and are responsible for their own progression in treatment.

5. Goal: To Create Optimism in the Clients

Rationale

By increasing a client's sense of hope and optimism, therapists can nurture clients' belief that they have the capability both to develop future plans and to achieve the goals they have set. Research by Beech and Fordham (1997) indicated that success in treatment is directly related to therapists' ability to communicate a sense of optimism about change to the group members (Beech and Fordham 1997). Thus by becoming more optimistic, Preparatory Program graduates achieve full participation more quickly in their next program, which in turn produces greater overall therapeutic benefits. Hope theory (Snyder 2000) suggests that if a person can be convinced that he has the capability of achieving his goals and can develop plans for doing so, his feelings of hope will be maximized and his chances of attaining success will be higher.

Method

A number of approaches are useful toward achieving this goal. A primary approach is a focus on ensuring that the therapists display empirically validated, positive therapeutic characteristics. According to Drapeau (2005), good sexual offender therapists are seen by clients as honest, respectful, nonjudgmental, available, caring, confident, competent, and persuasive. Beech and Fordham (1997) and Marshall et al. (2002, 2003) have shown that a more respectful and empathic approach to working with sexual offenders facilitates the attainment of within-treatment goals. That approach, for clients, accomplishes such goals as reducing distortions, providing recognition of victim harm, increasing coping skills, improving relationship style, and improving identification of offending patterns. Fernandez et al. (1999) found that successful participation in treatment was related to warm, genuine, and empathic non-confrontational challenges by therapists. These findings indicate that treatment style has a significant impact on the motivation of group members in sexual offender treatment. A sense of optimism is also engendered through early discussions of approach goals and the elements of a good life. Therapists seek to establish a supportive and collaborative relationship with clients where we help to motivate them to change by accepting them as whole people with strengths, but ones who have engaged in unacceptable behaviours. This approach is also based on the motivational model described by Miller and Rollnick (2002). Working collaboratively requires being fully open with clients about all aspects of treatment, therapeutic strategies, timescales, possible outcomes, and implications (Shingler and Mann 2006). It communicates to clients that the therapist believes they are capable of understanding and solving their own problems, and it helps to foster an increased sense of optimism for the future. Therapists keenly watch for skills and strengths in clients and identify these positive attributes to them. This approach starts the process of having clients define goals and plans for goal attainment.

6. Goal: To Enhance Clients' Self-Esteem

Rationale
Evidence from the general psychological literature demonstrates that improving clients' self-esteem facilitates their active participation in treatment, enhances their belief in their own capacity to change, and increases their commitment to change (Marshall, Anderson, and Champagne 1997). Levels of self-esteem in this client population is substantially below the normative average (Marshall, Champagne, Brown, and Miller 1997; Marshall and Mazzucco 1995), so in order to enhance client optimism and motivation, therapists work to enhance the self-esteem of those clients whose deficits of their self-worth adversely affect them. A recent study has also shown self-esteem to be a criminogenic need (Thornton, Beech, and Marshall 2004). In this study, self-esteem significantly predicted sexual recidivism (AUC = .69).

Method
Clients are asked to compile a list of their positive qualities (Marshall, Champagne, Sturgeon, and Bryce 1997). Therapists encourage them to increase the range and frequency of their social activities, and to produce positive statements about themselves, which they should regularly read in order to remind themselves of their good qualities. In order to further distinguish the client as a person apart from his behaviour, therapists on the

Preparatory Program insist that each client not describe himself as a sexual offender, but as a person who has committed a sexual offence. Therapists also help raise the self-esteem of clients by treating them respectfully and by viewing them as whole people with strengths as well as deficits.

7. Goal: To Build a Therapeutic Alliance

Rationale
Building a therapeutic alliance is critical to the success of the program. It has the particular benefits of increasing clients' trust in the type of professionals that they will be working with in the future, it provides a positive early experience of treatment, and it assures clients that professionals are interested in them. Overall, this goal aims at demonstrating that treatment can be a positive experience.

Method
The keys to succeeding at this goal are dependent on the flexibility and responsivity of the therapists. Preparatory Program therapists focus primarily on their interactions with clients rather than on attaining typical treatment goals, such as overcoming denial. Therapists work to ensure that the treatment arena addresses the needs associated with a client's age, ethnic background, learning style, and personal life experiences. Importantly, within the Preparatory Program, therapists have the scope to adapt the content, teaching style, and pace of delivery to suit particular individuals. Therapists model respectful behaviour at all times with clients. In particular, they concentrate on treating clients with honesty, fairness, respect, and genuineness. This contributes to the clients having sufficient confidence in the ability of future treatment providers to help them to achieve their treatment goals.

Given that the program includes a range of different techniques—including discussion, role-play, between-sessions work, and behavioural skills practices—Preparatory Programs are well suited to the needs of clients who have had prior negative experiences with education or other learning programs. Where possible, therapists also attempt to make discussions as enjoyable as they can be, including using appropriate humor. This method also has a positive effect on engagement and motivation of the participants.

When clients bring "outside issues" into sessions (e.g., problems on cell blocks, family problems, work or home-life issues), the therapist encourages discussion about how these problems are affecting the clients. In so doing, the therapist turns these issues into learning and teaching points. This broad-based, humanistic approach enhances the therapeutic alliance, as does the manner in which clients are challenged. Any challenges are always done in a supportive, encouraging, and helpful manner designed to engender cognitive dissonance in order to motivate change. For example, as Prochaska and DiClemente (1992) suggest, therapists should ask questions in the spirit of genuine enquiry if the client is at an early stage of change. Therapists can be more direct at a later stage.

8. Goal: To Increase Clients' Trust

Rationale
Without sufficient trust in the treatment provider at the first meeting of the Preparatory Program, a client is unlikely to commit to entering the program. Lack of trust may have the effect of reducing motivation. It is therefore critical that the treatment team make a positive impression on potential new clients from the outset.

Method
The group therapist interviews each prospective group member prior to his joining the program. This interview is relatively short and covers only a few basic areas so as not to overwhelm the client. The therapist outlines the purpose of the program and the value that other group members have found in attending. In addition, the client receives some brief information about the possible positive effects that engaging in all available programming may have for him in terms of moving to a lower-security institution or obtaining early parole. Even if, as is often the case, the client indicates that he is keen to start the program, it is made clear that joining it is his choice. On the rare occasion that a client declines to join the program, the therapist reassures him that

this decision is acceptable and that making that choice is his prerogative. The client is told, however, that if he should change his mind, he is free to contact the therapist to arrange another meeting. Occasionally, clients voice particular concerns about joining the program. These must be dealt with patiently. Therapists need to validate and accept clients' concerns without defensiveness. Where applicable, therapists may feed competing factors back to the client so that he can make a more informed decision. Therapists work to avoid having a client later feel that he has been misled into participation.

It is important to note that as far as therapists are concerned, motivation is motivation. The therapist may still be concerned about a client's motivation for joining the program. It often is for self-betterment, but an equally acceptable reason is a desire to gain earlier parole or to have increased time out of his cell. The important thing is that the client experiences some desire to attend and to engage in the program. Once the client enters the program, it is then up to the therapist to motivate the client toward the achievement of the goals of treatment.

9. Goal: To Build Group Cohesion

Rationale
One of the most important factors in the creation and maintenance of a positive and motivational group environment is the focus on the development of group cohesion. Cohesion refers to group members' feelings of involvement, participation, commitment to the group, and concern and friendship for each other. Beech and Fordham (1997) found that the most successful sexual offender groups "were highly cohesive, well-organized and well-led, encouraged the open expression of feelings, produced a sense of group responsibility and instilled a sense of hope in its members" (Beech and Fordham 1997). Further, Beech and his colleagues (Beech and Fordham 1997; Beech and Hamilton-Giachritsis 2005) found that the group climate has an effect on treatment changes. Using Moos's (1986) Group Environment Scale, these researchers found that cohesion was positively related, at significant levels, to a composite measure of treatment gains.

Method

One of the methods for attaining the goal of cohesion is to immediately orient new participants to work within a group setting. The therapist introduces a new participant to the other more senior group members and invites the existing group members to tell the new client what differences they believe the program has made for them. This inclusive approach has the dual effects of having the more senior group members elicit self-motivational statements, and of helping the new client to learn more about the program and its benefits from relatively trusted sources. It also provides an opportunity to illustrate that the therapist is a professional who can be trusted and who seeks feedback. Such pro-social modeling by more senior group members contributes to the development of pro-social change and a cohesive atmosphere.

The therapist or group members may ask the new client some general questions about himself, such as where his hometown is, what he did for a living before coming to jail, and what his leisure interests are. This introduction helps to get him contributing in a relatively non-threatening way and feeling an important part of the group from the start.

It is frequently the case that in such an open environment the new client will take the opportunity to share his negative experiences of the legal system and incarceration. The therapist validates these, where appropriate, thereby showing that the therapist has concern and empathy for the client. It also often provides an opportunity for the new client to receive sympathy and support from others in the group who may well have had similar experiences, again promoting group cohesion.

In many cases, the focus will then shift away from the new group member and onto a general discussion of the work of another, more senior, group member. That said, the therapist attempts to ensure that the new client participates in these discussions as much as possible. If the client cannot think of anything to say, then he is reassured that this is acceptable, but that he will be expected to contribute in the future. Therapists will seek opportunities to positively reinforce any attempts that new group members make in order to maximize their contributions. Greater use of positive reinforcement is generally made with newer group members in order to encourage their contributions.

Occasionally, early in treatment, newer clients will voice continued reservations about engaging in treatment. It is common for the other group members to address these reservations with the new client since it is likely that they once had similar thoughts. The therapist ensures that by the end of this discussion the group has acknowledged that change can be difficult, that the client has already taken the first important step—that programming is unlikely to make him worse—and that it is normal to be uncomfortable when considering making changes to one's life.

10. Goal: To Encourage Expressiveness

Rationale
Again, Beech and his colleagues (Beech and Fordham 1997; Beech and Hamilton-Giachritsis 2005) found another aspect of group climate that has an effect on treatment outcome. Using Moos's (1986) Group Environment Scale, these researchers found that expressiveness was positively related at significant levels to a composite measure of treatment gains. Expressiveness is defined by Moos (1986) as "the encouragement of freedom of action and the expression of feelings within the group."

Method
Therapists in the Preparatory Program focus their efforts on setting up the climate of the group to welcome and encourage the expression of feelings and a high level of participation. Frequently, discussions within the Preparatory Program take place only when the therapist occasionally directs and prompts the flow. The more senior members typically take a greater role in these discussions, reflecting their acquired expressiveness and modeling this behaviour to the newer clients. They often outline the benefits of change for the newer group members, which increases the new clients' expressiveness. These more senior members also tend to reflect on their own progress, leading to the production of further self-motivational statements. Therapists also outline some of the ways that group members can succeed in treatment programs, including specifically explaining that being an active, involved, and expressive group member increases their chances of success and allows the

therapist to write them a more favourable report. This kind of group-led structure increases levels of motivation, involvement, and commitment to the program.

Once a client shares an assignment with the group, the therapist asks each other group member for comments solely about the positive aspects of the assignment. The feedback helps group members to understand the goals of the assignments in a non-threatening way and further shapes them toward satisfactory participation and expressiveness. The emphasis on positive reinforcement of all such work also has a strong motivational effect on clients. The refusal rate for assignments is virtually zero, and in fact many clients cannot wait to get working on their next piece of work.

11. Goal: To Normalise Offending Processes

Rationale
Research indicates that clients are concerned that treatment is likely to focus too much on their offending (Mann and Webster 2002). It is our experience that clients can make damaging, negative evaluations of themselves, judging themselves as being significantly different from others. This attitude can lead to the experience of shame (i.e., "I am a bad person") rather than guilt (i.e., "I did a bad thing"). Shame is a block to effective treatment engagement whereas feelings of guilt can motivate change (Marshall, Marshall, Serran, and O'Brien forthcoming; Tangney and Dearing 2002).

Method
By explaining Finkelhor's Pre-condition Model (Finkelhor and Araji 1986), with general examples, therapists can help clients to begin exploring patterns in offending. It directs clients to consider why they offended, how they created the opportunity to offend, how they overcame the resistance of the victim, and how they justified their actions to themselves. This process helps clients to gain an early understanding of some of the key factors underlying their offending, in much the same way that therapists normalise the process by showing that all of us at certain times do things that are not acceptable, and do so because of the choices that we make.

12. Goal: To Enhance Clients' Self-Disclosure

Rationale

Once a client feels more at ease talking about himself, his life in general, and his offending, he engages with the treatment program in a more productive and effective manner. If he is able to achieve this level of comfort while in the Preparatory Program, he is likely to benefit more speedily from his next treatment program. As a result, the client becomes less anxious about making disclosures and is more comfortable with subsequent exploration of relevant issues.

Method

New group members can best get started by making relatively non-threatening self-disclosures in their early sessions. This approach serves the purpose of normalising and encouraging active participation and disclosure from the beginning. During a client's first session, the therapist can invite the new client to tell the group a few relatively innocuous facts about himself, such as his hometown, occupation prior to incarceration, hobbies, and key relationships. No challenge is given or invited at this stage so that early disclosures will be positive and rewarding experiences. The therapist also informs the client that in one of the next sessions he will be asked to give a disclosure of his offending to the group. The man is encouraged to share his feelings about doing this, and any concerns he has are addressed and validated so as to ensure that he is supported through this experience. The other group members provide reassurance that they will support him in this endeavor. They may also advise him on the best way to approach the exercise.

One way in which the group can help clients to develop their ability to be comfortable making self-disclosures in a group setting is for the therapist to make appropriate self-disclosures, thus providing a useful role-model for the clients. Given the rolling nature of the program, clients generally observe at least one or two other group members disclosing offence information before they are asked to do so themselves. This peer role-modeling is effective in convincing group members that disclosing can be a beneficial and positive experience. Typically, group members describe the feeling of a "weight being lifted from my shoulders" following their account of their offending.

The offence disclosure is the first exercise that group members complete because most expect they will have to provide one disclosure. Explaining it will come later, as they explore the psychological factors that contributed to their abuse. In our experience the longer clients wait to do so, the greater their anxiety level. Their initial disclosure helps clients feel that they can move on from this anxiety. It prepares them for future programs, and it can help the therapist to understand what, if any, resistance the client might have. As in all other phases of treatment, therapists must always be responsive to the needs of individuals. For example, the most anxious clients may be allowed to write down their disclosure and then read it aloud. Therapists stress that they want clients to explain what happened from *their* perspective. By doing this, therapists underline their intention to focus on the clients. This reassurance also conveys a respect for the client, underscores the importance for them to complete this work, and shows that they are valued. The approach, understandably, contributes to an enhancement of motivation to engage in this process and in the program overall. Therapists focus on general factors that contributed to clients' offending and avoid a de-motivating and unnecessary focus on fine details, particularly of the actual offences. In each disclosure, therapists only allow positive comments from other group members on what the discloser did well. This fosters an important sense of teamwork, trust, and an environment led by positive reinforcement.

In the disclosure exercise, the focus is on building trust and developing the group members' beliefs that what the therapist cares about is helping the clients to change rather than be punished for offending. This support is perhaps more important at this stage than at any other, as it can be essential in creating a positive and motivating group atmosphere from the beginning, which in turn can maximize the achievement of later treatment goals.

The autobiography, or life-description assignment, which is generally set after a group member completes his disclosure, helps to confirm to the client that treatment is not going to focus solely on offence-related details. It serves, at this early stage in the process, to reassure clients that broader lifestyle issues and patterns of behaviour are taken into account. Coming after the disclosure, the autobiography session can provide clients with a welcome break from offence-related discussions. Therapists encourage group members to discuss their strengths as well as the problems they have encountered in life. Marshall et al. (1999) noted that, "Therapists spend far too much time focusing on clients' deficiencies and not enough time encouraging them to believe in their strengths and capacities to change." As such, therapists in the Preparatory Program focus on strengths and skills already in existence. This motivates clients to consider how to build more fulfilling lives for the future that exclude offending. When describing this assignment, therapists ask the more senior group members about their experiences when they completed the same assignment, and what they found was good to include in their descriptions. This technique has the effect of helping the more experienced clients to recognize the gains they have made, which then motivates them to continue making further treatment gains. After an individual reads out his assignment, which he will have completed in the style that best suits him, the other group members provide positive comments on what he did well. This method again serves to reward the client's self-disclosure.

13. Goal: To Provide Experience of Assignments in Future Programming

Rationale
Exposing the client in advance, to at least some degree, to assignments they will be expected to complete later reduces their anxiety. They are also likely to benefit more from this work when their turn comes, as they will have already given it some thought and preparation.

Method
In addition to the more standard disclosures and life-description assignments, therapists hold more general discussions around the topics of victim empathy, healthy sexuality, coping, supports, relationships, and attachment styles.

Program Efficacy

We are currently working on a second evaluation of the impact of our Preparatory Program, this time focusing on participation in subsequent comprehensive treatment programs. To date, we have received positive feedback from the therapists of the programs that Preparatory Program graduates subsequently attend. These therapists have said that offenders experienced more rapid involvement in treatment, improved self-disclosure, advanced understanding of risk factors, increased responsibility, and appropriate group behaviour, all of which can be seen to link to many of the goals outlined above. We have previously (Marshall, Marshall, Fernandez, Malcolm, and Moulden 2008) compared those sexual offenders who did participate in the Preparatory Program with those who did not. Both groups completed subsequent comprehensive treatment programs. We found that the Preparatory Program participants displayed greater treatment readiness, were more likely to be accepted for a subsequent lower-intensity program, received earlier parole, and were less likely to be returned to custody or to reoffend. The sexual recidivism rate for Preparatory Program sexual offenders was found to be 1 percent compared to 5 percent for the matched group who received full treatment but did not participate in the Preparatory Program. The increased extent to which Preparatory Program clients were motivated to engage fully in their ongoing treatment may account for much of the difference in these rates. This study also demonstrated other significant changes within sexual offender participants in the Preparatory Program (Marshall, Marshall, Fernandez, Malcolm, and Moulden 2008). Clients in the Preparatory Program moved from what Prochaska and DiClemente (1992) call the contemplation stage of change to the action stage of change, and reported higher self-efficacy and greater hope as a result of their participation in the program.

Conclusions

The authors of this chapter developed a preparatory treatment program for sexual offenders. The program includes a series of specific goals designed to encourage clients' motivation and commitment to change, rationales behind each goal, and methods to target each. Research has shown this approach to be effective in promoting more rapid involvement in treatment, improved self-disclosure, an advanced understanding of risk factors, increased responsibility, and lower recidivism. Consequently we wholeheartedly encourage other professionals in the field working with convicted sexual offenders to adopt a similar pre-treatment intervention that targets the same goals and employs similar methods to address each.

REFERENCES

Annis, L. V., and D. F. Perry. 1977. Self-disclosure modeling in same-sex and mixed-sex unsupervised groups. *Journal of Counseling Psychology* 24:370–72.

———. 1978. Self-disclosure in unsupervised groups: Effects of videotaped models. *Small Group Behavior* 9:102–8.

Beech, A. R., and A. S. Fordham. 1997. Therapeutic climate of sexual offender treatment programs. *Sexual Abuse: A Journal of Research and Treatment* 9:219–37.

Beech, A. R., and C. E. Hamilton-Giachritsis. 2005. Relationship between therapeutic climate and treatment outcome in group-based sexual offender treatment programs. *Sexual Abuse: A Journal of Research and Treatment* 17:127–40.

Conyne, R. K., and R. J. Silver. 1980. Direct, vicarious, and vicarious-process experiences: Effects on increasing therapeutic attraction. *Small Group Behavior* 11:419–29.

Corder, B. F., T. Haizlip, R. Whiteside, and M. Vogel. 1980. Pre-therapy training for adolescents in group psychotherapy: Contract, guidelines, and pre-therapy preparation. *Adolescence* 15:699–706.

Curran, T. 1978. Increasing motivation to change in group treatment. *Small Group Behavior* 9:337–48.

Drapeau, M. 2005. Research on the processes involved in treating sexual offenders. *Sexual Abuse: A Journal of Research and Treatment* 17:117–25.

Fernandez, Y. M., G. Serran, and W. L. Marshall. 1999. *The reliable identification of therapist features in the treatment of sexual offenders*. Paper presented at the 18th Annual Research and Treatment Conference of the Association for the Treatment of Sexual Abusers. Orlando, FL.

Finkelhor, D., and S. Araji. 1986. Explanations of pedophilia: A four factor model. *Journal of Sex Research* 22:145–61.

Garrison, J. 1978. Written vs. verbal preparation of patients for group psychotherapy. *Psychotherapy: Theory, Research, and Practice* 15:130–34.

Hanson, R. K., A. Gordon, A. J. R. Harris, J. K. Marques, W. D. Murphy, V. L. Quinsey, and M. C. Seto. 2002. First report of the Collaborative Outcome Data Project on the Effectiveness of Psychological Treatment of Sex Offenders. *Sex Abuse: A Journal of Research and Treatment* 14:169–95.

Heitler, J. B. 1973. Preparation of lower-class patients for expressive group psychotherapy. *Journal of Consulting and Clinical Psychology* 41:251–60.

Linehan, M. M. 1993. *Cognitive-behavioral treatment of borderline personality disorder*. New York: Guilford Press.

Looman, J., J. Abracen, and T. Nicholaichuk. 2000. Recidivism among treated sexual offenders and matched controls. *Journal of Interpersonal Violence* 15:279–90.

Mann, R. E., and S. Webster. 2002. *Understanding resistance and denial*. Paper presented at the 21st Annual Research and Treatment Conference of the Association for the Treatment of Sexual Abusers. Montreal, Canada.

Marques, J. K., C. Nelson, J.-M. Alarcon, and D. M. Day. 2000. Preventing relapse in sex offenders: What we learned from SOTEP's experimental treatment program. In *Remaking relapse prevention with sex offenders: A sourcebook*, ed. D. R. Laws, S. M. Hudson, and T. Ward, 321–40. Thousand Oaks, CA: Sage.

Marshall, W. L., D. Anderson, and F. Champagne. 1997. Self-esteem and its relationship to sexual offending. *Psychology, Crime & Law* 3:81–106 and 161–86.

Marshall, W. L., D. Anderson, and Y. M. Fernandez. 1999. *Cognitive behavioural treatment of sexual offenders*. Chichester, UK: John Wiley & Sons.

Marshall, W. L., F. Champagne, C. Brown, and S. Miller. 1997. Empathy, intimacy, loneliness, and self-esteem in non-familial child molesters. *Journal of Child Sexual Abuse* 6:87–97.

Marshall, W. L., F. Champagne, C. Sturgeon, and P. Bryce. 1997. Increasing the self-esteem of child molesters. *Sexual Abuse: A Journal of Research and Treatment* 9:321–23.

Marshall, L. E., W. L. Marshall, Y. M. Fernandez, P. B. Malcolm, and H. M. Moulden. 2008. The Rockwood Preparatory Program for sexual offenders: Description and preliminary appraisal. *Sexual Abuse: A Journal of Research and Treatment* 20:25–42.

Marshall, L. E., and H. Moulden. 2006. Pre-treatment and psychotherapy with sexual offenders. In *Sexual offender treatment: Controversial issues*, ed. W. L. Marshall, Y. M. Fernandez, L. E. Marshall, and G. A. Serran. Chichester, UK: John Wiley & Sons.

Marshall, W. L., L. E. Marshall, G. A. Serran, and Y. M. Fernandez. 2006. *Treating sexual offenders: An integrated approach*. New York: Routledge.

Marshall, W. L., L. E. Marshall, G. A. Serran, and M. D. O'Brien. Forthcoming. *Sexual offender treatment: A positive approach*. Psychiatric Clinics of North America.

Marshall, W. L., and A. Mazzucco. 1995. Self-esteem and parental attachments in child molesters. *Sexual Abuse: A Journal of Research and Treatment* 7:279–85.

Marshall, W. L., and J. McGuire. 2003. Effect sizes in treatment of sexual offenders. *International Journal of Offender Therapy and Comparative Criminology* 46:653–63.

Marshall, W. L., G. A. Serran, Y. M. Fernandez, R. Mulloy, R. E. Mann, and D. Thornton. 2003. Therapist characteristics in the treatment of sexual offenders: Tentative data on their relationship with indices of behaviour change. *Journal of Sexual Aggression* 9:25–30.

Marshall, W. L., G. Serran, H. Moulden, R. Mulloy, Y. M. Fernandez, R. E. Mann, and D. Thornton. 2002. Therapist features in sexual offender treatment: Their reliable identification and influence on behaviour change. *Clinical Psychology and Psychotherapy* 9:395–405.

Mayerson, N. G. 1984. Preparing clients for group therapy: A critical review and theoretical formulation. *Clinical Psychology Review* 4:191–213.

Miller, W. R., and S. Rollnick. 1991. *Motivational interviewing: Preparing people to change addictive behavior*. New York: Guilford Press.

———, eds. 2002. *Motivational interviewing: Preparing people to change addictive behavior*. 2nd ed. New York: Guilford Press.

Moos, R. H. 1986. *Group environment scale manual*. 2nd ed. Palo Alto, CA: Consulting Psychologists' Press.

Prochaska, J. O., and C. C. DiClemente. 1992. Stages of change in the modification of problem behaviors. In *Progress in behavior modification* 28, ed. M. Hersen, R. M. Eisler, and P. M. Miller, 183–218. Wadsworth Publishing Company.

Shingler, J., and R. E. Mann. 2006. Collaboration in clinical work with sexual offenders: Treatment and risk assessment. In *Sexual offender treatment: Controversial issues,* ed. W. L. Marshall, Y. M. Fernandez, L. E. Marshall, and G. A. Serran, 225–39. Chichester, UK: John Wiley & Sons.

Snyder, C. R., ed. 2000. *Handbook of hope: Theory, measures, and applications.* New York: Academic Press.

Strupp, J., and A. L. Bloxom. 1973. Preparing lower class patients for group psychotherapy: Development and evaluation of a role-induction film. *Journal of Consulting and Clinical Psychology* 41:373–84.

Tangney, J. P., and R. L. Dearing. 2002. *Shame and guilt.* New York: Guilford Press.

Thornton, D., A. Beech, and W. L. Marshall. 2004. Pretreatment self-esteem and post-treatment sexual recidivism. *International Journal of Offender Therapy and Comparative Criminology* 48:587–99.

Whalen, C. 1969. Effects of a model and instructions on group verbal behaviors. *Journal of Consulting and Clinical Psychology* 33:509–21.

A Hopeful Approach to Motivating Sexual Offenders for Change

Heather M. Moulden and William L. Marshall

Many clinicians working with sexual offenders have recognized the impact of motivation on the quality and efficacy of sexual offender treatment. How to engage the client in a process that he often denies, resists, or resents has been a challenge and an ongoing uncertainty. In a review of motivation in sexual offenders, Tierney and McCabe (2002) stated that no empirical investigation has been done on the effectiveness of treatment on the motivation of sexual offenders to change their offending behaviour. In fact, what motivates sexual offenders for treatment remains largely unknown. The implications of poor motivation for change are significant, however, given the impact it has on participation and engagement in treatment, and the resulting benefits and applications of skills to offence-free living. For this reason, many clinicians have introduced motivational techniques into treatment protocols or have used those same techniques as pre-treatment interventions. Positive motivational approaches have been addressed by the many publications devoted to the application of positive psychology concepts to sexual offender treatment, as well as the development of sexual offender–specific theories for change. In spite of a lack of direct empirical evidence, these many publications suggest that motivational and positive approaches to change are increasingly relevant to sexual offender treatment. Indeed the publication of this book illustrates the growing interest and support for increasing positive and motivation-enhancing strategies in our work with sexual offenders.

How do we transmit to our clients a belief in the usefulness of change and convey a sense of ownership of that change to them? Positive approaches to sexual offender therapy are rooted in the belief that individuals working toward change will be more successful and will maintain those changes longer than those working toward lives based on avoidance (Mann 2000). Implicit in this assertion is the belief that individuals will be more motivated to increase positive aspects of their lives than to avoid negative consequences. Positive and motivational approaches are, for all practical purposes, inextricably linked. For those working with sexual offenders, motivation for treatment and change has been central to efforts designed to improve treatment efficacy and to understand what engages clients in the change process (Garland and Dougher 1991; Ginsburg, Mann, Rotgers, and Weekes 2002; Marshall and Moulden 2005). Many theories of motivation have been applied to offenders' engagement in various types of treatment and behaviour-modification interventions.

In this chapter, we propose hope theory as a theory of motivation that is conceptually similar to aspects of sexual offender treatment. Therefore, the approach lends itself well to the integration with theory, research, and treatment protocols for sexual offenders. This chapter will summarize hope theory and its components (i.e., agency, pathways thinking, and goals), and will review the research on its correlates and use with nonoffender samples. Second, the chapter reviews the application of hope theory to sexual offender treatment, and preparatory treatment specifically, and provides some preliminary research that applies this theory to offender populations. The objective of this review is not only to contribute to the general literature on motivation in sexual offenders, but also to further advance our understanding of the role of hope in behavioural change.

Hope Theory

Early conceptualizations of hope defined it as the positive expectancy of goal attainment (Menninger 1959; Stotland 1969). Defined this way, hope seems universal, relevant to all therapies and all modes of change. In fact, Frank (Frank 1989; Frank and Frank 1991) has argued that hope is better conceptualized as a meta-theory, common to all theoretical perspectives, rather than a unique theory of motivation. This definition of hope may explain why we have found it to compliment other therapeutic approaches so well (e.g., cognitive–behavioural therapy, Good Lives). Snyder (2000) has clearly articulated this overarching concept and operationalized measurable components. This process has allowed researchers and clinicians alike to assess the elemental factors, which may in turn account for the effects of a hopeful perspective.

Hope as a theory of motivation is comprised of cognitive, affective, and behavioural experiences that one attends to in the evaluation of one's goals. Snyder and his colleagues have defined hope as "a positive motivational state that is based on an interactively derived sense of successful (a) agency (goal-directed energy) and (b) pathways (planning to meet goals)" (Snyder, Irving, and Anderson 1991). Pathways thinking is characterized by planning the means for goal attainment and linking present behaviours or strategies to future goals (Cheavens, Feldman, Woodward, and Snyder 2006). Agency refers to aspects of freedom, capability, and responsibility for personal decisions and behaviours. It is the belief that the individual is capable of and responsible for the attainment of his/her goals. According to this definition, hope can be divided into three interdependent parts: goals, pathways thinking, and agentic thinking. When paths are successful and goals are attained, the individual's belief that future paths will also be successful increases, thus enhancing agency and pathways, which continue to influence each other, and therefore the overall experience of hope. Based on the relationship between the components (goals, pathways thinking, and agentic thinking), the hopeful person is able to set goals for him/herself, is able to identify realistic plans to attain those goals, and is confident that he/she is capable of attaining those goals.

Although similar, hope has been shown to be distinct from conceptually similar concepts such as optimism or self-efficacy. Agentic thinking, one component of hope theory, includes the assumption that goal-related outcomes are an important aspect of motivation. This position is very similar to Bandura's (1982, 1997) theory of self-efficacy. These theories, however, can be differentiated in two ways. The first is that self-efficacy places emphasis on situation-specific experiences, whereas hope theory argues that goal-directed energy can be both goal-specific and cross-situational. The second is that hope theory places equal emphasis on pathways thinking and goals, along with agentic thinking. In predicting well-being, hope accounted for variance that was independent of self-efficacy, suggesting a unique construct (Magaletta and Oliver 1999). Aspects of hope theory share many elements with other motivational theories, such as control theory and self-esteem. Like self-efficacy, however, research has demonstrated that hope is a distinct theory, contributing unique variance to the explanation of behaviour (see Carver and Scheier 2002; Snyder, Cheavens, and Michael 1999).

Historically, avoidance goals have been overemphasized in sexual offender treatment and relapse prevention. Initially, this emphasis seemed to make intuitive sense, given that treatment focused on reducing problematic behaviours and avoiding high-risk situations. Recently, however, we have come to understand that behaviour can be changed in many different ways, and thus treatment can allow people to strive for a broad variety of goals. Hope theorists have proposed four categories of hopeful goals. They include: (1) approach goals (moving toward a desired outcome); (2) forestalling negative-outcomes goals (deterring or delaying unwanted outcomes); (3) maintenance goals (sustaining the status quo); and (4) enhancement goals, which augment an already positive outcome (Snyder, Feldman, Taylor, Schroeder, and Adams 2000). Therapists identify both approach and avoidance goals, thereby presenting a more realistic version of the types of goals toward which clients are working. Furthermore, when therapists and clients can conceptualize multiple types of goals, the process acknowledges that various modes of behaviour are motivated by different goals, contingencies, and assumptions. Cheavens et al. (2006) explained that hope can be increased and pathological symptoms can be decreased simultaneously, rather than having an exclusive focus on the elimination of negative symptoms. A positive and defining aspect of this approach is that clients are encouraged to map healthy treatment targets, thereby allowing them to focus on the benefits of treatment and thus on the development of internal motivation.

In a previous article addressing the application of hope theory to sexual offender treatment, we discussed the importance of goal setting and pathways thinking for sexual offenders (Moulden and Marshall 2005). Most sexual offenders begin treatment with the global or primary goal of not offending, and although the goal is appropriate and has a worthwhile end, the pathways to get there are oftentimes avoidance-based and poorly defined. Given that hope is comprised of not only goal setting, but also the identification of appropriate pathways and agentic thinking, applying this theory to help motivate clients works in two essential ways. It provides a concrete conceptualization of change and it illustrates how and why motivation improves. Primary goals, such as non-offending, however, still need to be differentiated into more manageable sub-goals.

Snyder (1994) has argued that individuals high in hope have an ability to separate large goals into multiple small goals that are easier to define and that are associated with a greater likelihood for success. In our treatment programs for sexual offenders, we attempt to enhance hope by helping clients identify attainable sub-goals. With each positive experience, the offender's belief that future attempts will also be successful increases, and that success in turn influences future goal setting and improves the flexibility and development of subsequent pathways. Breaking primary goals into sub-goals, and identifying the type of goal as approach, avoidance, maintenance, or enhancement, has been associated with increases in hope and thus motivation to engage in treatment for change. For sexual offenders, this approach to goal setting presumably improves internal motivation, and also fits conceptually with positive approaches to sexual offender treatment as one pathway toward non-offending.

The Role of Hope Theory in Change

Research has demonstrated that hope theory can be operationalized into three distinct concepts that can be reliably measured and assessed. Hope theory also correlates with other related concepts of interest, such as coping, problem solving, and well-being or mental health. Snyder and his colleagues developed tools to measure the construct of hope in adults and children. These instruments assess hope as both a state and a trait and boast good psychometric properties (Snyder 2000).

Hope theory has been applied to explanations for post-traumatic stress disorder, eating disorders, and recently, criminal populations (Sympson 2000;

Irving and Cannon 2000; Moulden and Marshall 2005). Empirical studies examining the effect of hope have shown that increased hope is associated with many varied positive outcomes. Hopeful interventions have improved quality of life and have enhanced recovery from depression in the elderly (Cheavens and Gum 2000) and have been linked to enhanced athletic performance in amateur and professional athletes (Curry and Snyder 2000). Increased hope, in conjunction with cognitive–behavioural approaches, has contributed to symptom reduction in anxiety, panic (Michael 2000), and depression (Cheavens 2000). Hope has also been examined with respect to physical conditions and has been linked to positive coping for individuals diagnosed with breast cancer (Taylor 2000) and AIDS (Moon and Snyder 2000), as well as their family members.

Interestingly, research has found that the enhancement of hope is linked to increases in solution or task-focused coping (Walter and Peller 1992; Snyder, Cheavens, and Michael 1999; Snyder, Ilardi, Michael, and Cheavens 2000). Chang (1998) studied the correlates of hope in non-clinical adult samples. He found that those with high levels of hope demonstrated greater problem-solving skills when compared to low-hope individuals. He also found that high-hope individuals were less likely to use disengaging coping strategies, defined as social withdrawal and problem avoidance. Given that pathways thinking—the ability to define paths and strategies for goal attainment—is a component of hope, it is promising that pathways thinking is related to self-reported use of successful problem-solving techniques and negatively related to avoidance-based coping strategies. For sexual offenders and child molesters especially, emotion or avoidance-focused coping has been identified as problematic and associated with sexual coping. In fact, both child molesters and rapists are more likely than non-offending men to report the use of fantasy or actual sexual abuse to cope with negative emotions and situations (Cortoni and Marshall 2001; Serran, Firestone, Marshall, and Moulden 2007). Furthermore, research by Serran et al. examined the effects of a cognitive–behavioural program on the self-reported use of child molesters' coping strategies in high-risk situations. The researchers' results showed that compared to a waitlist group, treated child molesters identified more effective strategies evidenced by improved general coping techniques, and specific use of task-focused coping and social-diversion strategies. This research provided evidence that coping can be modified in sexual offenders. Given that hope is also associated with enhanced coping, increasing hope seems particularly relevant to the treatment of sexual offenders in that by enhancing hopeful thinking, these clients may be increasingly capable of employing task-focused strategies when confronted with high-risk situations.

Given that hope is related to various positive outcomes, and has been shown to be correlated with behavioural mechanisms implicated in change, such as problem solving and coping, it is likely that increases in hope, as an intervention, would enhance positive psychological changes. Hope theory has been proposed as part of effective preparatory programs, and also recently applied to cognitive therapies (Cheavens et al. 2006). In their review, Cheavens et al. illustrate the similarities between cognitive therapy and hope theory, and argue that hope may complement cognitive interventions. Cognitive therapy focuses on appropriate goal-setting (goals), problem-solving techniques (pathways), and positive self-talk (agency). Cheavens et al. compare Snyder's hope theory and Beck's hopelessness theory, and argue that despite some similarities, these concepts are not simply the inverse. As with sexual offender therapy, which is based on cognitive–behavioural treatment, the authors offer suggestions for how hope theory can be incorporated into cognitive therapy for depression. What is most striking and relevant to sexual offender treatment is the place for identification and elaboration of positive goals. Cheavens et al. highlight the importance of identifying strengths and positive-approach goals as a way of treating negative symptomology.

The Application of Hope to Sexual Offending

Support for the application of hope theory to sexual offender treatment is based on two premises. As discussed above, hope is a motivational theory that is conceptually consistent with existing positive approaches to sexual offender treatment. The research on hope is also consistent with etiological and maintenance factors implicated in sexual offending. In a previous article, we reviewed the theoretical convergence between the etiology and treatment of sexual offenders and hope (Moulden and Marshall 2005). In that paper, we hypothesized about how and why problems with hope may be related to sexual offending. We reviewed three factors believed to be associated with sexually offensive behaviour, giving particular attention to the overlap those factors had with hope theory, namely developmental factors, coping strategies, and negative mood.

Developmental factors such as hostile and insecure childhood environments have been identified as contributing to criminal behaviour. We hypothesized that such factors may predispose sexual offenders to having low hope (characterized by poor goal definition), restricted pathways generation, and a lack of agentic thinking. Specifically, negative early childhood experiences, such as abuse, insecure attachment, and inconsistent discipline, interfere with both learning and emotion regulation. Consistency and predictability provide children with a template for the cause-and-effect relationship of behaviour. When consistency is lacking, children may be deprived of the opportunity to understand this relationship, and thus that they are responsible for and capable of formulating plans and affecting change (Snyder 2000).

Coping was identified earlier as playing an important role in sexual offending and it has been shown to relate to hopefulness in non-clinical samples, as well. An inverse relationship has been found, such that disengaging, or avoidance coping is negatively related to high hope, and task or solution-focused coping is positively related to high hope. Since research has shown that sexual offenders engage in more emotional or avoidance-based types of coping—sexual coping specifically—we can deduce that by increasing hope (e.g., agency, pathways, goals), sexual offenders may engage in more appropriate coping strategies. This assumption, however, remains an unanswered empirical question.

A third potential explanation for how hope may impact sexual offending is based on a suggestion by Snyder and his colleagues. They posited that emotional responses are a function of an individual's analysis of goal pursuits (Snyder et al. 1996). A characteristic of hopeful individuals is their ability to respond positively when confronting obstacles to their goals. These individuals remain optimistic and draw upon agentic thinking and their ability to flexibly redefine pathways. For low-hope individuals, however, such barriers can produce negative emotional states, and they may respond by using ineffective coping strategies or simply by giving up (Snyder 1994). In research on the relationship between coping and mood state in sexual offenders, we found that for some sexual offenders, negative mood states were associated with the tendency to use sex as a coping strategy (Marshall, Marshall, and Moulden 2000; Serran, Marshall, Moulden, and Marshall 2001) and many clients reported negative effect and/or conflict prior to offending. Although seeming to be indirect, hope, mood, and coping skills appear related in inverse proportion to sexual abuse. It may be that by enhancing hope and, as a consequence, the ability to overcome barriers to goal pursuits, offenders may be less vulnerable to negative mood states and associated tendencies toward poor coping. These are some of the domains we have reviewed in our examination of the relationship between hope theory and sexual offending. At this point, they remain hypotheses to be tested, but we believe they hold promise for understanding the link between hope theory and sexual abuse, thus improving our ability to conceptualize resistance and improve motivation.

Support for Hopeful Approaches in Forensic Populations

The application of hope to forensic populations is a relatively new endeavor. Despite a prominent role in medical and psychological practice, and the theoretical convergence of hope theory and sexual offender treatment, hope has been late in its application to criminology and forensic domains. Rising interest in positive psychology approaches to rehabilitation are evident in the correctional services of countries such as the United Kingdom, Australia, and Canada. In fact, research has shown that many of the factors that call for motivational and positive techniques (e.g., poor knowledge, ability, and motivation; weak commitment to change; limited goals; and poor judgment) mediate the identified relationship between resistance to treatment and risk for future sexual reoffending (Doren 2004).

Martin and Stermac (2007) suggest that by applying hope theory, criminal behaviour can be conceptualized as choosing inappropriate pathways and having limited agency for desired outcomes. Indeed, both criminal behaviour and low levels of hope have been related to poor problem solving, inappropriate coping skills, and increased psychopathology (Chang 1998). In a study of 50 male and 50 female adult Canadian inmates, Martin and Stermac (2007) administered self-report questionnaires about hope and problem solving to investigate the nature of hope in criminal offenders in relation to their past and future criminal behaviour. The researchers collected information about demographics, criminal history, and risk of recidivism. The researchers found that lower levels of hope were related to poorer problem-solving skills, and that overall, the offenders studied exhibited weaknesses with respect to problem solving. The inmates were characterized by poor decision making and faulty solution implementation. Despite the fact that the respondents were able to generate methods of solving problems, their choices were not the most effective, and the inmates often failed to consider the long-term consequences of their decisions. Of particular relevance to offender populations was the finding that low hope was directly related to a larger percentage of inmates' involvement in the criminal justice system, and presented as a greater risk for reoffending compared to individuals who rated themselves more highly on hope. This finding is not surprising, given the above noted relationship to poor problem solving and coping.

Specifically, the authors (Martin and Stermac 2007) found that hope was negatively correlated to the Level of Service Inventory–Ontario Revision (LSI-OR) ($r = -.26$, $p < .05$), which is an actuarial risk/needs tool. This finding suggests that high hope is associated with lower risk for reoffending, and fewer criminogenic needs. Interestingly, only the agency subscale of hope correlated with risk levels, not pathways thinking. This relationship is particularly important, because it suggests that teaching skills to the inmates and having them learn the means to achieve their goals is not sufficient to lower risk; a client must also recognize his responsibility to and capacity for change. To further examine the influence of hope on relative risk for future reoffending, the authors performed a regression analysis. The results demonstrated that, in this sample at least, only agency, problem solving, and ethnicity account for unique variance in the explanation of risk for future reoffending.

Given the association between hope (and agency in particular) and the risk for recidivism in a sample of non-sex offenders, it seems likely that hope would also play a role in the risk management of sexual offenders. Although this relationship has not been investigated directly as of yet, research on the application of hope in the treatment of sexual offenders lends support to this hypothesis. In 1997, a preparatory program was introduced at the Millhaven Assessment Unit, an induction centre in the Ontario Region of the Correctional Service of Canada. The goal of this program was to begin addressing issues of resistance, motivation, and engagement in sexual offender treatment. The model of the program is grounded in positive approaches to therapy, building on foundational theories, such as motivational interviewing (Miller and Rollnick 2002), self-efficacy (Bandura 1982, 1997), and the literature on positive therapeutic process (Marshall et al. 2002). Other positive approaches have been introduced and integrated into the mode of therapy implemented in this program, such as the Good Lives model (Ward and Marshall 2004) and hope theory (Moulden and Marshall 2005; Snyder 2000).

In 2002, a study was undertaken to determine if the Millhaven Preparatory Program enhanced hope and increased motivation and readiness for change in sexual offenders (Marshall, Marshall, Malcolm, Fernandez, and Moulden 2007). This pilot study included 26 adult males who had been convicted of sexual offences against children and/or adults, and who were sentenced to two or more years. Participants completed the Dispositional Hope Scale (Snyder et al. 1991), State Hope Scale (Snyder et al. 1996), Self-Efficacy Scale (Sherer et al. 1982), and the University of Rhode Island Change Assessment (URICA; McConnaughy, Prochaska, and Velicer 1983) upon entering the treatment program and again when they completed treatment approximately six to eight weeks later. The researchers also collected demographic and criminal history information on the study subjects.

Results from this study showed significant changes from pre- to post-treatment on the overall scores for each of the hope measures, as well as on the agentic thinking subscale of trait hope. Self-efficacy was also significantly improved, as were scores on the URICA, which showed a dramatic decrease in contemplation and an increase in action stages. Finally, the researchers examined the relationship between the various measures to better understand how hope and change are related. Trait hope was positively related to state hope, and to contemplation and action subscale scores on the URICA. Trait hope was negatively associated with precontemplation scores and state hope was positively correlated with self-efficacy.

These findings suggested that participants in the preparatory program showed consistent and significant improvements in their overall hopefulness and in their beliefs about their capacity for beneficial change. The participants also more fully recognized the need for change than previously, and many demonstrated a shift into the action stage of change. This research, although preliminary, offered some support for the assertion that levels of hope can be increased through engagement in preparatory programs, and suggested that such programs are an effective means of increasing hope, motivation, and readiness for change.

Participants from the preparatory program graduate to a full treatment program, and we wondered what the long-term impact of improved hope, increased motivation, and readiness for change might be on subsequent treatment engagement, performance, and ultimately recidivism. The research of Martin and Stermac (2007) showed that agentic thinking is the component of hope most relevant to the risk of future offending. Indeed, participants in the preparatory program evidenced the most change, based on this aspect of hope. Therefore, it seems likely that sexual offenders who had benefited from a pre-treatment program, which successfully increased agentic thinking, might also do better in full treatment and on release to the community.

To investigate the outcome of those offenders who had participated in the preparatory program, we (Marshall et al. 2007) compared these offenders to a closely matched group that had also received a full-treatment program but had not participated in the preparatory program. We found that those individuals who had participated in the preparatory program were likely to be placed in a less secure institution, and they showed significantly reduced recidivism after a three-year follow-up.

The data presented here represent preliminary investigations of the relationship between hope and the treatment of offender populations. On their own, the results are modest and we must be cautious about overextrapolating. Taken together, however, the convergent findings suggest that motivational interventions, and hope specifically, are associated with many positive outcomes, such as increased agency and reductions in risk and recidivism.

Incorporating Hope Theory and Treatment for Sexual Offenders

Hope has previously been applied to pre-treatment intervention designed to motivate individuals for various types of behavioural change. Pre-treatment programs are an effective way of enhancing appropriate thinking about plans to achieve goals so that clients will be more prepared and internally motivated once they begin treatment proper (Mayerson 1984; Zwick and Atkinson 1985). A study by Irving et al. (1997) examined the impact of pre-treatment on measures of overall well-being, including levels of hope. High- and low-hope individuals were randomly assigned to either a five-week pre-treatment orientation, or a waitlist. Compared to participants with pre-orientation high hope, low-hope participants showed greater responsiveness to the pre-treatment orientation as measured by well-being, level of functioning, and state hope. Thus, the clients who were initially lowest in overall hope benefited the most from pathways thinking that was taught and reinforced in the pre-treatment orientation.

Often sexual offenders agree to participate in treatment based on external motivators such as the eligibility for early release or the possibility of residing at a treatment-oriented facility. However, the external motivation to refuse treatment is also very strong. In fact, in prison settings, offenders may be focused strictly on the potential negative consequences of participating in treatment (e.g., being identified by other inmates as a sexual offender). It is important to recognize that our clients, unlike most others, have not sought our services and may not recognize the problematic nature of their behaviour. In many sexual offender treatment programs, a notable amount of time is devoted to reducing resistance, increasing motivation, and engaging clients in the therapeutic process. As such, the benefits to clients are limited, because their initial resistance directly impacts on the quality and quantity of time spent addressing identified treatment targets and risk factors.

The focus of preparatory treatment is on the individual's readiness for change and motivation for treatment. Part of what makes someone prepared to engage in the treatment process is his belief that therapy will be beneficial to him. The matching of treatment intervention to motivation to change is well documented (DiClemente and Prochaska 1998; Prochaska and Norcross 2002). There are a number of basic goals for pre-treatment with sexual offenders (see Marshall and Moulden 2006). Here, we examine these goals from a hope-theory perspective. The first is to increase agency. Some strategies aimed at increasing agentic thinking include discussing the therapy process and revealing to clients what therapy will be about. In doing so, we make explicit the process of change and the client's responsibility for that change.

Another technique is to observe skills and strengths and identify them with clients. For some clients, recognizing the skills they possess is a new task, and may be difficult at first. This exercise provides clients with a sense of personal control, responsibility, and agency. It also demonstrates that as part of therapy, we are also interested in strengths, skills, and goals associated with enhancing clients' lives.

A second aim of pre-treatment is to reduce resistance. As sexual offenders, many of our clients see treatment as something forced upon them, and from which they will derive few, if any, benefits. Part of reducing resistance is to begin to personalize the general treatment plans and exercises. For example, many clients may share the primary goal of living offence-free, but each client will have individualized sub-goals, and ideas about the best way to achieve those goals. In doing so, the personal benefits are highlighted, and the client begins to take ownership of the treatment goals. A third and related goal of pre-treatment with sexual offenders is to identify goals, and sub-goals. Some of these goals are imposed, such as not reoffending, but many clients, when given the opportunity, are able to identify important and clinically relevant sub-goals, and possibly "stretch goals" such as anger-management, intimacy issues, or personal-growth issues. Lastly, pre-treatment is a time to discuss the potential pathways to the goals clients have defined. These pathways are the plans for how the offender will achieve his goals in subsequent full-treatment programs. Examples of pathways include participating in treatment programs, applying for employment upgrading, or finding a relationship. Client deficits and risk factors are emphasized in the form of assessment reports, and previous clinical documentation. Information about client skills, strengths, and personal pathways must be explored and uncovered within the treatment milieu. Given the benefits of acknowledging and incorporating strengths and approach goals into motivational techniques and, ultimately, treatment, we suspect that these benefits could be revealed from initial client assessment.

As described in the hope literature, hope techniques can be incorporated into existing treatment protocols in a variety of ways. Below are suggested applications for sexual offender treatment that focus on improving hope and thus internal motivation for change. The enumeration of past goal attainments and highlighting the individual's skills and successes conveys to the client that therapy will be about moving toward positive changes as well as away from negative patterns. The therapist works with the client to identify strengths. This process not only improves agentic thinking but also helps the therapist with treatment planning, the allocation of resources, and the management of waitlists. Many offenders possess skills and strategies that have contributed to offence-free periods, or even instances when they resisted offending. Building on those resources provides a template for useful pathways thinking later on in treatment. Cheavens et al. (2006) described stretch goals, which encourage the clients to set their sights beyond the attainment of the primary goal. For example, for sexual offenders, a primary goal may be to be offence-free. One sub-goal may be to improve the quality of social relationships, with further sub-goals including increased contact with family members, participation in social activities, and improved social skills. The stretch goal invites the client to look beyond the primary goal to a more challenging goal that builds upon the previous goals, such as developing romantic and intimate relationships. Continuously setting and meeting stretch goals teaches clients the process of striving and encourages individuals to move toward a more positive, strength-based lifestyle. Stretch goals are related to the concept of enhancement goals described above; they encourage clients to look beyond their goals. It is important for treatment providers to plan out the paths associated with each goal, however, and to demonstrate for offenders how the achievement of one goal provides the foundation for reaching subsequent goals.

One strategy for delineating such a plan is the use of goal hierarchies, a process that organizes sub-goals, primary goals, and stretch goals (Cheavens et al. 2006). This type of goal-mapping naturally leads clients to consider associated pathways, which are congruent with both sub-goals and primary goals, and which provide a bridge between the various levels. Explicitly defining the goals and processes this way demonstrates pathways, focuses on strengths, and instills in the client a sense of agency. Cheavens et al. demonstrated that because hope theory is in many ways a uniting theory of motivation and change, it is easily integrated into existing treatment protocols, such as cognitive therapy. This is precisely what we have found in the application of hope theory to sexual offender treatment.

Assessing for Strengths to Motivate Clients

Assessment of sexual offenders has primarily focused on the identification of skill deficits and risk factors implicated in the original decision to offend or on etiological theories and predictors of relapse and recidivism. These targets are clearly appropriate to the goal of decreasing problematic behaviours. Treatment models such as the Good Lives approach, however, have highlighted the importance of broad lifestyle improvements in reducing future sexual offences. In a recent study, Wakeling, Webster, Moulden, and Marshall (forthcoming) interviewed incest offenders about what factors informed their decisions to offend and also their choices to refrain from offending. Respondents reported that not only did proximal factors such as victim supervision and victim rebuff deter them, but the responders also identified important factors present during offence-free periods. Offence-free periods were characterized by social integration, employment, and positive mood. These offenders demonstrated to us that they possessed skills to achieve these components of greater life satisfaction at some point in their lives, and identified such factors themselves as protective. Interestingly, inquiries about protective and positive factors are virtually never incorporated into comprehensive sexual offender assessments. Furthermore, to our knowledge, this study represented one of the only attempts to investigate protective factors in sexual offenders (Wakeling et al. forthcoming).

The inclusion of strength-based queries in sexual offender assessments can benefit program administrators and therapists, as well. Previously in this chapter, we reviewed a study by Irving et al. (1997) who found that pre-treatment intervention had the greatest impact on low-hope individuals. These participants came to the intervention with internally low motivation characterized by poor definition of goals and pathways, and a limited belief in their capacity for change. These features are characteristic of many sexual offender clients. Therefore, by including measures of hope or other measures of motivation, programming can be personalized, based on the specific strengths and weaknesses of each offender, and can be offered to those most in need of motivational enhancement.

Future Directions

The application of hope theory to sexual offenders provides additional support for positive approaches to change. It also offers the benefits of motivational enhancement with this population. Much of the work on hope among forensic populations has been theoretical and at this point, research has not investigated the direct link between hope and sexual offender treatment and subsequent recidivism. In this chapter, however, we have attempted to review research and theory, which may guide program development and implementation. Further research is needed to assess the effectiveness of enhancing hope in sexual offenders. Our research has suggested two possible outcomes of hope. The first suggests that hopeful therapeutic intervention can have an impact on motivating clients for change and improving self-efficacy. As described above, however, our preparatory program incorporates elements from a number of positive approaches, in addition to hope theory. Despite efforts to highlight hope in the treatment program, it is not possible to attribute all benefits to hope alone. A useful follow-up would be to replicate our preparatory program study while more exclusively adhering to hope theory. In evaluating the role of hope, it would be very useful to include process and outcome measures to better understand what aspects (i.e., pathways, goals, and agency) exert the greatest influence on motivation, and through which mechanisms (e.g., problem solving, self-efficacy, coping, and responsibility) they have their greatest effect.

Research on hope is also needed to elucidate the very promising, but conservative finding that individuals who graduated from the preparatory program recidivated at a lower rate than those who had not participated in this program. Again, hope may be one of many factors contributing to the success of the participants. This study suggests, however, that in sexual offenders, hope may not only improve motivation and enhance engagement in the treatment, but hope may also exert more distal effects, through reduced recidivism.

Clinically, hope theory provides a well-articulated and elegant model for motivational enhancement. It is intuitively appealing in many ways, and it mirrors many aspects of effective treatment programs for sexual offenders. It is consistent with other empirically supported cognitive approaches, and shares assumptions with humanistic and experiential theories of change. This may account for why Frank (1989) suggested that hope, as a concept, is more accurately described as a meta-theory. It is this quality (i.e., hope's similarity to so many other psychological theories of change), however, that allows it to be incorporated both conceptually and in an applied sense to existing interventions. As a preparatory technique, hope has found support in enhancing motivation with a variety of clinical samples, including forensic and non-forensic populations. In offender populations, hope has also proven to be associated with improved readiness for change, and positive, long-term outcomes. Incorporating hopeful techniques into conventional sexual offender treatment improves motivation, and emphasizes skills, strengths, and a future-oriented focus.

The origins of sexual offending fit with what is known about the failure to develop hope and support the ways hope interacts with coping, mood, and problem solving. As reviewed here, many clinical applications of hope theory are consistent with therapeutic techniques for sexual offenders. Fundamentally, hope theory provides another example of how positive approaches more effectively engage individuals in the process of making change. The theory provides a clearly defined explanation for how change happens, how as therapists we can assist in the process, and how our clients make change happen.

REFERENCES

Bandura, A. 1982. Self-efficacy mechanism in human agency. *American Psychologist* 37:122–47.
———. 1997. *Self-efficacy: The exercise of control.* New York: Times Books.
Carver, C. S., and M. F. Scheier. 2002. The hopeful optimist. *Psychological Inquiry* 13:288–90.
Chang, E. C. 1998. Hope, problem-solving ability, and coping in a college student population: Some implications for theory and practice. *Journal of Clinical Psychology* 54:953–62.
Cheavens, J. 2000. Hope and depression: Light through the shadows. In *Handbook of hope: Theory, measures, and applications,* ed. C. R. Snyder, 321–40. New York: Academic Press.
Cheavens, J., D. B. Feldman, J. T. Woodward, and C. R. Snyder. 2006. Hope in cognitive psychotherapies: On working with client strengths. *Journal of Cognitive Psychotherapy: An international quarterly* 20:135–45.
Cheavens, J., and A. Gum. 2000. Gray Power: Hope and Older Adults. In *The Handbook of Hope Theory: Measures and applications,* ed. C. R. Snyder, 201–22. San Diego, CA: Academic Press.

Cortoni, F. A., and W. L. Marshall. 2001. Sex as a coping strategy and its relationship to juvenile sexual history and intimacy in sexual offenders. *Sexual Abuse: A Journal of Research and Treatment* 13:27–43.

Curry, L. A., and C. R. Snyder. 2000. Hope takes the field: Mind matters in athletic performances. In *Handbook of hope: Theory, measures, and applications*, ed. C. R. Snyder, 243–60. New York: Academic Press.

DiClemente, C. C., and J. O. Prochaska. 1998. Toward a comprehensive, transtheoretical model of change: Stages of change and addictive behaviors. In *Treating addictive behaviors, 2nd ed.*, ed. W. R. Miller and N. Heather, 3–24. New York: Plenum Press.

Doren, D. 2004. Toward a multidimensional model for sexual recidivism risk. *Journal of Interpersonal Violence* 19:835–56.

Frank, J. D. 1989. Non-specific aspects of treatment: The view of the psychotherapist. In *Non-specific aspects of treatment*, ed. M. Sheppard and N. Satorius, 95–114. Toronto: Hans Huber.

Frank, J. D., and J. B Frank. 1991. *Persuasion and healing.* Baltimore, MD: Johns Hopkins University Press.

Garland, R. J., and M. J. Dougher. 1991. Motivational intervention in the treatment of sex offenders. In *Motivational interviewing: Preparing people to change addictive behaviour,* ed. W. R. Miller and S. R. Rollnick, 303–13. New York: Guilford Press.

Ginsburg, J. I. D., R. E. Mann, F. Rotgers, and J. R. Weekes. 2002. Motivational interviewing with criminal justice populations. In *Motivational interviewing: Preparing people for change*, 2nd ed., ed W. R. Miller and S. R. Rollnick, 333–46. New York: Guilford Press.

Irving, L. M., and R. Cannon. 2000. Starving for hope: Goals, agency, and pathways in the development and treatment of eating disorders. In *Handbook of hope: Theory, measures, and applications,* ed. C. R. Snyder, 261–83. New York: Academic Press.

Irving, L. M, C. R. Snyder, L. Gravel, J. Hanke, P. Hilberg, and N. Nelson. 1997. *Hope and effectiveness of a pre-therapy orientation group for community mental health center clients.* Paper presented at the Western Psychological Association Convention. Seattle, WA.

Magaletta, P. R., and J. M. Oliver. 1999. The hope construct, will and ways: Their relative relations with self-efficacy, optimism, and general well-being. *Journal of Clinical Psychology* 55:539–51.

Mann, R. E. 2000. Managing resistance and rebellion in relapse prevention intervention. In *Remaking relapse prevention with sex offenders*, ed. D. R. Laws, S. M. Hudson, and T. Ward, 187–200. Thousand Oaks, CA: Sage.

Marshall, L. E., W. L. Marshall, P. B. Malcolm, Y. M. Fernandez, and H. M. Moulden. 2007. *Effectiveness of a preparatory program for sexual offenders.* Manuscript submitted for publication.

Marshall, L. E., W. L. Marshall, and H. M. Moulden. 2000. *Mood induction with sexual offenders.* Paper presented at the 19th Annual Treatment and Research Conference of the Association for the Treatment of Sexual Abusers. San Diego, CA.

Marshall, L. E., and H. M. Moulden. 2006. Preparatory programs for sexual offenders. In *Sexual offender treatment: Controversial issues,* ed. W. L. Marshall, Y. M. Fernandez, L. E. Marshall, and G. A. Serran, 199–210. Chichester: John Wiley & Sons, Ltd.

Marshall, W. L., G. Serran, H. M. Moulden, R. Mulloy, Y. M. Fernandez, R. Mann, and D. Thornton. 2002. Therapist features in sexual offender treatment: Their reliable identification and influence on behaviour change. *Clinical Psychology and Psychotherapy* 9(6):395–405.

Marshall, W. L., T. Ward, R. E. Mann, H. M. Moulden, Y. M. Fernandez, G. A. Serran, and L. E. Marshall. 2005. Working positively with sexual offenders: Maximizing the effectiveness of treatment. *Journal of Interpersonal Violence* 20(9):1096–1114.

Martin, K., and L. E. Stermac. 2007. *Measuring hope: Is hope related to problem solving and criminal behaviour in offenders?* Poster presented at the North American Corrections and Criminal Justice Psychology Conference. Ottawa, Ontario, Canada.

Mayerson, N. H. 1984. Preparing clients for group therapy: A critical review and theoretical formulation. *Clinical Psychology Review* 4:191–213.

McConnaughy, E. N., J. O. Prochaska, and W. F. Velicer. 1983. Stages of change in psychotherapy: Measurement and sample profiles. *Psychotherapy: Theory, Research and Practice* 20:368–75.

Menninger, K. 1959. The academic lecture on hope. *The American Journal of Psychiatry* 109:481–91.

Michael, S. T. 2000. Hope conquers fear: Overcoming anxiety and panic attacks. In *Handbook of hope: Theory, measures, and applications*, ed. C. R. Snyder, 301–20. New York: Academic Press.

Miller, W. R., and S. Rollnick. 2002. *Motivational interviewing: Preparing people for change*. 2nd ed. New York: Guilford Press.

Moon, C., and C. R. Snyder. 2000. Hope and the journey with AIDS. In *Handbook of hope: Theory, measures, and applications*, ed. C. R. Snyder, 341–54. New York: Academic Press.

Moulden, H. M., and W. L. Marshall. 2005. Hope in the treatment of sexual offenders: The potential application of hope theory. *Psychology, Crime & Law* 11:329–42.

Prochaska, J. O., and J. C. Norcross. 2002. Stages of change. In *Psychotherapy relationships that work: Therapist contributions and responsiveness to patients*, ed. J. C. Norcross, 303–13. London: Oxford University Press.

Serran, G. A., P. Firestone, W. L. Marshall, and H. M. Moulden. 2007. Changes in coping strategies following treatment in child molesters. *Journal of Interpersonal Violence* 22:1199–1210.

Serran, G. A., L. E. Marshall, H. M. Moulden, and W. L. Marshall. 2001. *An exploration of mood state, coping, and sexual compulsivity in sexual offenders.* Paper presented at the 20th Annual Treatment and Research Conference for the Association for the Treatment of Sexual Abusers. San Antonio, TX.

Sherer, M., J. E. Maddux, B. Mercandante, S. Prentice-Dunn, B. Jacobs, and R. Rogers. 1982. The Self-Efficacy Scale: Construction and validation. *Psychological Reports* 51:663–71.

Snyder, C. R. 1994. *The psychology of hope: You can get there from here*. New York: Free Press.

———, ed. 2000. *Handbook of hope: Theory, measures, and applications*. New York: Academic Press.

Snyder, C. R., J. Cheavens, and S. T. Michael. 1999. Hoping. In *Coping: The psychology of what works*, ed. C. R. Snyder, 205–51. New York: Oxford University Press.

Snyder, C. R., D. B. Feldman, J. D. Taylor, L. L. Schroeder, and V. Adams III. 2000. The roles of hopeful thinking in preventing problems and promoting strengths. *Applied and Preventive Psychology: Current Scientific Perspectives* 9:249–69.

Snyder, C. R., S. Ilardi, S. Michael, and J. Cheavens. 2000. Hope theory: Updating a common process for psychological change. In *Handbook of psychological change: Psychotherapy practice for the 21st century,* ed. C. R. Snyder and R. E. Ingram, 128–53. New York: John Wiley & Sons.

Snyder, C. R., L. Irving, and J. R. Anderson. 1991. Hope and health: Measuring the will and the ways. In *Handbook of social and clinical psychology: The health perspective,* ed. C. R. Snyder and D. R. Forsyth, 285–305. New York: Pergamon Press.

Snyder, C. R., S. C. Sympson, F. C. Ybasco, T. F. Borders, M. A. Babyak, and R. L. Higgins. 1996. Development and validation of the State Hope Scale. *Journal of Personality and Social Psychology* 2:321–35.

Stotland, E. 1969. *The psychology of hope.* San Francisco: Jossey-Bass.

Sympson, S. C. 2000. Rediscovering hope: Understanding and working with survivors of trauma. In *Handbook of hope: Theory, measures, and applications,* ed. C. R. Snyder, 285–300. New York: Academic Press.

Taylor, J. D. 2000. Confronting breast cancer: Hopes for health. In *Handbook of hope: Theory, measures, and applications,* ed. C. R. Snyder, 355–72. New York: Academic Press.

Tierney, D. W., and M. P. McCabe. 2002. Motivation for behavior change among sex offenders: A review of the literature. *Clinical Psychology Review* 22:113–29.

Wakeling, H. C., S. Webster, H. M. Moulden, and W. L. Marshall. Forthcoming. Decisions to offend in men who sexually abuse their daughters. *Journal of Sexual Aggression.*

Walter, J. L., and J. E. Peller. 1992. *Becoming solution focused in brief therapy.* New York: Brunner/Mazel.

Ward, T., and W. L. Marshall. 2004. Good Lives, aetiology and the rehabilitation of sex offenders: A bridging theory. *Journal of Sexual Aggression* 10:153–69.

Zwick, R., and C. C. Atkinson. 1985. Effectiveness of a client pre-therapy orientation program. *Journal of Counseling Psychology* 32:514–24.

Motivational Interviewing in the Treatment of Sexual Abusers

David S. Prescott

> *"Always give the patient every opportunity to resist."*
> —Milton Erickson

In his later years, celebrated hypnotherapist Milton Erickson recalled growing up on a Wisconsin farm and encountering a resistant calf:

> *One winter day, with the weather below zero, my father led a calf out of the barn to the water trough. After the calf had satisfied its thirst, they turned back to the barn, but at the doorway the calf stubbornly braced its feet, and despite my father's desperate pulling on the halter, he could not budge the animal. I was outside playing in the snow and, observing the impasse, began laughing heartily. My father challenged me to pull the calf into the barn. Recognizing the situation as one of unreasoning stubborn resistance on the part of the calf, I decided to let the calf have full opportunity to resist, since that was what it apparently wished to do. Accordingly I presented the calf with a double bind by seizing it by the tail and pulling it away from the barn, while my father continued to pull it inward. The calf promptly chose to resist the weaker of the two forces and dragged me into the barn.*

People who have sexually abused are not cattle, yet reluctant behavior appears everywhere. How is it that some people who have sexually abused are able to make it all the way through treatment and find real value along the way, while others fall by the wayside or even cheat their way through? It is clear that individual disposition is important, but what can the clinician do to help clients stay the course? How can professionals help build healthier lives as well as safer communities?

Rick, aged 29, walks in for his first individual session with his clinician. He was convicted of molesting an 11-year-old girl, his niece. He accepted a plea agreement to avoid what could have been a lengthy prison sentence. There is little question that Rick engaged in the behavior for which he entered the legal system. However, he feels two ways about being in treatment. While he is motivated to live a better life and avoid getting into further trouble, he is also motivated to keep his family together. He wonders what would happen if he entered treatment and acknowledged having caused sexual harm. Would his family leave him? He believes he is different from those whose mug shots he has seen on television news programs. While there is little doubt that his motivation to change will wax and wane throughout treatment, his initial commitment as he enters a treatment program will be particularly important. Motivation can change throughout the treatment experience. While Rick's initial motivation is to meet the demands of the legal system and not lose his family, he may well find that changing becomes more important as he moves further into a treatment program.

For Rick, treatment will be like a swimming pool. He will stay at the shallow end where he can feel some degree of safety before venturing out where his feet no longer touch the bottom, and he is more likely to need help when things get difficult. In fact, should anyone try to impose change on him, he will quickly become resistant. Why should Rick be any different from other human beings? After all, the research on personal change clearly shows that most people who enter treatment are not necessarily thinking about genuine change. Yet many sexual-abuser treatment programs behave as if they are.

Motivational interviewing is a person-centered counseling approach in which the practitioner uses a guiding style to enable the client to build and strengthen his or her own motivation for change. Although Miller (1983) and Miller and Rollnick (1991) first coined the term, many others have helped to develop motivational interviewing into its current form (e.g., Moyers, Martin, Manuel, Miller, and Ernst, draft manuscript). This chapter describes ways that professionals can use motivational interviewing in their work with people who have sexually abused. It is by no means the final word on the topic, and appears with the hope that readers will explore this topic further through training and other venues where they can receive helpful feedback on their practice. Since most treatment with this population takes place in group therapy settings, a separate chapter with specific applications appears in this volume (i.e., Prescott and Ross).

As one reads the literature about it, motivational interviewing appears easy to do, but it becomes more complex in actual practice. Professionals commonly believe they already know how to do it. In fact, they usually do. The problem is that many professionals who know how to use motivational interviewing do not actually use it in practice as much as they think. As a result, they may be helping clients less than they believe.

Before describing motivational interviewing further, it helps to engage in a self-assessment exercise. Many trainees experience this exercise as a helpful means of establishing an understanding of how they respond differently before and after exposure to motivational interviewing. Take out a piece of paper and write down your responses to these typical statements that indicate client resistance. Make sure to write your responses on the left side of the paper. When you have finished this book, you can then write out your new responses on the right-hand side and compare them, having studied (and hopefully practiced) the motivational interviewing style and skills described below:

1. I'm only here because of the court. I don't believe in treatment.
2. How long are you going to keep asking me questions?
3. I attended a treatment program in prison and it was no good.
4. My private life is none of your business.
5. All this talking is wasting my time. You need to tell me exactly which behaviors you want me to change.
6. You can't change me. No one's going to change me. I'm not a robot.

7. What exact credentials do you have to do this work? Where did you go to school?
8. Go ahead and do what you're going to do; you're going to do it anyway.
9. I don't think I belong in treatment. I'm not like your other clients.
10. You know, we could hit it off nicely under other circumstances.

Style and Spirit

Central to motivational interviewing is the professional's capacity for collaboration, evocation, and support of the client's autonomy. This approach is more challenging than it might seem. Many of us work with clients who appear to have little investment in change or willingness to participate in treatment. Clients enter many settings ready, willing, and able to do legal battle with their therapist. Under these conditions, professionals understandably might resort to tactics aimed at gaining short-term compliance with treatment or supervision expectations. However, these same tactics, such as a harsh, confrontational approach, are more likely to meet the momentary needs of the professional than the long-term needs of the client and community (Garland and Dougher 1991). Of particular concern, these short-term tactics may come remarkably easily to professionals while research has found them to be less effective than approaches delivered with a warm, empathic, rewarding, and directive style (Marshall 2005).

How is it that people in the helping professions can so quickly revert to short-term, compliance-based tactics? There are likely many reasons, although motivational trainees have typically provided a number of common ones. These include fear of appearing "soft" on offenders, concerns that a warm approach leaves them open to easy manipulation, and a sense that others demand immediate gains. In some cases, it seems that healthy professionals engage in unhealthy practices because their clients tacitly encourage them to do so. This last reason deserves further attention.

One motivational interviewing training exercise encourages participants to play either the role of a client entering treatment or the treatment provider.

In this exercise, the treatment provider receives explicit instructions to provide the "client" with reasons to change, strategies for change, and encouragement that will allow the client to change. The clients, whose only instruction is to be ambivalent about change, invariably become defensive and resistant. Participants playing the clients often report that they find this role simple to adopt and easy to maintain. In fact, it is easier to play a waiting game of reluctance to change than it is to discuss change. Meanwhile, participants role-playing the therapist typically report that the exercise is exhausting and that they worked too hard for very little gain. Just the same, these professionals frequently experience an intense sense of responsibility for clients' change processes.

Practitioners often refer to this sense of responsibility for the clients' change as an example of "the righting reflex." This reflex results from that all-too-frequent response human beings have wherein they feel they must fix things or set something right. This urge to remediate can be key to survival (for example, the effective parent of a disease-stricken child knows to seek medical assistance rather than to engage in psychotherapeutic discussions). However, it can stop client change in its tracks, since prompting this reflex is often the client's intent. In its most obvious forms, it can appear as therapists scold, attempt to educate, or generally talk at clients when they are unwilling or not ready to listen. Common reactions to the righting reflex include feeling misunderstood, angry, insulted, disrespected, and defiant. Thus, it is no surprise when these clients deny, minimize, or justify their behavior.

Motivational interviewing does not require professionals to abandon these concerns. Rather, professionals can simply put their concerns on the side while they await the client's incentives or reasons for change. Professionals can be at their most effective by entering each interaction with an explicit agenda of collaboration, which means that clinicians abandon attempts to fix problems or issue directions. It means asking questions, offering reflections, and providing summaries of what the client says in order to demonstrate that the clinician is listening. From here, the client can make his or her own case for change. These actions receive further discussion later. The vital thing to keep in mind, as the research shows, is that people who perceive themselves as having some degree of choice in an endeavor often become more compliant with it (Bem 1972; Ryan and Deci 2000).

Along the same lines, professionals are most effective when they respect a client's autonomy. Often clients are unwilling and unready to change. A shift in behavioral patterns is something that only a client can decide to make. In some cases, the willingness to make change defines the line between where a client finds himself and his future. To use motivational interviewing techniques as a means of manipulating someone to change against his will is unethical and likely ineffective (Miller and Rollnick 2002). Ultimately, adopting the style and spirit of motivational interviewing involves being aware of and setting aside one's righting reflex, maintaining a position of collaborating with the client, supporting the client's autonomy as he considers change, evoking and eliciting his thoughts and actions, and—above all—listening.

Good Listening

Many professionals believe they are listening when they are not. For purposes of this chapter, truly good listening includes entering each interaction with undivided attention, curiosity, appreciation, and wonder. It involves listening with the heart as well as the ears. Most importantly, good listening requires demonstrating to the client that the professional is listening, and soliciting feedback as to how well they are listening (Miller, Hubble, and Duncan 2007). In the practice of motivational interviewing, good listening does not involve agreeing, advising, persuading with logic, arguing, sympathizing, or consoling. Professionals working with sexual offenders commonly find these clients defensive, reserved, or argumentative. Simply taking extra time at the beginning of each interaction to demonstrate that one is listening can alter the tone of the interview dramatically. The challenge is that in many cases, good listening involves reflecting back statements that reflect antisocial attitudes. The professional will doubtless be tempted to provide feedback on these attitudes, but doing so too early disrupts the conversation and demonstrates that the professional is more interested in fixing the client than listening to him or her. There should be plenty of time to ask questions and offer feedback later in the session.

Self-assessment exercise: Ask a friend, colleague, or client if she would be willing to speak with you about any topic of her choice. It could include what her hopes and dreams are for the next several years. Have her speak to you for one to three minutes on this topic while you simply listen with interest. How do you demonstrate interest while saying as little as possible? What non-verbal indicators do you use? If you have a strong reaction to anything she says, how can you keep it to one side while you continue to listen? When your speaker is finished, offer back a summary of what she has said. Think of her statements as flowers that you will arrange into a bouquet, or pearls that you will arrange into a necklace. Finally, ask if you heard it all correctly.

One beauty of this exercise is that there is no penalty for not capturing everything. If you haven't listened, your speaker will let you know, and you can have another chance. The key is asking whether you understood. It is easy to skip this step in an effort to be efficient. After all, there are numerous times throughout the day when we commonly don't ask people close to us whether we understood what they were saying.

In the final analysis, it is tempting to believe that sexual offender treatment providers have an obligation to "lay it on the line" or otherwise scold their clients into a more prosocial stance. By doing so, it is easy to create interpersonal conflicts rather than motivate your client to make his own case for change.

Ambivalence

Ambivalence is inevitable in motivational interviewing and sexual offender treatment. Although many clients present themselves as having very little they need to change in their lives, an astute professional who understands sexual offenders can find numerous areas where a given client feels ambivalent. For the purposes of this chapter, ambivalence simply means feeling two ways about something. Here are a few examples:

- On the one hand, I really want to build a better life for myself and on the other hand, I'm not sure I have it in me to change.
- On the one hand, I really want to give this treatment program my very best, and on the other hand, I don't want to talk with others.

- On the one hand, I really want to stop getting in trouble and on the other hand, I don't want to give up my sexual fantasy life.
- On the one hand, I want to make connections with my group members, and on the other hand, I am concerned about whether I can trust anyone.
- On the one hand, I want to explore my life and on the other, I don't want to think that maybe my dad wasn't who I thought he was.
- On the one hand, I want to talk about what I've done, and on the other hand, I don't know if I can handle the feelings it will bring up.
- On the one hand, I want to feel like I've accomplished something in treatment, and on the other hand, I'm not used to much in my life besides failure.

One way to size up a client's ambivalence is to draw upon the experiences of other clients and then make an educated guess: "This sounds like a real dilemma. If I'm reading this right, you'd really like to participate more in group, on the one hand, and you're really concerned about trusting people, on the other." Notice that the conjunction used between the two sides of the ambivalence is an "and" instead of a "but." This choice in words is the better one because when you use "but," it risks highlighting the client's ambivalence. Using "and" highlights that the client holds these contrary sides simultaneously. Outside of treatment, professionals can imagine themselves in the place of clients who at times are lying awake and unable to sleep. What ambivalence might clients be trying to resolve in their own minds at that point?

Four Principles

Miller and Rollnick (2002) provide four basic principles in motivational interviewing: expressing empathy, developing discrepancy, rolling with resistance, and supporting self-efficacy. As with other aspects of learning motivational interviewing, it is often tempting to think that we already work within these principles; we might continue to think that, until and unless we receive direct feedback from others.

Expressing Empathy

Empathy has received significant attention in offender treatment in recent years (c.f., Fernandez 2002). For purposes of this chapter, it may help if professionals view empathy as their ability to enter and understand their clients' worlds. Professionals should express clear and deep understanding of their clients' perspectives, including both what the clients say and what they have not yet said (Moyers, Martin, Manuel, Miller, and Ernst draft manuscript). While it is clear that sexual offenders are responsible for many of the consequences of their actions, that reality does not preclude professionals from actively expressing empathy with statements such as these:

- It's hard for you to talk about this topic.
- You're wondering what this situation is going to mean for your family.
- You really miss your loved ones.
- You're concerned that discussing your past might get you into more trouble.
- It's not easy coming to these groups.
- Having to trust others in treatment is really new to you.
- You're wondering if anything is ever *really* going to change.

Empathy is clearly not the same thing as sympathy. While it may be tempting to sympathize with clients ("I hear you. Being on the sex offender registry is no fun"), this approach does little to support their autonomy and is potentially harmful. It is much different to provide treatment in a fashion that we believe to be empathic. Actively providing empathic statements throughout each interaction can be a much greater challenge for the clinician, but far more helpful to the client.

Developing Discrepancy

Discrepancy is the difference between where someone currently is, with respect to a given issue, and where he or she wants to be. Depending on the individual circumstances, identifying discrepancy can be done relatively easily. Almost no one wants to be identified as a sexual offender. Demonstrating meaningful change in the factors that contributed to one's offending can be a long and difficult journey. Developing discrepancy can include exploring what a better life would be like ("Tell me about some times when things were going well and you weren't engaged in this behavior"). It can also include exploring specific issues ("On the one hand, you believe it wasn't that big of a deal, and on the other hand, your family has expressed concern about your coming home").

Rolling with Resistance
The term *resistance* can be misleading. It is important to consider what the client is resisting and what his or her motivation for resisting actually is. Is the client genuinely uninterested in changing some area of his life? Or is he resisting the professional's attempts to engage him in a change process? Whatever the case, a professional gains nothing by combating resistance. Many practitioners have concluded that resistance is an interpersonal phenomenon. It is most likely to appear during interactions where the client feels misunderstood or unheard. When all else fails, the most human response can often be the best response ("So with all the reasons you have for not being here, what would be the most helpful way we can spend our time together?"). It is easy to forget that sometimes what appears to be resistance is actually an invitation to understand ("Since this is obviously a difficult conversation, can I just ask you something? You and I seem to be from different worlds. What's it like in your world?").

Supporting Self-Efficacy
Autonomy and choice are vital to change. It is very easy to assume that people who have sexually abused are unable to make good decisions for themselves. All too often, well-intended professionals attempting to help their clients by building safety into their lives end up restricting the clients rather than allowing them to explore and improve their decision-making skills. It is often the case that professionals experience a strong righting reflex when they feel responsible for their clients' actions. Of course, even the most prolific offenders are not abusing all the time and they will not have their treatment providers with them for every decision. Although direct intervention

in an emergent situation can become necessary at certain times, professionals will be most effective when they guide clients in making decisions rather than when they impose decisions or directions on clients. Many professionals have expressed concern during trainings that this method of treatment is time consuming. A helpful slogan at these times is to remind ourselves that, "The slower we go, the faster we get where we're going."

For many professionals, the four principles described above are a direct affront to their work. Many participants in motivational interviewing trainings offer responses that begin with, "Yes, but . . ." One helpful self-assessment exercise at this point might be to draw three columns on a sheet of paper. In one column, write a list of all the challenging aspects of your interactions with sexual abusers. In the next column, write a list of how these four principles would make your work more difficult. Finally, write a list of the ways in which these principles might be helpful.

Many professionals find that this exercise helps them explore their own ambivalence toward a truly different way of interacting with clients. These professionals often recall times when their historical style has worked, such as when a harsh and confrontational approach has brought short-term compliance with rules. However, it is common that these same professionals discover for themselves that motivational interviewing can help build long-term change and allow the client to make their own case for engaging meaningfully in treatment.

Basic Skills

Although proficiency at motivational interviewing can be a life-long endeavor involving many skills, four basic motivational interviewing "micro-skills" are vital for practitioners to utilize. These include open-ended questions, affirmations, reflections, and summaries. Together, many practitioners refer to them by their acronym, OARS.

Open-Ended Questions
Closed-ended questions require only yes/no responses or simple information (e.g., What is your name? Can I ask you a question?). Open-ended

questions require more thought, and forming these questions can be much more difficult than it might initially seem. It is tempting to ask at the start of a session, "Is there anything you'd like to discuss today?" However, this question risks an immediate response of, "No." Turning this question into a more open-ended one can produce more information: "What would you like to discuss today?" Alternatively, "I wonder what concerns you might have today?" In addition to providing more options to the client, it also introduces a refreshing, if slightly directive, component to the question. For example:

- What questions might you have for me?
- What concerns you about making a change in this area?
- What would it be like if you made this change?
- Why might others want you to make a change in this area?
- If you did make a change in this, how would you go about it?
- How might others have handled that?

It can be simple enough to open up closed-ended questions. The group therapist providing psycho-education can simply change "does anyone have any questions" into "I wonder what questions people might have?" Often, it only takes the open nature of the question to inspire further discussion. Consider the case of suicide assessment. Many students learn to ask, "Have you had any thoughts of hurting or killing yourself," to which experienced clients can easily answer, "No." Depending on circumstances, it can be more effective to ask, "Under what circumstances would you think of hurting or killing yourself?" While many treatment providers would not even think of asking whether their client will engage in future sexual harm (a closed-ended question), "Under what conditions would you do this again" might contribute to a productive discussion.

One way to practice opening up questions after-hours is to listen carefully to interviews on news broadcasts and identify the open-ended and closed-ended questions. How could opening up questions result in a better interview, particularly with image-conscious interviewees? Many newer practitioners believe that closed-ended questions are somehow "bad." They're not. The key is that open-ended questions can result in the client speaking more and the professional speaking less. This is a hallmark of both motivational interviewing and high-quality sexual offender assessment and treatment.

Affirmations

Affirmation is showing genuine appreciation for candor, effort, and accomplishment. It is most effective when it accompanies a deep understanding of the client's situation and worldview. Affirmations are not simply empty compliments or warm and fuzzy praise (e.g., "You're a good guy"). In fact, many sexual offenders—particularly those who have spent a number of years in prison—tend to interpret the latter as unhelpful and manipulative. More effective statements can be:

- I appreciate how difficult this has been for you.
- Your willingness to discuss this topic today is truly impressive, particularly under your current circumstances.
- It took courage for you to address this in front of the others.

As with the other micro-skills described in this section, it can be tempting for professionals to think they offer more affirmations than they actually do. A warm facial expression, engaged body posture, and friendly smile are not the same thing as an individualized, verbalized affirmation.

Reflections

This may be the most effective skill to elicit information and to demonstrate active listening. Reflective statements act as a mirror and build upon what the client has said. It may be a reflection of the client's actual statement, or a reflection of larger meaning or feeling. In fact, it can be helpful to think of a mirror when forming these statements. Which element of the client's statement do you wish to reflect back to him? Do you wish to understate or overstate that element, as reflections can call attention to different elements of a statement? The answer to that question can determine the direction of the conversation. Reflections can be powerful, and the most effective reflections involve the fewest words. Simple reflections almost always feed back what the client has actually said, while complex reflections feed back what they have not yet said.

Reflecting exact words means simply repeating back what the client has said. It is difficult to do harm with this kind of reflection, although many newcomers to motivational interviewing express concern that over-reliance on it can undermine attempts to form a therapeutic alliance. *Reflecting closely related words* is self-explanatory and applicable to situations where the practitioner is more comfortable taking a constructive risk.

Rick: Your treatment program is no good.
Practitioner: No good (exact words).
Rick: (emphatically) That's right.
Practitioner: You see nothing worthwhile about it (closely related words).
Rick: I'm only here because my probation officer told me he'd send me to prison.
Practitioner (reflecting slightly deeper meaning): The only reason you're even showing up is to keep him off your back.
Rick: You got it.

Please note that there is no right or wrong response when a client makes a statement such as, "Your treatment program is no good." Some responses will be more helpful than others. For example, "What do you mean by 'no good?'" runs a higher risk of building resistance than simply saying, "Tell me more about that." Repeating exact and closely related words can be a way for the clinician to get his or her bearings within an interaction. Like anything else, simply repeating a client's statements can become annoying and counterproductive quickly.

Continuing the paragraph is where the clinician is making a guess at the client's deeper meaning. It can be as though the client was making a statement and the clinician is continuing the paragraph for him. Miller and Rollnick (2002) recommend that clinicians think of this approach as first taking a question that starts with "Do you mean…" Next, rather than asking it as a question (where the clinician's voice would inflect upward at the end), take away the "Do you mean" and simply utter the question as a statement. For example, imagine a client says, "I'm only here because my probation officer sent me here." Rather than asking, "Do you mean you have no interest in treatment?" the clinician can simply say, "You have no interest in treatment."

Clinicians can also simply *reflect emotion*. In the preceding example, when the client says, "I'm only here because my probation officer sent me here," the clinician might simply observe, "And you're pretty frustrated about it."

These complex reflections, *reflecting emotion* and *continuing the paragraph*, can produce powerful results. Where simple reflections using exact and closely related words can be effective with minimally verbal clients, or when clinicians are not exactly sure how best to proceed, complex reflections can express interest, elicit more information, and can be very brief. Many clinicians are unaware of how many unnecessary words they use. Likewise, there is evidence that clinicians believe themselves to be more helpful than their clients do. Although all people want to be sure that others are listening, people who have sexually abused very often enter treatment with a long history of being discounted and unheard. By adding reflections to questions, the clinician can demonstrate that he or she is listening. In research studies, trained motivational interviewers average at least two reflections to every question. In practice, the ratio of questions to reflections is a clinical judgment for the clinician to make. Clinicians focusing exclusively on only one or the other can create an awkward interaction and are likely not meeting the client's needs.

Clinicians can guide conversational flow with complex reflections. For example, while clinicians may want to use simple reflections in uncertain situations, they can deliberately reflect meaning in order to elicit information, or reflect emotion to guide the client to a deeper place.

Rick: It wasn't my idea to come here to this stupid program.
Clinician: This program seems stupid (simple reflection).
Rick: The only reason I'm even here is because the court sent me.
Clinician: It was part of a plea agreement (continuing the paragraph).
Rick: That's right. Look, I'm sure this is a good program and nothing against you, but it's stupid that I have to be here. I can't be a part of treatment when it involves all these rapists and child molesters. There were a whole lot of problems with my court case and the only reason I pleaded guilty is I didn't want any hassle. This whole thing is stupid. What I really need is some kind of counseling that's going to show the court I'm not the kind of guy they need to worry about.

Clinician: So there's a lot about you that the powers that be don't understand (continuing the paragraph).
Rick: That's right. They were treating me like a common criminal.
Clinician: And it's not making sense to you that you have to be in a program like this with others whom you feel are coming from a different place (continuing the paragraph).
Rick: Yeah. Look, no offense to anyone, but I can't be around a bunch of rapists and child molesters.
Clinician: If you were to be in a treatment program, you'd need to be around people you knew you could trust (continuing the paragraph).
Rick: That's exactly right. I've got a lot riding on this, and I need to get back to my family, re-build my career, pay the rent, you know . . . .
Clinician: You love your family (reflecting emotion).
Rick: Well yeah! I have to find some way to get back with them.
Clinician: . . . And it's been a long time since you've all really been together (continuing the paragraph).
Rick: After everything the court and social services put us through, it's a miracle I still have them in my life at all (looking down, voice lowers).
Clinician: It's been a long road for all of you.
Rick: And now I have to do all this . . . like talking in some group just to please my probation officer.
Clinician: So this is a dilemma. On the one hand, you don't see any value in this for you, and on the other hand, you're thinking that being in treatment might get you to a place with your family and the law where you can get on with your life. Your family and freedom mean everything to you.
Rick: You got it.

In this example, the clinician is deliberately not responding to the comments about other group members, the program, or the client's apparent lack of accountability. To respond directly to these would likely only result in further resistance. Instead, the clinician is exploring the client's ambivalence and developing some discrepancy between where the client is in his life and where he would like to be.

The general rule in motivational interviewing is to offer two or more reflections for each question. This does not mean that questions are forbidden, just that offering reflections can be more helpful and in line with motivational interviewing's research base. Offering reflections can feel unusual at first, yet it becomes a habit with time.

Recognizing and Reinforcing Change Talk

Research (e.g., Amrhein, Miller, Yahne, Palmer, and Fulcher 2003) suggests that client statements indicating a willingness to make positive changes are the most important material for clinicians to explore and reinforce. Originally described as self-motivating statements, change talk signals readiness, ability, and willingness to change. All too often, it appears as one small pearl[1] in an ocean of resistance talk. The clinician focusing on the ocean will miss the pearl. Likewise, in working with sexual abusers, it is easy to imagine the clinician's work as resembling that of a goalie in ice hockey (although it is important to note that treatment is not competitive). In order to be effective, the dispassionate goalie must be aware of the fact that an entire team of athletes is approaching him rapidly (with sharp skates on, no less) and he needs, instead, to focus on the puck. In the goalie's field of vision, the opposing team is large, fast, and threatening. The puck is small, but the clear object of focus. Just as the goalie needs to attend to the opposing team, the focus is to get the puck and send it in the right direction. There is no disrespect of the other team—far from it—just a desire to focus on the puck and send it in the right direction.

Change talk generally consists of four types of statements, known by the acronym DARN:

- **Desire** ("I want to...")
- **Ability** ("I'm able to..." or "I could...")
- **Reason** ("I've got some good reasons to...")
- **Need** ("I need to...")

Clinicians will want to pay special attention to these statements. They can be the first indication that the client is motivating himself to change. Rather

---

1. The author is grateful to Steve Berg-Smith for this analogy.

than making the case for change, clinicians can be more effective by rolling with resistance and reinforcing change talk where they find it.

> *Clinician:* So this is a dilemma. On the one hand, you don't see any value in this for you, and on the other hand, you're thinking that being in treatment might get you to a place with your family and the law where you can get on with your life. Your family and freedom mean everything to you.
> *Rick:* You got it. I have to find a way to do this.
> *Clinician:* You're thinking it's time to make this happen.
> *Rick:* I really want my life back and my family back. I just don't see how I'm supposed to be in some group with these people.
> *Clinician:* It can be confusing getting going in this kind of program. You have a solid goal for your life and it's not clear how you're going to make it work with the others in this picture.
> *Rick:* It's like you said. I want to make sure that I can work with these other people.
> *Clinician:* Teamwork is going to be a big part of this.
> *Rick:* Yeah.
> *Clinician* (summarizing): So let me see if I have this right. You really want to show the judge, probation officer, and social services that you can and should stay in the community. You love your family and want to keep them together. You really want your life back and want to re-build your career and pay your mortgage. It's hard to get past the feeling that you don't belong in a treatment program, and you're really wondering what it's going to be like to be in a group with others who've been convicted of sex crimes. You're not happy about this, but you're determined to make it work somehow. Did I get it about right?
> *Rick:* Yeah.

In this instance, the clinician is responding primarily to those statements indicating that Rick desires, is able to, and has reasons or needs to get involved in the treatment program. At this point, Rick has spoken mostly of his desire to keep his family together, get on with his life, and be free of the restraints of the legal system. The clinician is aware that in order to meaningfully complete a treatment program, the client will likely need to find different motivations (such as a genuine desire to explore his life and make changes). However, rather than focusing on what needs to change, the clinician is reflecting back whatever willingness to change the client has to offer.

Commitment Talk

Statements involving desire, ability, reason, and need to change are vital. Clinicians will want to reinforce them, reflect, and look for more. It is even more vital to look for signs of commitment. These include stating a commitment to change and statements indicating that a person has taken steps toward change. Continuing the earlier conversation:

> *Clinician:* Did I get it about right?
>
> *Rick:* Yeah. Given what the court and social services have done to me, if I don't finish this program I might as well throw in the towel. After all, I've already been through an assessment, that pre-disposition process, and everything else. I don't like any of this, but I've been through hard times before. And who knows, maybe I can learn a few things that will help me with my family along the way.
>
> *Clinician:* You're committed to making this work and hope that you can use it to make your life better.

Below is a list of client resistance and change-talk statements. How would you respond to each of them? Keep in mind that change talk can appear as a small pearl in an ocean of resistance. The clinician's job is to collect these pearls and feed them back in a summary.

- This program is just the Department of Corrections in sheep's clothing.
- I don't like any of this.
- I have to do something to keep that probation officer off my back.
- How do you know this treatment stuff even works?
- What are you going to do, peel back my skull and look inside?

- You're trying to provide treatment for something I may do in the future?
- I need to do something to keep my job, not keep a journal.
- I don't think they'll ever let me go home.
- Give me a break. What do you do when you get bored?
- I got some of my treatment assignments done.

Another way to build skills for attending to change talk is to listen to the media. Pop singer Amy Winehouse, for example, offers a tragic account in her song, "Rehab." The song contains repeated reasons for not going into drug-abuse treatment ("no, no, no, I won't go, go, go"). It is only after several minutes of protest that she offers her internal motivation to change ("I don't ever want to drink again; I just need a friend"). Likewise, news media accounts, particularly those that interview public figures, can provide rich material for reflecting resistance and change talk in the moment, even in the absence of genuine conversation.

Providing Feedback

Many clinicians working with people who have sexually abused wonder how best to offer constructive feedback in a way that is consistent with the style and spirit of motivational interviewing. People who have abused often seem to invite clinicians to become aggressive in their provision of feedback. Some general tips involve the following:

Ask, don't tell. Asking permission to share feedback sets the stage for a more respectful interaction and ensures that the client has some responsibility in that by giving permission he or she has acknowledged a readiness to listen. Likewise, eliciting the client's response helps ensure that the client listens to the feedback.

No fixing things. Many clinicians may feel a strong urge to set the record straight or immediately fix a problem. It can be most helpful to think of feedback provision as an offering that the client must decide whether to use or not.

Style is everything. Providing feedback can be a particularly sensitive time in the course of any interaction. Maintaining a spirit of collaboration and respect for autonomy is vital. Providing feedback as described below can be many times more helpful than simply giving unsolicited advice.

Ask—Provide—Ask. This framework (also known as Elicit—Provide—Elicit) is an excellent anchor point for clinicians. It simply involves asking permission to provide feedback, providing the feedback, and asking what thoughts the client might have. For example:

> *Clinician:* Rick, after being in this evening's group, I have some thoughts I'd like to share with you. Would that be OK? (Closed-ended question emphasizes the yes/no nature of the inquiry.)
>
> *Rick:* Go ahead. You're just going to do it anyway.
>
> *Clinician:* Actually, I don't believe it would be helpful or respectful to speak with you about this if you're not willing to listen. I'm not just asking to be polite.
>
> *Rick:* OK, then, go ahead. I'm ready.
>
> *Clinician:* Rick, the other guys in the group have been telling me privately that they feel your behavior is disrespectful. They feel that it's not so obvious as to be openly disruptive or bring the group to a screeching halt. However, they do feel that they can't move forward with their own treatment unless you're an equal, productive member of the group. They've mentioned this privately because they feel you didn't take their concerns seriously when they brought them up in the group sessions. What's also important for you to know is that I have had the same concerns myself. You appear to view yourself as very different from and slightly superior to them. My observation is that although you are good at providing supportive and challenging feedback to them, it doesn't seem that you take their feedback seriously or consider it very much. As you know, I have a responsibility for the well-being of the entire group. It may be that if things continue along these lines, we may need to consider an alternative treatment situation for you. Just the same, you have my complete confidence that when you are ready to give this group your all, there will be very little that can hold you back. I wonder what thoughts you have about that?
>
> *Rick:* I'm going to have to think about that. It's like I said when I first started, it's hard to do group with others who have done worse things than I have.

Clinician: And where the others in group are investing themselves, it's hard for you to do the same. This is a real dilemma. You have concerns about them and they have concerns about you.
Rick: (after a pause) I hadn't looked at it that way.
Clinician: What do you think you might do?
Rick: I guess I could bring this up in group. I really want to finish that group and get on with my life. I think I've been unfair to them.
Clinician: As you think about this further, I'm confident you'll do a good job, if that's what you choose to do. See you in a few days!

In this instance, the clinician has left no doubt as to where the responsibility for treatment participation lies. The message is very clear and utterly respectful. Using Ask—Provide—Ask as an anchor point can lessen resistance, and may make the difference between the client's success and failure.

Conclusion

The desire to be heard, understood, and autonomous is universal, while resistance is largely an interpersonal phenomenon. Resistance to change is not the same thing as resistance to others peoples' attempts to change someone. At the start of this chapter, a young Milton Erickson recognized that the calf simply wanted to be resistant at that moment, and he rolled with it. His ability to enter the calf's world fostered a solution. Likewise, Rick's clinician, fearing the consequences should Rick not fully participate in treatment, might easily have resorted to a coercive solution that would have produced short-term compliance. Of course, this less-supportive approach might well have occurred at the expense of long-term change through meaningful participation in treatment.

The research on motivational interviewing is impressive (Hettema, Steele, and Miller 2005; Lundahl, Tollefson, Gambles, Brownell, and Burke forthcoming). But immersing one's self in its practice is harder than it seems. When the reader is ready, it may be useful to re-visit the questions at the start of this chapter, and write out responses on the other side of the sheet of paper for comparison purposes:

1. I'm only here because of the court. I don't believe in treatment.
2. How long are you going to keep asking me questions?
3. I attended a treatment program in prison and it was no good.
4. My private life is none of your business.
5. All this talking is wasting my time. You need to tell me exactly which behaviors you want me to change.
6. You can't change me. No one's going to change me. I'm not a robot.
7. What exact credentials do you have to do this work? Where did you go to school?
8. Go ahead and do what you're going to do; you're going to do it anyway.
9. I don't think I belong in treatment. I'm not like your other clients.
10. You know, we could hit it off nicely under other circumstances.

If you are like many who attend motivational interviewing trainings, you may find that your answers have become shorter and more helpful. You ask fewer questions and are better able to detect clues as to the client's internal motivation to change. By becoming a better listener, you can become a better agent of change.

This chapter results from the work of an entire community of professionals. I am grateful to the Motivational Interviewing Network of Trainers for their many ideas and resources. Particular thanks go to Bill Miller, Steve Rollnick, Terri Moyers, Denise Ernst, Marilyn Ross, and Chris Wagner. This chapter is dedicated to, and borrows heavily from, Steve Berg-Smith.

REFERENCES

Amrhein, P. C., W. R. Miller, C. E. Yahne, M. Palmer, and L. Fulcher. 2003. Client commitment language during motivational interviewing predicts drug use outcomes. *Journal of Consulting and Clinical Psychology* 71:862–78.

Bem, D. J. 1972. Self-perception theory. In *Advances in experimental social psychology* (Vol. 6), ed. L. Berkowitz, 2–62. New York: Academic Press.

Fernandez, Y. 2002. *In their shoes: Examining empathy and its place in the treatment of offenders.* Oklahoma City, OK: Wood'N'Barnes.

Garland, R., and M. Dougher. 1991. Motivational intervention in the treatment of sexual offenders. In *Motivational interviewing—preparing people to change addictive behavior,* ed. W. R. Miller and S. Rollnick, 303–13. New York: Guilford Press.

Hettema, J., J. Steele, and W. R. Miller. 2005. Motivational interviewing. *Annual Review of Clinical Psychology* 1:91–111.

Lundahl, B. W., D. Tollefson, C. Gambles, C. Brownell, and B. L. Burke. Forthcoming. A meta-analysis of motivational interviewing: Twenty-five years of empirical studies. *Research on Social Work Practice.*

Marshall, W. L. 2005. Therapist style in sexual offender treatment: Influence on indices of change. *Sexual Abuse: A Journal of Research & Treatment* 17(2):109–16.

Miller, S., M. Hubble, and B. Duncan. 2007. Supershrinks: Who are they? What can we learn from them? *Psychotherapy Networker* November 1:27–56.

Miller, W. R. 1983. Motivational interviewing with problem drinkers. *Behavioural Psychotherapy* 11:147–72.

Miller, W. R., and S. Rollnick. 1991. *Motivational interviewing: Preparing people to change addictive behavior.* New York: Guilford Press.

———. 2002. *Motivational interviewing: Preparing people for change. 2nd edition.* New York: Guilford Press.

Moyers, Martin, Manuel, Miller, and Ernst. Draft manuscript. *Revised global scales: Motivational interviewing treatment integrity 3.0 (MITI 3.0).* Retrieved May 25, 2009 from www.motivationalinterview.org.

Ryan, R. M., and E. L. Deci. 2000. Self-determination and the facilitation of intrinsic motivation, social development, and well-being. *American Psychologist* 55:68–78.

Using Motivational Interviewing with Sexual Abusers in Group Treatment

David S. Prescott and Marilyn Ross

People who have engaged in sexual abuse oppose significant concerns for community safety. Although recidivism rates for sexual offenders are lower than once thought (Bureau of Justice Statistics 2003; Hanson and Bussière 1998; Harris and Hanson 2004), professionals are nonetheless aware of the potential harm in even one instance of sexual assault. Treatment programs for sexual abusers have increased in number and scope over the past 30 years (McGrath, Cumming, and Burchard 2003), some more successfully than others (Furby, Weinrott, and Blackshaw 1989; Hanson, Broom, and Stephenson 2004; Marques, Wiederanders, Day, Nelson, and Van Ommeren 2005). Fortunately, research has documented increasingly positive results from cognitive–behavioral interventions with sexual abusers across the life span (Hanson, Gordon, Harris, Marques, Murphy, Quinsey, and Seto 2002; Lösel and Schmucker 2005; Reitzel and Carbonell 2006; Walker, McGovern, Poey, and Otis 2002). More recently, professionals have increased their attention to the confluence of treatment material and provider style (Levenson and Prescott 2007; Marshall 2005).

Hanson and Bussière's (1998) meta-analysis examined factors related to sexual recidivism and found that failure to complete treatment programs was associated with increased risk for subsequent sexual harm. Likewise, and Bussière's colleagues (2005) found that although a standard relapse-prevention program did not demonstrate significant reductions in recidivism, those offenders who *successfully completed* their treatment goals and who demonstrated that they "got it" re-offended at significantly lower rates. These findings have contributed to many professionals redoubling their efforts to engage sexual abusers meaningfully throughout their treatment experience (Marshall and Marshall 2007; Prescott 2007). As a result, treatment programs have emerged for treating a wide range of individuals, including those who categorically deny their sexually abusive behavior and appear to be poor candidates for treatment. Controversy, however, still surrounds denial's relevance to the likelihood of future sexual harm (Hanson and Bussière 1998; Lund 2000; Serran and O'Brien, see chapter 5).

The use of harsh, confrontational therapy techniques can hamper efforts toward substantively engaging sexual offenders in the treatment process. Even for offenders who acknowledge their culpability, confrontation can still impede meaningful participation in treatment by creating defensiveness (Marshall, Serran, Moulden, Mulloy, Fernandez, Mann, and Thornton 2002). Although professionals may feel pressure to use techniques that compel short-term compliance with rules, a harsh, confrontational style does not necessarily promote long-term behavior change (Garland and Dougher 1991).

Sexual offender treatment providers often face the challenge of delivering effective treatment in a shorter amount of time to meet the needs of community safety in an efficient, cost-effective manner. Although no current research demonstrates the superiority of group treatment, it has become the modality of choice with this population for practical reasons beyond the scope of this chapter (Jennings and Sawyer 2003; McGrath, Cumming, and Burchard 2003). Given the research indicating that the most effective sexual offender therapists are warm, empathic, rewarding, and directive (Marshall 2005), we offer the following ideas for integrating motivational interviewing principles and techniques into the group treatment of sexual abusers.

A Community-Based Pre-Treatment Group for Individuals Who Say They Have Not Abused

Individuals who deny engaging in the actions for which they have received criminal sanctions pose a problem for treatment providers and probation departments alike. Attempts to place them into action-oriented groups often result in angry, resistant clients who object to the diagnostic and legal labels imposed upon them, who have not yet been honest with those closest to them, and who are unprepared to look candidly at their own behavior. This attitude can bring about increasingly punitive consequences from those supervising or treating them, leading to a snowballing of behavior and consequences. Therapists may remove these offenders from treatment programs, possibly creating a greater risk of recidivism due to lack of treatment completion, as noted above (Hanson and Bussière 1998).

Professionals working with such individuals may feel stymied in identifying ways to address their supervision and treatment needs while simultaneously acknowledging that their clients are not prepared to take on the expectations of most treatment programs. In this situation, a pre-treatment group designed specifically for individuals who deny culpability may help relieve the pressures of an action-oriented program while at the same time preparing them for such treatment in the future.

A pre-treatment group allows referred individuals to explore the components of treatment in the context of the crime for which they entered the legal system, yet without the requirement of acknowledging harm. As such, they complete assignments as if the charges against them hypothetically were true. Throughout its process, the group presents and explores situations in a manner that emphasizes the discrepancy between the client's stated position regarding the charges made against him and the presumed reality of the case.

Pre-Treatment Group Format

The basic format of the pre-treatment group includes a pre-group interview, an introduction to treatment including brief modules that give an overview of treatment components, a post-group interview, optional assessments, and a second post-group feedback session. Information presented here reflects several outpatient pre-treatment groups with a mixture of clients including individuals on probation as well as those who have recently received parole.

The therapist can modify group content and length to adapt to needs and constraints of the program. The most important element is the group's capacity to engage its most ambivalent members. It is useful to follow the motivational interviewing "spirit" (Miller and Rollnick 2002) of collaboration, evocation, support for autonomy, and friendly neutrality at all times in order to facilitate openness and develop a positive working relationship. This attitude and approach can be more difficult in practice than it appears. It is particularly important for therapists in this setting to avoid using labels with their potential for binary perspectives that may increase resistance. Noteworthy examples include the words denier and offender, except in the case of one assignment described below. It is especially important to educate the referring sources to refrain from describing the program to potential members as a "denier's group."

Initial Interview

Referrals for the pre-treatment group may come from probation or parole departments or from therapists who have already had contact with the individuals. These clients are in the pre-contemplation stage of change (Prochaska and DiClemente 1982), and thus state that they have no problem with their sexual behavior. Indeed, if they did not think this, they would not be appropriate referrals for such a group.

The goals of the initial session include developing initial rapport with each client, understanding the official versions of the abuse, hearing each client's version of what happened, and learning the motivations each has, both for keeping to this position and possibly for shifting the position toward that reflected in the offense report. Opportunities to work collaboratively in the motivational interviewing spirit begin with the contact to schedule the initial appointment. Often, clients express much unhappiness about the referral. A therapist who responds with warmth and acceptance instead of engaging in limit-setting or argumentation sets the stage for a different type of relationship from the very beginning.

> *Client:* I've been referred to this pre-treatment group. What is the group anyway? I didn't do anything wrong, and now I'm being sent here. No offense, but I don't need this s***.
>
> *Therapist:* You're pretty unhappy about being sent to this program. May I give you some information about it?

If the client agrees to listen, he is one step closer to handling the information that the therapist gives him. At this point, many clients may want to discuss the details of their case with the therapist. The therapist assures the client of the importance of hearing his position on the charges and explains that part of the reason for the first appointment is to have a place where that can happen.

All along the way, the therapist can foster a spirit of collaboration and cooperation by giving the client as many choices as possible. For example, in the first phone call, the therapist can offer the client two alternative appointment times to choose between or can ask the client if he wishes to come in this week or next week. Throughout the program, the motivational interviewing skills of rolling with the resistance, and dancing rather than wrestling with the client, prove invaluable in maintaining an atmosphere that minimizes the likelihood of resistance.

The initial appointment begins with the client completing intake forms for the program. The therapist can start the contact with a smile and a warm handshake. Reviewing social history helps to start the appointment out on a note that is not emotionally charged. It allows the therapist to begin to establish rapport with the client.

When the therapist is ready to turn to a discussion of the abusive behavior, the client may choose to tell his version of the story of what happened. Ideally, the therapist has a copy of the offense report and can refer to it during the interview. In this situation, there will always be a discrepancy between the official version of what happened and the client's version. If there were not, the client would not have been referred to the program. The therapist reflects these discrepancies back to the client in a manner that is neutral, conversational, and pleasant. At no time should the therapist confront the client with the discrepancy or comment on the implausibility of the story presented.

When the client has completed his account, the therapist states, "From what you have told me here, it sounds as if you don't have a problem with your sexual behavior. If you should wake up one day and say, 'My sexual behavior *has* caused problems for me or someone else,' what not-so-good things would come of that?" Throughout the interview, the therapist has been making note of things the client has said that indicate potential problems in changing his position. Now, with this question, the therapist asks the client directly about it.

While a few individuals will respond that they cannot answer the question because they cannot imagine this possibility, most will give an answer. The answer to this question gives a hint regarding the roadblocks to change that exist for this client. Therapists may be surprised by the answers they receive when they ask this question, and they may be tempted to reassure the client that the imagined consequences will not occur. The best follow-up to the client's response, whatever it is, is a statement that this outcome would be difficult for the client to handle, if it did happen. The conversation allows the client to own his personal dilemma, and encourages further discussion. Reassurance at this point risks falling into the "expert trap," in which therapist and client both agree that the therapist is going to do the work—a process that may hamper change and increase resistance.

At the point where the therapist confirms the difficulty of handling the imagined situation, the client often responds in one of two ways. On the one hand, he may acknowledge that it would indeed be difficult, perhaps thanking the therapist for recognizing this. In this instance, the therapist may respond by acknowledging and affirming the statement that the client has made. On the other hand, the client may begin to shift his position a bit, stating that he may perhaps be able to handle this outcome after all. This change talk provides an opportunity for further exploration. The therapist may follow this statement by asking the client how he will be able to handle such an outcome and then listening for statements of self-efficacy. The therapist makes note both of these indices of self-efficacy as well as the motivation to change in response to this question, noting the roadblocks to change as stated in the response to the "not-so-good things" question asked earlier. Together, these factors mark the initial baseline for the client, and everything after that point will address these factors to continue to prepare the client for change.

The last part of the initial interview involves having the therapist review the elements of the group, including basic format, expectations, and practical matters such as fees, start dates, time, and location. Clients sign a treatment contract that lists expectations of the pre-treatment group, including the statement that they will not admit to any sex offense that they did not commit. The purpose of this statement is to emphasize that the focus of the group is not to overtly encourage the individual to shift his position but rather to "come alongside" (Miller and Rollnick 2002). This position works more effectively with those who are not yet contemplating change than action-oriented approaches.

The fees collected cover the group sessions and post-group assessments. Clients learn in the initial interview that if they decided to shift their position, they will not have the post-group assessment and then all fees collected for it will be refunded to them. Thus, the format creates a subtle though unspoken encouragement toward change.

Group Format

The group format may vary depending on the needs of the program. Therapists can modify the format to reflect current trends in treatment. This section provides a general overview of useful components with possible adaptations to suit treatment purposes.

The goals of the pre-treatment group are twofold. The primary goal is to provide an overview of treatment in a format that does not require clients to admit to any abusive acts. The second goal involves guiding the client from precontemplation (not thinking about change) into contemplation (thinking about change) or possibly into determination and preparation stages of change, helping him to become more amenable to treatment.

Basic components of current treatment generally include the client writing out his or her history of abusive behavior and general sex history. This involves identifying behavior chains that ended in abusive behavior and creating a plan for addressing these issues. Because the teaching of victim empathy has not been demonstrated to affect relapse (Seager, Jellicoe, and Dhaliwal 2004; Hanson and Morton-Bourgon 2005), it is not always required in some treatment programs. However, many clients have themselves stated that this has been an important component of treatment (Levenson and Prescott 2009; Levenson, Prescott, and D'Amora forthcoming). Many programs retain this component as a means for helping clients discover their own reasons to progress through treatment. At the end of the pre-treatment program, the therapist asks the individuals who attended to acknowledge what parts of the program helped them to shift their position. Many cite the victim empathy section of the program as having a significant impact on their decision to admit their actions. Although empathy does not correlate with decreased recidivism, it often leads to greater acceptance of responsibility for the abusive behavior of the individual, and thus can be a useful part of a program such as this one (Levenson and Prescott 2009).

Once the pre-treatment group gets underway, the components of such a group generally include the following:

1. The group begins with a brief presentation of the Holocaust with film footage from the liberation of a concentration camp, followed by a discussion of Holocaust denial and the reasons why people may wish to deny something in general.
2. The group learns about cognitive distortions or thinking errors, using *The True Story of the Three Little Pigs* (Scieszka and Smith 1996) to teach the concept.
3. The therapist introduces the concept of empathy with information about different types of victims through the use of films, group discussion, and abuse-specific thinking errors. Because group members generally show the greatest amount of distortion with acquaintance rape, the therapist presents this information first so that group members can generally show greater clarity of thinking as they progress through the types.
4. To mimic the sex history portion of a treatment program, each group member fills out information about his alleged offense, responding to statements such as, "If the allegations against you had been true, please describe all the things that you were reported to have done to your victim." Most clients will complete assignments worded in this manner. If an individual reports no knowledge based on being unaware of the charges (presumably due to not having engaged in the behavior), his pre-sentencing investigation report may be used to assist in obtaining the information. These assignments further ask the client to write about victim impact, and end by asking, "If the charges against you had

been true, what would be the likely result for a victim, if the perpetrator denied the offense?"

5. Finally, the group members learn about behavior chains that can result in abusive behavior. First, they pick a problem of their choice that has nothing to do with the offenses for which they are charged. Then they follow that problem as they learn the concepts. After doing this process, they then repeat the assignments, this time writing about their own alleged behavior. Again, the assignment asks, "If the charge against you had been true, what high-risk people, places, and things would you need to avoid in the future to prevent repeating the same behaviors?" Thus, they begin to create hypothetical safety plans.

By the end of the pre-treatment program, individuals have received a cursory introduction to most of the components of treatment, all worded in a manner that does not push them to admit an offense, while simultaneously underscoring the discrepancy between their position and the probable truth. In a friendly, non-pejorative manner, they discuss topics such as the reasons why someone might wish to deny this kind of behavior. Though not necessary, bringing in individuals who have graduated from a regular group program can be helpful early in the group series. As the graduates talk about their experiences with treatment, they provide one more source of gentle discrepancy to group members.

The pre-treatment program described here lasts 18 weeks. If time constraints require an abbreviated program, the therapist can shorten it by leaving out components, combining components, utilizing fewer types of vignettes, et cetera.

Post-Group Sessions

At the conclusion of the pre-treatment program, each participant schedules a post-group session to review the group experience with the therapist. During this session, the participants have the opportunity to discuss what they thought of the group, any ideas for improving it, what they found most useful, and the like. The therapist reminds them of the position they each gave before the group started and asks them about their current position regarding the charges made against them. The clients were told in the initial individual session that those who shifted their position would not have any post-group assessments, and that the fees that were collected to pay for these assessments will be refunded to them. At this point, some individuals shift their positions and the remainder of the post-group session involves discussing a referral to a regular treatment program.

A great many participants in these groups do not shift their positions in this session and elect to have the post-group assessments. The last minutes of the post-group session cover possible assessments of sexual interests and arousal, as well as polygraph examinations. Clients then schedule a second post-group session to review their assessment results. It is common for these clients to have displayed abuse-related interests and arousal patterns. It is also common that they have indicated deception on their polygraph examinations. As with other areas of the program, the therapist discusses these results in a matter-of-fact, informational manner, eliciting each client's thoughts about the feedback and listening with interest.

By continuing to point out discrepancies in the client's presentation in a manner that remains non-confrontational, collaborative, and concerned, the therapist helps each client to stay focused on the interaction between them. Clients receive no pressure to make any particular decision and can evaluate the choices before them with greater care. Again, the therapist can bring up the good things/not-so-good things question about changing their position regarding their sexual behavior. Historically, slightly more than half of clients do shift their position by or at this point in the program. Like those who shifted position at the first post-group individual session, the individuals who do so at this time receive referrals to standard treatment programs. Those who do not may receive a referral into harm-reduction programs. The therapist may notify a client's referral source, who may subsequently consider alternative placements. The majority of these latter individuals, though they do not admit to abusive behavior, show themselves to be more amenable to treatment, and some admit later on that they engaged in abusive behavior, after they are placed in a standard treatment program.

The Preparatory/Individualized Treatment Group

This group had its beginnings in Wisconsin's civil commitment center for high-risk sexual abusers. In many instances, these clients are unable, unwilling, or simply not ready to engage meaningfully in treatment. The individualized treatment group is where clients directly address treatment-interfering factors within a group treatment setting. This situation provides the benefits of feedback, questions, and discussion from other clients, and provides clients with the opportunity to practice having challenging discussions within a group context before delving into more serious issues.

Throughout the treatment experience in this inpatient setting, clients and therapists meet to discuss progress and the expectations of the program. Placement in an individualized treatment group follows a process in which each client meets with staff members involved in his treatment. The treatment team includes therapists, unit staff, and health service staff. The therapists typically include one psychotherapist and one unit supervisor. This helps to bring both perspectives into the group and to assure discussion of behaviors that occur on the living unit.

The team asks permission to discuss the individual's status in treatment and seeks his perspective on how he is doing. This dialogue can include a discussion of prior attempts to engage the client and agreements the client may have made. A therapist then outlines the treatment-interfering factors that have concerned the team. Although it is highly likely that various members of this team have discussed these issues with the client prior to this meeting, it is helpful to have representatives from as many departments as possible in attendance to prevent unnecessary blame being placed on absent team members (a device often referred to as "staff splitting").

It is most helpful when the team can focus on a few core elements of the treatment-interfering factors rather than a laundry list of irritating behaviors. Ideally, one to four goals for the individualized treatment group is optimal in order to maximize the client's ability to stay focused on them. This limitation may require team members to conceptualize single behaviors as part of larger areas of need. Often team members establishing these goals rely on the language of the barriers and tactics (Truthought 2001) or the six key areas of progress for the early phase of treatment.

Clients address diverse issues in individualized treatment groups. Beyond common challenges such as pervasive disruption, attention-seeking behavior, or reluctance to pay attention, clients can address such areas as their reluctance to provide a comprehensive account of their behavior or their sexual history. In some cases, clients have entered an individualized treatment group due to intense ambivalence about their relationships with other clients (and the effect of those relationships on their treatment progress). Other clients have come to address their low motivation for treatment and persistent reluctance to apply treatment material to their daily lives. These issues are all ideally suited to an individualized treatment group where other clients can provide support, thoughts, ideas, and feedback. For example, one client struggled for months to address his history of bestiality. Another client (who experienced different problems with respect to treatment) was able to relate that he had a similar history. This revelation started a group discussion that resulted in the client's eventual return to his original treatment group.

Once the team determines these areas of need, the needs can be written into an "options tool" (see Figure 1; Berg-Smith 2008). This process is as simple as drawing on a sheet of paper eight circles, like the ones that appear in Figure 1, into which the client or therapist can write a series of treatment-interfering factors, or other points of ambivalence regarding change. By writing these factors in the circles, the client has:

- a handcrafted document different in appearance from the usual formatting of clinical paperwork, including treatment plans;
- a tangible, visual roadmap whose structure does not necessarily imply a specific sequence of tasks;
- a menu from which he can choose for himself which area he will address first. This emphasis on choice is fundamental to the client's ability to make change for himself as well as to advance in treatment; and
- additional "circles" where he can add goals of his own.

Therapists should anticipate that the client will not agree with some or all of the goals. This response is to be expected; the team can note that the client

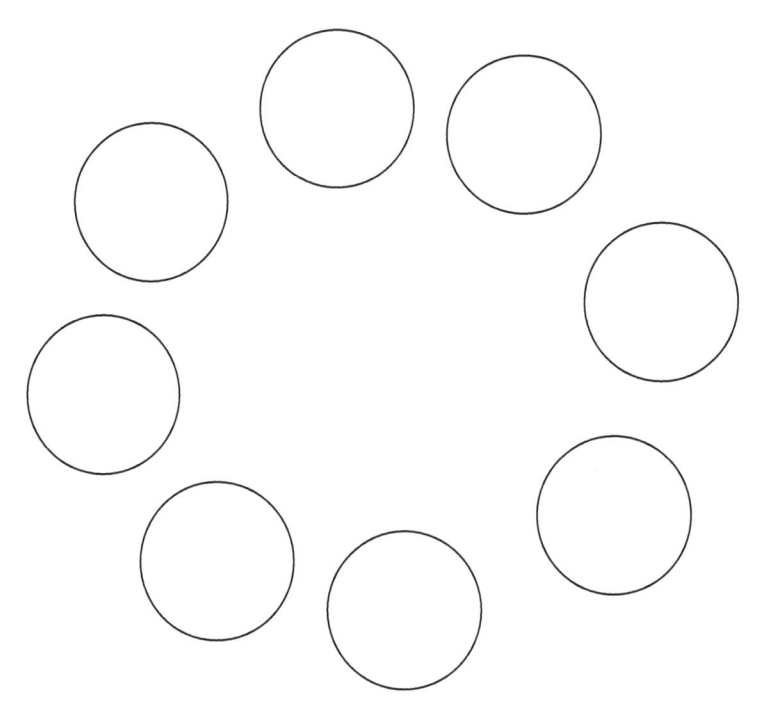

FIGURE 1: OPTIONS TOOL

did not agree with all of the treatment team's concerns and recommendations. Likewise, the therapists encourage the client to add concerns of his own. The guiding value is that the process is collaborative but includes the treatment team's concerns. After all, left alone, these treatment-interfering factors will prevent meaningful personal change. Therapists can address the client's strong resistance to addressing treatment-interfering factors during the course of the group.

Depending on the client's circumstances, his placement will either occur in tandem with other treatment activities (signaling a last effort to maintain his placement in various groups) or will occur as his sole treatment activity. Whatever the case, the team offers the individualized treatment group as a means to guide the client back on track. While many clients express a desire to continue their participation, the individualized treatment group should last only long enough to return clients to the rest of their treatment programs.

Upon establishing the goals for a client to work in the individualized treat-

```
+----+----+----+----+----+----+----+----+----+----+
0    1    2    3    4    5    6    7    8    9    10
```

FIGURE 2: READINESS RULER

ment group, therapists can next use a "readiness ruler" (see Figure 2; Miller and Rollnick 2002, p. 183; Berg-Smith 2006) to explore the client's motivation further.

Despite its apparent simplicity, the use of this ruler can produce fruitful discussion as well as a tangible visual aid. The therapist can ask, "On a scale of one to ten, how ready are you to consider addressing these areas?" When the client offers only a "four," the therapists can then ask why he did not choose a one or a two. Whatever the client's response, it will almost invariably involve some sort of strength, positive attribute, or belief in his ability to address the issue. The therapists can then affirm and explore these areas before asking, "What would need to happen for you to move up a half-step to a four and a half?" The client's answer will likely involve some sort of action that he and/or others can take and include what Miller and Rollnick (2002) call "change talk," invoking "the person's own reasons for and advantages of change." This process can provide considerable insight and direction for clients and team members alike. It also helps if each client considers possibilities for change rather than having those suggestions come from others.

The Group Process
The individualized treatment group is open-ended, and it provides the opportunity for newer clients to receive feedback from more experienced ones. Once involved in the individualized treatment group, clients receive the opportunity to review each of the issues outlined in their option tools, and then to discuss those issues with the whole group. The same process of assessing readiness with the readiness ruler is useful for exploring each area. In addition to eliciting "change talk," the process provides a forum in which other clients can ask open, thought-provoking questions and provide support.

Once the group begins exploring a relevant area, all of the members next examine the costs and benefits of each issue. For a client who is addressing disruptive group behavior, this discussion will involve what he gets out of being disruptive as well as what the costs are of that behavior (e.g., continued failure to progress). Key questions for this discussion include:

- How has this issue played a role in your past behavior?
- How does this issue play a role in your current behavior?
- What kinds of payoffs do you get from this?
- On the other hand, what kinds of difficulties is it bringing you?

Depending on circumstances, supplementary questions can include:

- What is happening when you decide to engage in this behavior?
- What do you want to happen and what will you get from it?
- How might this issue affect others?
- How might you approach situations where this issue might arise and get what you need without this issue happening?
- If you were in my (or someone else's) shoes, what might you think about this issue? (Other clients often have a number of contributions to add to this question.)

By exploring the benefits as well as the costs, each client can decide for himself how committed he is to making change in this area. It is important that he make these decisions free of coercion or the sales pitches of well-intentioned professionals. The client will need to rely on his own commitment in later stages of treatment.

Action Planning and Completing the Group
Therapists and clients monitor the referral issues both on the unit and within the group. Together these players design formal and informal action plans that vary according to the issues. For some, the action plans involve a demonstrated and agreed-upon pattern of reducing disruption; for others, the plan includes the completion of some task, such as an assessment process. In some cases, clients can return for additional work to consoli-

date the gains they have made. Others must work further to address issues incrementally. When each client is ready to leave, the group has a "send-off" discussion in which the members review that client's strengths and accomplishments.

Potential Traps

Working with clients who have been unsuccessful in other treatment settings, often for decades, presents no shortage of challenges. Clients who are resistant to change can disrupt the process of the group in many ways. The following are some, but not all, of the potential difficulties that therapists might experience. Professionals also might wish to review the motivational interviewing literature for other typical "traps":

Debate versus Dialog
Clients often enter group with an intense sense of grievance toward the legal system and mental health professionals. Therapists may sense that the client has brought abusiveness with them into treatment. It can be productive for the whole group to hear a client out and to encourage dialog with others who have moved beyond similar concerns. However, therapists should take care to maintain a focus on personal change.

Unrealistic Expectations
The treatment team must guard against expecting too much too soon. The purpose of the individualized treatment group is to help the client rejoin the mainstream treatment program. The treatment team can best prevent unrealistic expectations by outlining very clear goals at the outset.

Discrepancy Hurdles
Clients are sometimes ambivalent about discussing the discrepancies between their current and desired statuses. Under these conditions, therapists are at risk to argue for change, often by offering suggestions as to the advantages of change. Under these conditions, possible solutions include focusing on other clients and convening staff meetings to discuss alternatives.

Focusing on One Client to the Exclusion of Others

Some clients seek attention while others actively avoid scrutiny. It may be useful to develop and maintain a schedule with topics the group will determine and discuss, ensuring that all clients contribute. Therapists should invite input from the less-vocal group members.

The Negative Spotlight

Professionals with experience in diverse inpatient settings can understand how problems command attention far more readily than successes do. In some clients' cases, simply getting out of bed or maintaining a schedule represents success. Therapists should remain active in their attempts to highlight even small successes while recognizing the challenges that clients have yet to address. With no spotlight on success, clients have fewer avenues for exploring what has worked in their attempts to get back on track.

Etiology

Group members sometimes engage in lengthy discussions and other periods of reflection in which they explore how various issues in their lives came to be. Group members can certainly find great value in exploring their own life histories. In fact, they are often expected to compile autobiographies of their lives in subsequent treatment phases, but when a group member does a self-focused study in which he learns to understand the roots behind his need for treatment, it still is not the same as when he actually learns how to make changes in his life. It can be very easy for group members to substitute eloquent life narratives for acceptance of responsibility and demonstrated change. To prevent the etiology trap from taking time away from change, therapists can remind clients that they will have ample time to search out the causes of their behavior in other treatment venues.

Adverse Experiences and Trust

Although the literature describes varying levels of prior sexual victimization among those who have engaged in sexual aggression, a great many clients have experienced a wide range of other traumatic and adverse events in their lives. This background creates a number of potential challenges. First, therapists should recognize that treatment for sexual aggression addresses material that can be upsetting to clients on a number of complex levels. Many clients cannot meaningfully address their own actions until they come to terms with their own victimization. Others report histories of events that they do not perceive as traumatic, but that outside observers typically would (e.g., sexual abuse by female caretakers). Still other clients view this personal history as merely an excuse for their past behavior. As a result, some clients actually invent a fictitious history of trauma to serve that same purpose. Therapists typically find themselves balancing support and collaboration with their clients while remaining vigilant for signs of deception that can undermine treatment progress.

Adverse Experiences and Authority
The prior experiences of those who have engaged in sexual aggression can also influence their relationships with therapists. Many clients who grew up in abusive environments develop a belief that the world is a hostile place where people are either abusive or abused. Because clients often perceive their therapists as powerful or aligned with other authorities, clients often expect their therapists to become abusive and may be confused when they don't. In some cases, a therapist using motivational interviewing is one of the first warm and empathic people they have ever met. This new territory can create tension in clients, and some will deliberately become provocative to test the limits of their therapists. Some clients have said that their own confrontational style results from their being so anxious that the therapist will inevitably become abusive that they feel compelled to provoke an abusive response in the therapist rather than wait for it to happen.

Therapist Gender
Given the often brutal upbringing of many clients, many clients will respond differently to male vs. female therapists. Men who have sexually assaulted same-aged females often hold adversarial attitudes toward women in general. In many cases, this attitude translates into their expecting female therapists to betray them or to turn a blind eye to their distress in much the same way that their own mothers did when failing to stop abuse by their fathers. With a male therapist, clients who have engaged in violence may attempt to bully or intimidate the therapist, if he is using motivational interviewing. At these

times, it is helpful for the therapist to explore the client's perspective and recognize that while abuse of therapists is not acceptable, exploring these attitudes can have direct relevance to treatment of sexual aggression. Again, while a harsh and confrontational approach may bring about short-term compliance, it will not likely produce long-term client change.

Fear of Disclosure
Many localities have increased the severity of their responses to sexual abuse. Therapists using motivational interviewing will want to remain sensitive to the fact that disclosing instances of sexual aggression can have dramatic repercussions for clients. Therapists frequently find that clients have engaged in sexual aggression that went unreported, and will want to be sensitive to the ambivalence that this discovery creates (the desire to be honest directly conflicts with the desire to avoid further imprisonment).

Superficial Participation
Some people who have engaged in sexual aggression feign meaningful participation in order to please others. In many cases, these clients (who may have engaged in sexual aggression against peers, children, or both) appear to view their environment as one where others are in control of them, so that the best they can hope for is to adapt. In group treatment using motivational interviewing, this attitude can appear as a willingness to explore but not necessarily resolve ambivalence. Statements such as, "I'll have to think about that," or attempts to steer discussion in the direction of past events rather than current actions can signal clients' attempts to survive discussions rather than engage in change. In some cases, these clients speak directly about motivation and commitment in an apparent attempt to use the therapist's own words. Therapists will want to remember that people who have engaged in sexual aggression very often possess generally underdeveloped interpersonal skills. At the same time, they still very often have developed remarkable abilities to comply with expectations in order to avoid detection of harmful activities.

Not Sticking with the Style
People who have engaged in sexual aggression can present numerous challenges, whether directly (e.g., through intimidation) or indirectly (e.g., by

only appearing to participate meaningfully). Often, therapists feel some urgency to "fix" their clients or to respond harshly to evidence of wrongdoing. Very often, novice motivational interviewing practitioners quickly find themselves saying, "I tried that approach and it didn't work," only to experience subsequently heightened resistance. In these instances, it can help to remember the adage that, "The slower you go, the faster you get where you're going."

Group Engages in the Righting Reflex
At times, group members will give unsolicited advice in an attempt to fix another group member's problem. This can result in resistance on the part of the member receiving the advice and can also increase everyone else's frustration. Teaching the group to use the OARS micro-skills (Open-ended questions, Affirmations, Reflections, and Summaries) can help prevent these problems. When such instances do occur, the therapist may comment on the group's desire to help the member with his problem and the member's apparent desire to address the problem himself.

Conclusion

Facilitating group treatment using motivational interviewing can be a radically different experience for many therapists whose earlier training emphasized the need for tight control over treatment. However, the emerging research evidence shows that if professionals wish to reduce the likelihood of future sexual harm, it is essential to involve clients meaningfully in their own change process. Although it is convenient to use harsh and confrontational approaches to gain short-term compliance, professionals should not mistake this blunt, but seemingly effective, approach for building client capacity for long-term change.

REFERENCES

Berg-Smith, S. M. 2006. An introduction to motivational interviewing. Presentation at Sand Ridge Secure Treatment Center. Mauston, WI.

Berg-Smith, S. M. 2008. *An introduction to motivational interviewing*. Presentation at the National Wellness Conference. Stevens Point, Wisconsin.

Bureau of Justice Statistics. 2003. *Recidivism of sex offenders released from prison in 1994*. Washington, DC: U.S. Department of Justice.

Furby, L., M. Weinrott, and L. Blackshaw. 1989. Sex offender recidivism: A review. *Psychological Bulletin* 105(1):3–30.

Garland, R. J., and M. J. Dougher. 1991. Motivational intervention in the treatment of sex offenders. In *Motivational interviewing: Preparing people to change addictive behavior*, ed. W. R. Miller and S. Rollnick, 303–13. New York: Guilford Press.

Hanson, R. K., I. Broom, and M. Stephenson. 2004. Evaluating community sex offender treatment programs: A 12-year follow-up of 724 offenders. *Canadian Journal of Behavioural Science* 36(2):85–94.

Hanson, R. K., and M. T. Bussière. 1998. Predicting relapse: A meta-analysis of sexual offender recidivism studies. *Journal of Consulting and Clinical Psychology* 66:348–62.

Hanson, R. K., A. Gordon, A. J. R. Harris, J. K. Marques, W. Murphy, V. L. Quinsey, and M. C. Seto. 2002. First report of the collaborative outcome data project on the effectiveness of treatment for sex offenders. *Sexual Abuse: A Journal of Research and Treatment* 14(2):169–94.

Hanson, R. K., and K. E. Morton-Bourgon. 2005. The characteristics of persistent sexual offenders: A meta-analysis of recidivism studies. *Journal of Consulting and Clinical Psychology* 78(6):1154–63.

Harris, A. J. R., and R. K. Hanson. 2004. *Sex offender recidivism: A simple question* (No. 2004-03). Ottawa: Public Safety and Emergency Preparedness Canada.

Jennings, J. L., and S. Sawyer. 2003. Principles and techniques for maximizing the effectiveness of group therapy with sex offenders. *Sexual Abuse: A Journal of Research & Treatment* 15:251–68.

Levenson, J. S., and D. S. Prescott. 2007. Considerations in evaluating the effectiveness of sexual offender treatment: Incorporating knowledge into practice. In *Knowledge and practice: Challenges in the treatment and supervision of sexual abusers*, ed. D. S. Prescott, 124–42. Oklahoma City: Wood 'N' Barnes Publishing.

———. 2009. Treatment experiences of civilly committed sex offenders: A consumer satisfaction survey. *Sexual Abuse: A Journal of Research & Treatment* 21:6–20.

Levenson, J. S., D. S. Prescott, and D. A. D'Amora. Forthcoming. Sex offender treatment: Consumer satisfaction and engagement in therapy. *International Journal of Offender Therapy and Comparative Criminology*.

Lösel, F., and M. Schmucker. 2005. The effectiveness of treatment for sexual offenders: A comprehensive meta-analysis. *Journal of Experimental Criminology* 1:117–46.

Lund, C. A. 2000. Predictors of sexual recidivism: Did meta-analysis clarify the role and relevance of denial. *Sexual Abuse: A Journal of Research and Treatment* 12:275–88.

Marques, J. K., M. Wiederanders, D. M. Day, C. Nelson, and A. Van Ommeren. 2005. Effects of a relapse prevention program on sexual recidivism: Final results from California's Sex Offender Treatment and Evaluation Project (SOTEP). *Sexual Abuse: A Journal of Research & Treatment* 17(1):79–107.

Marshall, W. L. 2005. Therapist style in sexual offender treatment: Influence on indices of change. *Sexual Abuse: A Journal of Research and Treatment* 17(2):109–16.

Marshall, W. L., and L. E. Marshall. 2007. Preparatory programs for sexual offenders. In *Knowledge and Practice: Challenges in the Treatment and Supervision of Sexual Abusers*, ed. D. S. Prescott, 108–23. Oklahoma City: Wood 'N' Barnes Publishing.

Marshall, W. L., G. A. Serran, H. Moulden, R. Mulloy, Y. M. Fernandez, R. E. Mann, and D. Thornton. 2002. Therapist features in sexual offender treatment: Their reliable identification and influence on behavior change. *Clinical Psychology and Psychotherapy* 9:395–405.

McGrath, R. J., G. F. Cumming, and B. L. Burchard. 2003. *Current practices and trends in sexual abuser management: The Safer Society 2002 Nationwide Survey*. Brandon, VT: Safer Society Foundation, Inc.

Miller, W. R., and S. Rollnick. 2002. *Motivational interviewing: Preparing people for change*. 2nd ed. New York: Guilford.

Prescott, D. S. 2007. Getting Back on Track: Addressing treatment-interfering factors in a group setting. In *Knowledge and Practice: Challenges in the Treatment and Supervision of Sexual Abusers*, ed. D. S. Prescott, 201–21. Oklahoma City: Wood 'N' Barnes Publishing.

Prochaska, J. O., and C. C. DiClemente. 1982. Transtheoretical therapy: Toward a more integrative model of change. *Psychotherapy: Theory, Research & Practice* 19(3):276–88.

Reitzel, L. R., and J. L. Carbonell. 2006. The effectiveness of sexual offender treatment for juveniles as measured by recidivism: A meta-analysis. *Sexual Abuse: A Journal of Research and Treatment* 18:401–21.

Scieszka, J., and L. Smith. 1996. *The true story of the three little pigs*. Victoria, BC: Puffin.

Seager, J. A., D. Jellicoe, and G. K. Dhaliwal. 2004. Refusers, dropouts and completers: Measuring sex offender treatment. *International Journal of Offender Therapy and Comparative Criminology* 48(5):600–12.

Truthought. 2001. Truthought corrective thinking process. Treatment materials prepared by Truthought, Inc. Available at www.truthought.com.

Walker, D. F., S. K. McGovern, E. L. Poey, and K.E. Otis. 2002. Treatment effectiveness for male adolescent sexual offenders: A meta-analysis and review. *Journal of Child Sexual Abuse* 13:281–94.

Supervising Clinicians Using Motivational Interviewing

David S. Prescott

Introduction

Many professionals emerge from training in motivational interviewing (MI) enthusiastic about applying its style, spirit, and techniques to diverse areas of their lives. Bill Miller (2006) has written about the frustrations of professionals returning to settings whose climates are inconsistent with MI. Only a handful of specialized training exists for those interested both in using MI with supervision and in supervising MI practitioners. Unfortunately, even an outstanding two-day training cannot address the potential complications in making one's supervisory practice more consistent with the principles of motivational interviewing (referred to below as "MI-consistent"). This chapter explores the integration of motivational interviewing principles and techniques into clinical supervision. It emphasizes that high-quality treatment requires high-quality supervision and ethical integrity at all levels of the program in which it happens.

Background

Those who have supervised newer clinicians may be familiar with challenging situations such as the following:

> *You supervise staff in a residential treatment center for adolescents who have sexually abused. A new clinician describes the fabulous work he has just done. The clinician went to a living unit where his client was involved in an incident requiring physical management. While a staff was physically restraining the client, the clinician engaged the youth in a conversation about the youth's family. The young man became agitated and struggled more while the staff continued to restrain them on the floor; other staff attempted to re-direct the other clients, who were by now watching and commenting. The clinician encouraged the youth to get his concerns out in the open, and the youth complied, becoming exhausted from the experience, withdrawn, and ultimately motionless in the process. The clinician is reporting success in exploring the etiology of the young person's behavior problems. The staff members are reporting that the clinician's intervention placed everyone present at increased risk for physical injury. Your immediate thoughts are that this situation can never, ever happen again.*

In another instance:

> *You supervise a therapist who is treating a man convicted of First Degree Sexual Assault. The therapist has expressed some suspicions that the man was falsely accused and convicted. You discover that the therapist has just contacted the prosecutor and probation officer to express concern that the man should never have been arrested in the first place. You are now in the position of requiring that the therapist stop all contact with these representatives of the legal system. The therapist says he is simply advocating for his client, while you are aware that the situation is not anywhere near as simple as the therapist seems to think.*

Finally:

> *You are supervising a new clinician assigned to treat an 11-year-old boy with sexual behavior problems who has also experienced severe physical abuse by his now-absent stepfather. The clinician reports success in getting the child to express his emotions. In fact, the child tore the office to shreds, breaking toys and knocking over a bookcase. Although no one questions that expressing emotions can be healthy, this was an unsafe situation likely to cause more problems than it solved.*

Many supervisors have encountered situations like these. Each one most likely requires some degree of overt direction from the supervisor. Matters can become complicated for supervisors attempting to use and model motivational interviewing during the course of supervision. The ethical use of MI involves collaboration and support for autonomy. Supervisors can find themselves in situations where the ethical use of MI does not seem possible (e.g., enforcing workplace rules) or where MI techniques would be inappropriate (e.g., asking an employee to describe the positive aspects of absenteeism).

What Is Supervision?

An Internet search quickly shows many definitions of clinical supervision and no shortage of resources for providing it—many more than this article can cover. Common activities of clinical supervisors include providing support, guidance, direction, encouragement, education, and consultation. In practice, however, clinical supervisors typically provide administrative supervision as well, particularly in settings that provide treatment for sexually abusive behavior. Supervisory activities range from understanding a specific case to providing specialized treatment, and from managing caseloads to completing paperwork and following rules and protocols. Supervisors can adopt directing, guiding, and following styles depending upon circumstances. Because supervisors are often responsible for many aspects simultaneously (e.g., quality assurance and performance evaluation as well as support, ideas, and encouragement), supervisory dilemmas can occur on short notice, making supervisors uncertain how best to proceed as they strive to be MI-consistent.

Getting Started with MI-Consistency

Moyers (2006) observed that many practitioners become skilled at MI but when providing supervision, they can wind up distorting or diluting MI in order to meet the needs of the immediate situation. In the end, what they are actually doing is either MI-inconsistent or an unethical use of motivational interviewing. Moyers goes on to remind trainees that, "It's OK not to use MI." By this, she means that it is better not to use MI than it is to use a distorted version in the name of being MI-consistent. Giving permission not to use motivational interviewing also provides choice and autonomy to the supervisee, which is itself an element of motivational interviewing. There are, after all, occasions when one has an urgent need to give firm directions rather than explore and resolve ambivalence about the process of receiving direction. Having permission not to use MI often has a paradoxical effect: supervisees become more dedicated to using it for themselves and not because their supervisor demands it.

It is also possible to establish a clinical setting in such a way that minimizes the need for MI-inconsistent supervision practice. One place people can start is with themselves. To what extent do professionals have an unexplored *righting reflex* (that urge to intervene in a client's life and make things "right") when they are providing supervision? To what extent does that reflex prevent therapists from seeing opportunities for creating a more motivational interviewing–consistent workplace? In some cases, it may be easier for the therapist to guide the client's exploration and to assist his resolution of ambivalence than it is to understand our ambivalence as supervisors. In other cases, our righting reflex may signal challenges in the set-up of our program.

Miller (2006) suggests that organizations can become more MI-consistent by promoting its spirit and practice. He notes that key opinion leaders can promote MI principles such as collaboration, support, and autonomy and can have teams of individuals encourage one another. He also highlights the importance of hiring MI-consistent staff (e.g., using demonstrated empathy as a criterion for hiring) and suggests that this kind of organizational climate may help with staff retention. There are other things professionals can do to ensure a more MI-consistent workplace as well.

Mission Statements, Job Descriptions, and Supervisory Identity

First, supervisors can ensure that treatment programs develop MI-consistent mission statements. Although mission statements can be deceptively simple, some agencies do a better job of describing their missions than others do. For agencies seeking to incorporate the style and spirit of MI, the mission statement is an important place to start. Depending on circumstances, those seeking to refine their mission statement might frame this task by describing what is proven by research and then show how it works effectively in influencing long-term change. Mission statements can also contain a more overt shift away from harsh and confrontational treatment practice. For example, Schladale (2007) described the mission statement that was written for a program for youth who had sexually abused. The supervisors created the program's mission statement in collaboration with those young clients. For others who hope to become more MI-consistent, it may be helpful for them to make sure that the core values of a treatment program are as explicit as possible.

One benefit of attention to an agency's mission statement is that supervisors can rely on it instead of on their righting reflex. The MI-consistent mission statement becomes a compass by which supervisors can assess the direction of supervision issues. When a supervisee is heading in an unhelpful direction, the supervisor can explore and reflect back to that staff person the discrepancy between agency mission, values, and protocols rather than point to the discrepancy between what the supervisor wants and what the supervisee is doing. In addition to helping ensure program fidelity, such an approach also reduces the likelihood that discussions take on an unnecessarily personalized tone; the impatient supervisor can follow an internal script of, "This is not about me; it's about the mission, purpose, style, and policies of this agency."

Additionally, agencies do not always rely on the job descriptions of clinicians as often as they might. The poorly defined roles in these settings can create confusion, leading to the risk of having these treatment programs become reflections of the strongest personalities within them. Programs that establish job descriptions reflecting MI values leave little reason for supervisors to be unnecessarily harsh in providing direction, because those supervisors can reframe any given situation by the discrepancies that exist between job description and actual performance. Such clearly defined roles can serve as the stars for supervisors to steer by in difficult times.

When all else fails, supervisors can always fall back on the MI technique of elicit-provide-elicit so that they can give difficult feedback in the most respectful possible fashion. Closely related in approach is the feedback sandwich, where the supervisor provides areas for improvement in between affirmations and praise (Dohrenwend 2002). Supervisors need to take care to provide affirmations that are clear, specific, personal, and honest. Feedback must be respectful to its core. Simply providing adjectives and vague praise (e.g., "nice job") is less helpful than specific examples (e.g., "Did you notice how that client got tears in his eyes when you provided that reflection? He really understood that you were listening."). Feedback is likely most helpful when it focuses on one specific area at a time. For example, in the vignette involving the therapist contacting the prosecutor and parole officer, the supervisor might wish to say:

> *You are committed to your clients and you work hard to go over and above expectations. If you come to me with these kinds of concerns first, we can discuss the most effective ways to handle them. That way, the prosecutor and parole officer won't be concerned that you're acting outside the mission and methods of our agency. I'm impressed that you're willing to take such initiative! What do you think about what I've said?*

Ethical Considerations

Miller and Rollnick (2002) outline three areas of ethical complexity that apply to supervisors' attempts to be MI-consistent. These areas are as follows:

- The person's aspirations are dissonant with the supervisor's opinion as to what is in the supervisee's best interest.

- The supervisor has a personal investment in the supervisee's actions.
- The nature of the relationship includes coercive power of the supervisor to influence the directions the supervisee takes.

Ultimately, the supervisor must be prepared for and accepting of a supervisee's decision to terminate employment. Using MI to coerce supervisees into actions they do not want to take is clearly outside the scope of its ethical use. A key element of the above approach is that supervisors provide a framework for preventing MI's use for controlling their clinicians. All supervisors will experience situations that occur where using MI is inappropriate to the situation (e.g., imminent danger). Instead of asking how one can always use MI in supervision, supervisors might do better to ask how best to prepare their environment to be as MI-consistent as possible. This approach could involve explicitly developing goals for supervision in collaboration with the supervisee.

Traps to Avoid

The general traps that can hold mental health practitioners back from the most effective motivational interviewing practice also hold true for supervision. They include the question-answer trap, taking-sides trap, labeling trap, premature-focus trap (particularly with respect to the stages of supervision described below), and blaming trap (Miller and Rollnick 2002). Likewise, it can be easy to forget that changing professional behavior can be as difficult as changing personal behavior. Supervisors can overlook the fact that supervisees often place themselves in a position of considerable vulnerability with each session. After all, their very livelihood can depend on their performance evaluation. A particularly destructive trap is the expert trap, where a supervisor attempts to convey the impression that he or she has all the answers (Miller and Rollnick 2002). One possible solution in settings where a number of clinicians work is to invite the supervisee to collect thoughts and ideas from their colleagues.

Professional pride can also be a potential trap in MI-consistent supervision; such supervision can resemble a hybrid of the expert role and righting reflex. Some supervisors need others to perceive them as experts, and so they often try to provide answers before adequately asking questions or assessing situations that arise. The unspoken power needs of a supervisor in these situations can result in bringing an end to genuine dialog. One option is for the supervisor to acknowledge that the best answer will come from continued discussion and then, through that process, see what unfolds. Should this approach not become productive, the supervisor can then ask permission to share additional ideas, provide suggestions, and ask for feedback. This method requires a supervisor to see herself in the role of guide rather than an esteemed expert with all the answers.

People become supervisors for a variety of reasons. Some are competent clinicians for whom supervision is a means to expand or diversify their attempts to help others. Some simply enjoy being in charge of others, while many provide supervision out of a sense of obligation to their programs or agencies. Sadly, few educational programs are available for training supervisors (Rich 2007), and those few programs that do exist offer virtually no guidance in the field of sexual offender treatment. In order to be MI-consistent, all supervisors will want to be clear on their values in order to be truly collaborative, evocative, and supportive of the autonomy of supervisees.

A Supervisory Trajectory

In spite of the paucity of training programs, numerous other resources are available for supervisors of all backgrounds. Many of these resources share common elements with MI. Many others extend beyond supervision and explore the differences between management, leadership, and command (e.g., Gittell 2003). John C. Maxwell, for example, defines leadership as influence—nothing more and nothing less—and describes "laws" for those that lead others. Among his axioms is, "No one cares how much you know until they know how much you care." He also emphasizes that those who follow must know that they are on solid ground with those who lead (Maxwell 2007).

Blanchard, Zigarmi, and Zigarmi (1985) have described four leadership and management styles that can inform supervisors. They include *directing, coaching, supporting,* and *delegating.* These styles make intuitive sense, correlate with the successful development of a supervisee, and may provide useful anchor points for supervisors aiming to be MI-consistent. Each stage of those four management skills asks for varying levels of direction and support. Like the transtheoretical stages of change model (Prochaska and DiClemente 1982), this management approach may be best used as a rough guide. In line with criticisms of the stages of change model (e.g., Sutton 1996), supervision may need to move from one stage to another in response to situational needs. Professional development takes place within the context of the employment situation and various life events.

Directing involves providing specific instructions and close supervision of task accomplishment. Affirming, listening, and facilitating processes are all vital means by which these take place, and it is not difficult to see how the MI skills of Elicit-Provide-Elicit will be particularly helpful at this phase of supervisee acclimation and development. Supervisors can use Denise Ernst's recommendations for when to provide brief advice as a working foundation (Miller and Rollnick 2002):

- The supervisee asks for information.
- The supervisor has information that might be helpful.
- The supervisor feels ethically compelled to provide advice.

The astute supervisor can frame each of these exchanges within a course of asking permission and eliciting responses (for example, "Can I make a suggestion?"). This phase of the supervisory relationship has many features in common with Phase I of MI, and supervisors can use many of the same MI techniques to teach MI. These techniques can include options menus and variations on the readiness ruler (Miller and Rollnick 2002). One can expect that supervisees may experience ambivalence and discrepancy in a number of areas such as the following:

- I feel two ways about having my supervisor directly assessing my motivational interviewing skills.
- I have never been very good at this area of the job. Do I really want to expend the effort to improve?

- I do not really feel like a part of this team yet and am not sure what to make of it.
- I am more comfortable with some members of my team than others.
- I enjoy providing services in one aspect of my work, but I am not so sure about this other aspect.
- I am not sure yet how open I can be with my supervisor.
- I feel two ways about having to accept explicit direction. The sooner I can be left alone the better.
- Conversely, I know my supervisor has faith in me, but I think I need more direct oversight than what I'm getting.
- I have done this work a long time, but now I am in a new situation. I am a good therapist, but I am not so sure about some of these methods.
- I am torn between wanting to improve my performance and not wanting to give up my old work habits.

Ultimately, the supervisee's developmental task is acclimating to a new environment and taking his or her first steps within it. Virtually all supervisees have a wish for mastery over their work and lives with some discrepancy between where they are and where they want to be. Assuming that no ethical issues surface, supervisors can then watch for change indications such as expressed desire, ability, reason, and need to improve in the negotiated areas.

Coaching involves direction and close supervision of task accomplishment. It also requires that supervisors explain decisions, solicit suggestions, and support progress. Here, supervisors will wish to be sensitive to issues around leading, guiding, and following. The developmental task of supervisees is to take their first independent steps in their new work situations. Possible indications of readiness for this supervisory style can include a stated commitment to and steps taken toward improvement in job duties. At this stage, supervisors will wish to be cautious about attempting to strengthen commitment in sensitive areas too quickly or trying to adhere too rigidly to a manualized approach in supervision (Hettema, Steele, and Miller 2005), in order to prevent further ambivalence or resistance. Rather, classic examples of developing discrepancy can include questions such as, "What went well in the session today?" and "What would you do differently?" In this way, the supervisee can make the argument for change (Murphy and Ford 2006).

Several responses are possible in the chapter's first vignette, when a therapist could easily make a bad situation worse by trying to provide treatment during a physical restraint. The first would be to explore the good and not-so-good elements of this approach and provide reflections and amplifications. Depending on whether the supervisee comes to understand the physical dangers involved, the supervisor may also wish to:

- ask permission to share feedback;
- describe the inherent dangers of trying to provide therapy during physical management;
- describe the agency policy on physical restraint;
- elicit a response; and/or
- express confidence that the supervisee is able to work within the boundaries and job descriptions that the program has established.

Although each job description and agency mission statement can provide clear-cut goals for supervision, pursuing a long-term plan that considers the supervisee's total experience can be beneficial. In the criminological world, Tony Ward and his colleagues (Ward and Stewart 2003; Yates 2007) have described a Good Lives model for offender rehabilitation that has relevance for supervision, particularly in criminal justice situations (where the model is gaining currency).

In essence, the Good Lives model holds that all people are motivated by primary goods that make life more meaningful. They argue that treatment will be more effective when clients use it to pursue meaningful goals rather than to avoid unpleasant outcomes. In this way, supervisors may wish to gain a clear understanding of who their supervisees want to be in their professional lives and how they hope to get there. To some extent, all human beings want to pursue competence in life (health, functioning, etc.); some kind of mastery at work (and at play); autonomy and self-directedness; inner peace (e.g., feeling safe in the workplace, emotional equilibrium, etc.); a sense that they are part of their surrounding community; meaning and purpose in their work; creativity; and a general sense of happiness. Depending on the situation, supervisors can negotiate to include one or more of these areas into an options menu as part of a professional development plan. One way to do this might be to present these themes and other potentially relevant ones as an options menu and ask which, if any, of them the supervisee would care to work toward during the course of his or her supervision. Although this approach will not be to everyone's liking, it can make supervision more satisfying and provide a sense of collaboration beyond adherence to agency expectations.

Possible areas of supervisee ambivalence and discrepancy can be the same as in the first stage. These areas can also include themes related to the pace of professional development as well as the supervisee's personal sense of confidence and importance of each issue in his/her job description and agency mission.

Supporting means upholding and facilitating the efforts of the supervisee toward the accomplishment of tasks and goals and sharing responsibility for making decisions. The developmental task of the supervisee is to take on more responsibility for decisions and treatment provision and to become more active in collaboration with his or her supervisor. This stage has elements in common with Phase II of MI, in which professionals strengthen commitment and engage in action planning. Possible points of discrepancy and ambivalence at this stage include:

- Do I really want to take on more responsibility for the success and failure of treatment?
- Is this where I want to put my energies for the future?
- I've done well up to this point; do I really want to share the things that are still bothering me?

These are serious questions deserving of supervisory consideration. Remaining MI-consistent means not taking sides in what are very important decisions for the supervisee. MI techniques such as coming alongside the reluctance can be particularly helpful here.

Delegating means turning over responsibility for making decisions and solving problems. The developmental task for the supervisee involves demonstrating increased competence and developing new ideas. Possible points of discrepancy and ambivalence at this stage include:

- Do I really want to go to my supervisor with questions? Conversely, do I really want this degree of independence?
- Do I really want to branch out or advance into different areas?
- Do I really want to share my experiences with those who are newer to this work?
- My supervisor thinks I'm doing well, but I'm not so sure. I'm not sure how comfortable I am talking about that seeming discrepancy.

These stages are all excellent opportunities for listening to supervisees and for demonstrating MI spirit and techniques, including reflections, summaries, open questions, and affirmations. Techniques such as querying extremes and agreeing with a twist can also extend supervisory discussion and goal setting along the way.

Conclusion

Providing supervision to professionals in mental health settings is a great—and often underrated—honor. Making one's agency and supervisory style consistent with the style and spirit of MI is valuable for many different reasons. Miller (2006) notes that the benefits of utilizing MI may include improved staff retention. It seems clear that if MI works in part because it taps the inherent need of all people to experience someone listening to them, then any progress that supervisors can make in the MI direction is a step in the right direction. Further, the business world has been providing us with an emerging consensus that organizational leadership involves many of the same principles as MI. For example, Collins (2001) identifies four basic leadership skills that improve performance for all. These skills are leading with questions and not answers, engaging in dialogue and debate without coercion, conducting debriefings without blame, and requiring discussion of sensitive information to prevent ignoring or shortchanging it.

Ultimately, supervisors seeking to be as MI-consistent as possible will want to prepare themselves for those times when it may not be possible to handle situations in this way. It even is permissible in certain situations, and in many circumstances actually more ethical, not to use MI. However, the above suggestions may be helpful to some supervisors as they move forward with making their therapeutic and work environments more MI-consistent. In the final analysis, we can likely:

- learn best from our supervisees how to use MI in supervision;
- learn to appreciate our supervisees' resistance, as it can teach us how to be better supervisors and how to improve our programs;
- stay closer to the mission of our work by dancing more and wrestling less; and
- continue to learn patience with all populations we work with; after all, treatment professionals have as much ambivalence about change as any other human beings.

REFERENCES

Blanchard, K., P. Zigarmi, and D. Zigarmi. 1985. *Leadership and the one-minute manager.* New York: Morrow.

Collins, J. 2001. *Good to great: Why some companies make the leap… and others don't.* New York: Harper Collins.

Dohrenwend, A. 2002. Serving up the feedback sandwich. *Family practice management news letter.* Retrieved December 30, 2007, from http://www.aafp.org/fpm/20021100/43serv.pdf.

Gittell, J. 2003. *The Southwest Airlines way: Using the power of relationships to achieve high performance.* New York: McGraw-Hill.

Hettema, J., J. Steele, and W. R. Miller. 2005. Motivational interviewing. *Annual review of clinical psychology* 1:91–111.

Maxwell, J. C. 2007. *The 21 irrefutable laws of leadership.* 10th ed. Nashville, TN: Thomas Nelson.

Miller, W. R. 2006. Can organizations be MINTy? *MINT bulletin* 13:1–4. Retrieved December 30, 2007 from http://motivationalinterview.org/mint/MINT13.2.pdf.

Miller, W. R., and S. Rollnick. 2002. *Motivational interviewing: Preparing people for change.* New York: Guilford.

Moyers, T. 2006. *Motivational interviewing supervisor training*. Workshop conducted with William Miller and Denise Ernst. Albuquerque, NM.

Murphy, B., and L. Ford. 2006. MI and supervision workshop. *MINT bulletin* 13:40–42. Retrieved December 31, 2007 from http://motivationalinterview.org/mint/MINT13.1.supplement.pdf.

Prochaska, J. O., and C. C. DiClemente. 1982. Transtheoretical therapy: Toward a more integrative model of change. *Psychotherapy: Theory, research and practice* 19(3):276–88.

Rich, P. 2007. *Clinical supervision of therapists in the treatment of sexually abusive youth*. Manuscript under review.

Schladale, J. 2007. Integrating best business practices into residential programs for youth. In *Knowledge and practice: Challenges in the treatment and supervision of sexual abusers*, ed. D. S. Prescott, 345–78. Oklahoma City: Wood'N'Barnes.

Sutton, S. 1996. Can "stages of change" provide guidance in the treatment of addictions? A critical examination of Prochaska and DiClemente's model. In *Psychotherapy, psychological treatments and the addictions*, ed. G. Edwards and C. Dare, 189–205. Cambridge, UK: Cambridge University Press.

Ward, T., and C. A. Stewart. 2003. The treatment of sexual offenders: Risk management and Good Lives. *Professional Psychology: Research and Practice* 34:353–60.

Yates, P. M. 2007. Taking the leap: Abandoning relapse prevention and applying the self-regulation model to the treatment of sexual offenders. In *Knowledge and practice: Challenges in the treatment and supervision of sexual abusers*, ed. D. S. Prescott, 143–74. Oklahoma City: Wood'N'Barnes.

CLOSING REMARKS
David S. Prescott

For some readers, this book may have confirmed their attitudes and beliefs about the treatment and supervision of people who have sexually abused. There are probably yet other readers who resonate with the text and feel they need much more practice in order to claim proficiency.

As I close this book, may I ask a few questions for you to consider?

- What was the most helpful part of this book?
- What is one part of this book (either a chapter or a message) that you could have done without?
- What is one part of this book that really surprised you?
- What is one part of this book that you can take with you back to work?
- Given how important it is to get the context right for treatment, understand client readiness, prepare for change, remain hopeful, and awaken inner motivation, which of these are you most motivated to do?
- How ready are you to consider making changes to the way you practice your work?
- How confident are you that you can make those changes?
- What would make you more confident?

When you have considered all of these, can I please ask you to consider:

- What is the most respectful way you can interact with sexual offenders even when they are not respectful to you?

- What are your professional and personal hopes and dreams for the next five years?
- Knowing that our work has many difficult aspects, what is the best thing for you about working with sexual offenders?
- And when you have considered that, what is the most fun thing about working with sexual offenders?
- If you stopped working with sexual offenders today, what kinds of things would be at stake?
- Why might others want you to keep working with sexual offenders?

And finally…

- What is the number one reason you should keep working respectfully with sexual offenders?

My hope for all readers is that you are in contact with others who do this work. Besides the quality-assurance aspects, our teamwork proves the Sotho saying that, "Alone I go faster. Together, we go further."

APPENDIX

The Violence Treatment Readiness Questionnaire (VTRQ)

(from chapter 2)

		Strongly Disagree	Disagree	Unsure	Agree	Strongly Agree
1.	Treatment programs are rubbish.	1	2	3	4	5
2.	I am not able to do treatment programs.	1	2	3	4	5
3.	Treatment programs are for wimps.	1	2	3	4	5
4.	I want to change.	1	2	3	4	5
5.	Stopping my offending is really important to me.	1	2	3	4	5
6.	Treatment programs don't work.	1	2	3	4	5
7.	When I think about my last offence, I feel angry with myself.	1	2	3	4	5
8.	I feel ashamed about my violence.	1	2	3	4	5
9.	I am upset about being a corrections client.	1	2	3	4	5
10.	Being seen as an offender upsets me.	1	2	3	4	5
11.	I regret the offence that led to my last sentence.	1	2	3	4	5
12.	I feel guilty about my offending.	1	2	3	4	5
13.	Others are to blame for my violence.	1	2	3	4	5
14.	I don't deserve to be doing a sentence.	1	2	3	4	5
15.	I am to blame for my violence.	1	2	3	4	5
16.	When I think about my sentence, I feel angry with other people.	1	2	3	4	5
17.	I am well organized.	1	2	3	4	5
18.	I have not acted violently for some time now.	1	2	3	4	5
19.	I hate being told what to do.	1	2	3	4	5
20.	Generally, I can trust other people.	1	2	3	4	5

ABOUT THE AUTHORS

Sharon Casey, PhD, is program director of the Forensic Psychology Masters Programme at the University of South Australia in Adelaide.

Robyn L. Langlands, BA (Hons), MA, is a clinical psychology student and PhD candidate at Victoria University of Wellington, New Zealand. She was awarded a Top Achiever Doctoral Scholarship from the Tertiary Education Commission to investigate the emotional, cognitive, and situational factors that precipitate deliberate self-harm behaviors in adolescents and young adults.

Ruth Mann, PhD, worked for Her Majesty's Prison Service in England and Wales for over 20 years and is now employed by the new National Offender Management Service in England and Wales. Initially employed as a prison psychologist and sex offender treatment manager, Ruth moved into a national program management role in 1994. She is responsible for sex offender treatment policy for prison and probation services in England and Wales, as well as cognitive skills program and interventions research. Ruth has a PhD from the University of Leicester and has published approximately 40 scholarly articles on the topic of sex offender assessment and treatment.

Liam E. Marshall has been conducting research on sexual offenders and has been treating offenders for 13 years. He has delivered trainings for correctional services and for those who work with sexual and violent offenders in 14 countries. Liam has authored many publications, including a co-edited and a co-authored book. He is on the editorial board of the journals *Sexual Aggression* and *Sexual Addiction and Compulsivity*. Liam has helped develop and has been a therapist for a variety of sexual offender treatment programs, including preparatory, regular, maintenance, deniers, and low-functioning programs. He also works in anger management and domestic violence programs. He is currently the research director for Rockwood Psychological Services and research chair and co-supervisor of core treatment programs at a secure treatment unit for incarcerated, seriously psychiatrically disordered offenders.

William L. Marshall is professor emeritus of Psychology at Queen's University and director of Rockwood Psychological Services. He has been working with sexual offenders for 40 years and has over 360 publications in print, including 18 books. Bill is, or has been, on the editorial boards of 16 international journals. In recognition of his scientific contributions, Bill was elected a Fellow of the Royal Society of Canada in 2000. In 2006, he was appointed an Officer of the Order of Canada for his international contribution to the safety of society.

Heather M. Moulden, PhD, completed her doctorate in clinical psychology at the University of Ottawa in 2008, and her clinical residency at St. Joseph's Healthcare in 2007. She is a clinical psychologist at St. Joseph's Healthcare, and an assistant professor with the Department of Psychiatry and Behavioural Neurosciences at McMaster University in Hamilton, Ontario, Canada. Heather has provided sexual offender treatment, and has designed and implemented motivational preparatory treatments in forensic settings. She has authored peer reviewed publications, invited chapters, and has presented at scholarly conferences in Canada and the United States. Heather's research interests include risk assessment, evaluating and enhancing treatment efficacy, and diagnostic issues relevant to risk and treatment.

Matt D. O'Brien, MA, MSc, has worked directly with sexual offenders in correctional settings for more than 12 years. He was the head of the Department of Psychology at HMP Wandsworth, UK, where his responsibilities as lead therapist included managing, supervising, and running the full range of sexual offender programs as determined by risk. He then transferred to HMPS Headquarters where he was employed to assess the quality of program delivery, provide clinical advice to treatment managers, and design and deliver new programs. Matt has trained therapists from a wide range of different services in the delivery of sexual offender programs. He is currently delivering preparatory, maintenance, and deniers programs in Canadian Federal institutions for Rockwood Psychological Services.

David S. Prescott, LICSW, is currently president of the Association for the Treatment of Sexual Abusers (ATSA), and clinical director of the Minnesota Sex Offender Program in Moose Lake. Prior to that, he was treatment assessment director at Sand Ridge Secure Treatment Center, Wisconsin's civil commitment program. Since 1987, David has consulted to programs and has worked directly with youth who have sexually abused. He has authored and edited many books, chapters, and articles on the assessment and treatment of sexual abusers.

Marilyn Ross is a sociologist and psychotherapist with a private practice near Austin, Texas. She has directed inpatient children's psychiatric and eating disorder programs and has worked for more than 20 years with people who have sexually abused. Through the past decade, she has applied her knowledge as a motivational interviewing trainer to develop and facilitate treatment groups for these clients, including groups for adjudicated individuals who deny committing an offense.

Geris A. Serran, PhD, graduated with a doctoral degree in clinical psychology from the University of Ottawa in 2003. As a registered psychologist, she is currently employed at Rockwood Psychological Services as the clinical director of the Sexual Offender Treatment Programs at Bath Institution (a medium-security, federal penitentiary) and assessment/intervention with juvenile sex offenders. In addition to her clinical work, Geris's research interests include therapeutic processes, coping strategies, maladaptive schemas, and treatment of sexual offenders. She has authored several book chapters and journal articles, co-edited and co-authored books, and presented at international conferences. Geris has offered consultation services internationally. She is also on the editorial board for the *Journal of Sexual Aggression*. Outside of sex-offender-specific work, Geris provides part-time supervision for behavioural psychology students at St. Lawrence College, Kingston.

About the Authors

Tony Ward, DipClinPsyc, is professor of clinical psychology at Victoria University of Wellington, New Zealand. His research interests include cognitive processes in offenders, rehabilitation models, and ethical issues in forensic psychology. His most recent books are *Rehabilitation: Beyond the Risk Paradigm* (2007), and *Morals, Rights and Practice in the Human Services* (2008).

Robin J. Wilson, PhD, ABPP, is a researcher, educator, and board certified clinical psychologist who received his PhD in applied cognitive science from the University of Toronto in 1996. He has worked with sexual offenders and other offenders in institutional and community settings for 25 years. He is presently the clinical director of the Florida Civil Commitment Center in Arcadia, Florida. Robin's current interests are focused on the collaborative model of risk management and restoration utilized as persons who have sexually offended are moved from institutional to community settings. He has published and presented widely on the diagnosis and treatment of social and sexual psychopathology, and was the recipient of the Association for the Treatment of Sexual Abusers' (ATSA) 1996 Graduate Research Award. Robin is presently the editor of the *ATSA Forum*.

Pamela M. Yates, PhD, RD Psych, is a private consultant in sexual offender research, specializing in the assessment and treatment of sexual offenders at Cabot Consulting and Research Services. She has worked as a clinician, researcher, and program developer since 1987 with adults and youth, sexual offenders, violent offenders, individuals with substance abuse problems, and victims of violence. Her research interests include risk assessment, treatment of sexual offenders, the Good Lives and Self-Regulation Models, and treatment effectiveness evaluation. Her published works, presentations, and consultative work include offender rehabilitation, sex offender assessment and treatment, psychopathy, sexual sadism, phallometric assessment, treatment evaluation, and program development and accreditation.

INDEX

A

adverse experiences of clients, effect on treatment of, 200–201
affirmation, as interviewing technique, 172, 203
agency/agentic thinking, 141–143, 147–148, 151–153
alternative behaviors, healthy, 21–23
Andrews, D. A., 9, 29. *See also* risk-need-responsivity (RNR) model
anger-management programs, 42
approach goals, 84–85, 91–92, 124, 142, 152
assuming the worst. *See* hostile intent, attributing to others
Australia
    Corrections Victoria Treatment Readiness Questionnaire, 39–41, 47, 49
    crime statistics, 42
autonomy
    of client, respecting, 165, 169, 187
    client responsibility and, 123
    as primary human good, 78–80, 86–87, 89
avoidance-based coping strategies, 144, 146
avoidance goals, 84–85, 91, 142–143
awareness of problem, offender's, 21. *See also* denial; disclosures of previous deviant behavior or accusations

B

barriers to change. *See* obstacles to entering treatment; resistance to treatment; treatment interfering factors
Bath Institution Deniers' Program. *See* Deniers' Program
Beech, A. R., 128, 130
behavior modification, 74. *See also* cognitive-behavioral treatments
    assuming impossibility of, 37
    motivational interviewing and, 89
    treatment readiness and, 47–48
black offenders, concerns of, 59
blaming others, 37–38
Bonta, J., 9, 29. *See also* risk-need-responsivity (RNR) model

C

Cage Your Rage, 15
change. *See also* motivation to change
    barriers to (*See* obstacles to entering treatment; resistance to treatment; treatment interfering factors)
    hope theory, role in, 143–145
    preparation for (*See* treatment readiness)
    Thinking for a Change (T4C), 18–20
change-talk statements. *See* motivational interviewing (MI)
Cheavens, J., 142, 144, 145, 153
choices within treatment, offering, 64, 70, 164–165, 169, 188, 198. *See also* coercion

civil commitment, 7, 17–23
client responsivity. See responsivity
client-therapist relationship. See therapeutic relationship
clinical supervision
  importance of, 47
  motivational interviewing, for clinicians using (See motivational interviewing (MI), supervising clinicians using)
coaching, as supervisory style, 215–217
coercion. See also choices within treatment, offering
  group, participation in, 198
  in therapeutic relationship, perceived, 37
  into treatment, 48
cognitive-behavioral treatments, 184. See also behavior modification
  coping strategies, effects on use of, 144–145
  Good Lives Model, 74, 77, 83, 91
  hope theory and, 145, 155
  motivational interviewing and, 89
  treatment readiness and, 47–48
cognitive dissonance
  as motivation to change, 127
  between self-image and offending behavior, 119
cognitive distortions, 8, 20
  primary self-serving, 36–37
  secondary self-serving, 36–38
  treatment readiness, determination of, 20, 36–38
cognitive distortions and treatment readiness, 36–38
cognitive shutdown by offenders, 7
cognitive skills educational programming, 19–20
cognitive traits and treatment readiness, 38

communications
  creating optimism in clients through, 125
  information on treatment program, provision to offenders of, 66, 120–122, 151–152
  treatment aims, communicating to offenders and public of, 65–66
competing priorities of treatment refusers, 58
comprehensive treatment programming for offenders, 11–25
  Florida Civil Commitment Center, Comprehensive Treatment Program of, 17–23
  problem identification and treatment readiness, 13–15, 18
  treatment readiness programming as part of, 15–17
context for treatment, improving, 55–73. See also obstacles to entering treatment
  choice, providing, 70
  experience of offenders, recognizing, 64
  families, working with, 68
  graduates of treatment, utilizing, 66, 69–70
  information on treatment methods/ outcomes, effective, 66
  intrinsic motivators, use of, 68–69
  listening to offenders, 63–64
  myths concerning treatment, identifying and countering, 65
  non-treatment staff, educating, 67
  personal relationships between staff and offenders, enhancing, 64–65
  perspective, recognizing, 64
  referrals for treatment, effective, 66
  risk assessments taking account of treatment progress, 66–67
  self-actualization, 56–58
  strength-based treatment aims, communicating, 65–66

support network, working with, 68
therapist leadership for pro-
  social modelling and supportive
  environment, 68
treatment staff motivations,
  exploring and monitoring, 70–71
coping strategies
  Deniers' Program, 103–104, 110
  hope, role of, 144–147
Corrections Victoria Treatment
  Readiness Questionnaire (CVTRQ),
  39–41, 47, 49
CTP. *See* Florida Civil Commitment
  Center, Comprehensive Treatment
  Program of
Cullen, Murray, 15–16
cultural influences, effect of, 8
CVTRQ. *See* Corrections Victoria
  Treatment Readiness Questionnaire
  (CVTRQ)

D

Day, A., 38–39, 41–47, 49–50
decision-making skills, 89, 169–170.
  See also choices within treatment,
  offering; self-efficacy
delegating, as supervisory style,
  217–218
denial, 5–6, 8
  adaptational model of, 64
  recidivism, relation to, 14, 98–99, 101
  righting reflex and, 164
  treatment readiness, effect on,
    97–98
denial, treatment for offenders in,
  13–15, 96–117, 185. *See also*
  Deniers' Program
  overview, 96–99
  Rockwood treatment approach, 100
  treatment outcomes, 13–14, 98–101
  treatment readiness/pre-treament
    programs, 13–17, 48, 97–98,
    122–123, 185–193

deniers
  family and friends, effect of, 61–62
  perspective and experience, effect
    of, 64
  treatment for (*See* denial, treatment
    for offenders in)
Deniers' Program, 100–114
  case study, 105–112
  coping strategies and emotion
    management component,
    103–104, 110–111
  disclosure component, 102
  intimacy and relationships
    component, 103, 109–110
  life story component, 102–103,
    108–109
  outcome, 100–101
  preparatory sessions, 101–102
  problem analysis component,
    104–105, 107–108
  professional concerns and
    questions, 112–113
  recommendations to clinicians,
    113
  release planning, 105, 111–112
  self-esteem assignment, 102, 110
  self-management component,
    105, 111
  victim harm component, 104, 111
developmental history of offenders,
  13, 146
directing, as supervisory style,
  214–215
disabled offenders, concerns of, 59
disclosures of previous deviant
  behavior or accusations
  deniers, programs for, 97–98, 102,
    107–108, 112–113
  in Florida Comprehensive
    Treatment Program, 21
  in motivational interviewing, 202
  requiring of sexual offenders, 6, 8,
    55–56

in Rockwell preparatory program, 132–133
treatment readiness and, 112
discrepancy between client's current status and goals, 168–169, 199–200
distrust. See also trust
  of correctional system and people in it, 61
  of treatment providers by treatment refusers, 59–61, 119, 201

E

effective interventions. See also recidivism, sexual; treatment completion
  describing treatment efficacy to clients, 120–121
  design and implementation of treatment, importance of, 15–16
  overview, 9–11
  treatment refuser concerns about, 57–58
ego defense mechanisms, 8
emotion coping strategies, 144, 146
emotion reflections, as interviewing technique, 174
emotional awareness and regulation skills, developing, 22, 103–104, 110
empathy
  developing offenders' empathy skills, 22, 190–191
  of treatment provider for offender, 64, 75, 124–125, 129, 163, 168, 185, 201
employment, preparation for, 23
enhancement goals (hope theory), 152, 153
ethnic minorities, concerns of, 59
etiology, group treatment, 200
experiences of offenders, treatment provider's recognition of, 64
expressiveness, encouraging, 130–131

F

families
  deniers, effect on, 61–62
  involvement in treatment, value of, 68
feedback
  as interviewing technique, 179–181
  supervisor/clinician, 211
Florida Civil Commitment Center, Comprehensive Treatment Program of, 17–23
  Phase I, preparation for change, 17–21
  Phase II, awareness, 21
  Phase III, healthy alternative behaviors, 21–23
  Phase IV, maintenance and comprehensive discharge planning, 23
Florida Involuntary Civil Containment for Sexually Violent Predators' Treatment and Care Act, 17
Fordham, A. S., 128, 130
friends
  deniers, effect on, 61–62
  involvement in treatment, value of, 68

G

Gannon, T., 76
gay offenders, concerns of, 59
gender of therapist, issues of, 201–202
goal-directed energy (agency), 141–143, 147–148, 151–153
goals
  approach and avoidance goals, Good Lives Model, 84–85, 91–92, 124
  deniers' pre-treatment group, 190
  discrepancy between client's current status and goals, 168–169, 199–200

Good Lives Model, treatment goals
  of, 78, 81–82
 in hope theory, 141–143, 146–147,
  151–153
 human goods, in Good Lives
  Model, 9–10, 77–81, 86–87, 90
 preparatory/individualized
  treatment group, 194–196, 199
Good Lives Model (GLM), 13, 46,
 74–95, 124
 approach and avoidance goals,
  84–85, 91–92, 124
 case conceptualization, 82–83
 deniers, treatment of, 100
 goals of treatment, 78, 81–82
 human goods (goals), 9–10, 77–81,
  86–87, 90
 motivation and, 82, 88–92
 overview, 76–81
 pre-treatment assessment, 82
 problems of offenders, 79–80
 risk-needs-responsivity model and,
  10–11, 65–66
 supervision of clinicians, applying
  to, 216–217
 treatment using, 81–88
graduates, treatment. *See* treatment
 graduates
group, expressiveness within, 130–131
group cohesion, building, 128–130
group norm and rules, establishing,
 85, 101–102, 121–122
group participants, mentoring/
 leadership of, 23, 69–70, 97,
 129–130, 134
group treatment, motivational
 interviewing used in. *See*
 motivational interviewing (MI)
 used with offenders in group
 treatment
guilt
 admission of, 6, 14–15 (*See also*
  denial)

 as change motivator, 131
 treatment readiness, determination
  of, 35–36

H
Hanson, R. K., 98–99, 120, 184
healthy alternative behaviors, 21–23
histories of offenders
 developmental history, 13, 146
 life stories, 102–103, 108–109,
  133–134, 200
 sexual history, 190, 195
HM Prison Service, 56, 66, 67
hope theory of motivation, 139–159
 change, role in, 143–145
 definition of hope, 140–141
 forensic populations, support for
  hopeful approaches in, 147–150
 future directions, 155–156
 goals, 141–143, 146–147, 151–153
 incorporation into existing offender
  treatment programs, 150–153
 offender assessments as motivation
  tool, 154
 overview, 140–143
 pre-treatment programs, 150–152,
  154, 155
 sexual offending, application of
  hope to, 145–147
hostile intent, attributing to others,
 37, 38, 61, 201
hostility of other prisoners toward
 sexual offenders, 6–7, 61, 68
Howells, K., 35–36, 38–39
human goods, 9–10, 77–81, 86–87, 90

I
improving context for treatment. *See*
 context for treatment, improving
impulsivity, 80
institutional settings
 hopelessness of offenders in, 7–8

risks to offenders in, 6–7, 61, 68
treatment takeup in, 64–65
interventions. *See* effective
interventions; pre-treatment
assessments/interventions;
treatment programs
interventions, effective. *See* effective
interventions
interviews
    to assess treatment readiness, 43, 44
    motivational (*See* motivational
      interviewing (MI))
    pre-treatment group, initial
      interview for, 187–190
    Rockwood preparatory program,
      prior to entering, 127–128
intimacy
    Deniers' Program treatment,
      103, 109–110
    in Good Lives Model, 78–79,
      86–87, 91
    sexual behavior, intimate nature
      of, 6
Involuntary Civil Containment
    for Sexually Violent Predators'
    Treatment and Care Act (Florida), 17
Irving, L. M., 151, 154

J
Jones, L., 58
Judeo-Christian morals, 8

K
Kansas Sexually Violent Predator
    Act, 17
Kansas v. Hendricks, 17

L
leadership
    clinician supervision, 213–216
    treatment participants/graduates,
      mentoring/leadership by, 23,
      69–70, 97, 129–130, 134

by treatment provider for pro-
    social modelling and supportive
    environment by, 68
learned helplessness, 7
life stories, offender, 102–103, 108–109,
    133–134, 200
lifestyle management issues, 14–16
listening
    as motivational interviewing
      technique, 165–166
    to treatment refusers, effect of,
      63–64

M
Mann, R. E., 61, 119–120
Marshall, W. L., 13–17, 99
Martin, K., 147–148, 150
masculinity
    as component of minimization, 38
    demasculinization, treatment
      refuser's concerns about, 58–59
mental disorders, effect on treatment
    readiness of, 38–39
mentoring, by treatment participants
    and graduates, 23, 69–70
Miller, W. R., 64, 123, 209. *See also*
    motivational interviewing (MI)
Millhaven Preparatory Program,
    149–150
minimization, 5–6
    as cognitive distortion, 37–38
    factors in, 7–8
    recidivism, relation to, 14
    righting reflex and, 164
    treatment outcomes, effect
      on, 98
mislabeling, 37
mood states and coping, 146–147
moral decision-making skills, 19–20
Moral Reconation Therapy (MRT),
    18, 19
MORM. *See* Multifactor Offender
    Readiness Model (MORM)

Index **237**

motivation to change, 20, 31, 119.
See also hope theory of motivation;
motivational interviewing (MI)
ambivalence concerning, 166–167, 202
cognitive distortions, effect of, 36–37
extrinsic motivators, use of, 68–69
Good Lives Model (GLM) and, 82, 88–92
group members, discussion by, 130
guilt, role of, 131
individual needs, therapist's duty to meet, 46
intrinsic motivators, use of, 68–69
measurement of, 39
pre-treatment interventions, effect of, 45, 47–48, 151–152
Rockwood preparatory program goal, 123–125
self-disclosures, role of, 134
treatment efficacy and, 120
treatment readiness differentiated, 31–32
Treatment Readiness for You (TRY) goal, 16–17
unmotivated offender, placement in treatment program of, 48
motivation to participate in treatment, 24, 75–76
cognitive distortions, effect of, 37
external motivators, 151
motivational interviewing and, 161
positive reinforcement, role of, 131
preparatory/individualized treatment group, 195
Rockwood preparatory program, 119, 124, 128, 135
self-disclosures, role of, 133
treatment readiness differentiated, 31–32
motivational interviewing (MI), 47, 63, 160–183

affirmations, 172, 203
ambivalence of clients, 166–167, 202
change talk, recognizing and reinforcing, 123, 129, 130, 176–179, 189, 197
choice given to client, 70, 164–165, 169, 188, 198
commitment talk, 178–179
deniers, treatment readiness of, 98
feedback, providing, 179–181
Good Lives Model and, 88–91
group treatment, used with offenders in (*See* motivational interviewing (MI) used with offenders in group treatment)
listening technique, 165–166
open-ended questions, 170–172, 203
principles of, 64, 70, 167–170
reflections, 172–176, 203
righting reflex and, 164, 203, 209
Rockwell preparatory program and, 123
role-playing training exercise, 163–164
self-assessment training exercises, 162–163, 165–166, 170, 181–182
short-term, compliance-based tactics, 163, 185, 203
style and spirit of, 163–165, 187, 202–203
supervision of clinicians using (*See* motivational interviewing (MI), supervising clinicians using)
violent offenders, treatment readiness of, 47–48
motivational interviewing (MI), supervising clinicians using, 206–220
background, 207–208
consistency with MI, 209–212
ethical considerations, 211–212
leadership and management styles for, 213–216

supervision, definition of, 208–209
traps to avoid, 212–213
motivational interviewing (MI) used with offenders in group treatment, 184–205
   adverse experiences of offenders, effects of, 200–201
   components of group, 191–192
   debate *vs.* dialog, 199
   deniers, pre-treatment group for, 185–193
   disclosure, fear of, 201
   discrepancy hurdles, 199
   etiology, 200
   group format, 186–193
   initial interview, 187–190
   negative *vs.* positive focus, 200
   post-group sessions, 192–193
   potential traps in, 199–203
   preparatory/individualized treatment group, 194–199
   righting reflex used by group, 203
   single client, focus on, 200
   style and spirit of MI, using, 187, 202–203
   superficial participation in group, 202
   therapist gender as issue, 200–201
   treatment contract signed by offender, 189–190
   unrealistic expectations, 199
Moyers, T., 209
Multifactor Offender Readiness Model (MORM), 33–39
   clinical supervision, importance of, 47
   Corrections Victoria Treatment Readiness Questionnaire measurement factors, 40
   literature review, 35–39
myths associated with treatment programs
   identifying and countering, 65, 120, 121
   as obstacle to entering treatment, 58, 65

N

needs. *See* risk-need-responsivity (RNR) model
non-treatment staff, educating, 67
normalisation of offending processes, 131

O

obstacles to entering treatment, 56–63, 119–120
   competing priorities, 58
   distrust of key professionals, 59–61, 119
   friends or family, pressure from, 61–62
   hostile responses from other prisoners, expectation of, 37, 38, 61
   ineffectiveness of treatment, beliefs concerning, 57–58, 120
   responsivity of program, concerns about, 34–35, 59, 120
   side effects, concerns about, 58–59, 120, 121
   stigma, fear of, 62–63
   uninformed about treatment aims, 57–58
offending processes, normalising, 131
offense analysis, Deniers' Program, 104–105, 107–108
optimism, creating client, 124–125

P

participation, culture of, 122, 130–131
pathways thinking, 141–144, 147–148
personality disorders, effect on treatment readiness of, 38–39

perspective of offender, treatment provider's recognition of, 64. *See also* responsivity
pharmacological treatments, refuser concerns about, 58–59
polygraphs, 6, 21, 113, 193
pre-treatment assessments/interventions. *See also* Rockwood preparatory program for sexual offenders
  for categorical deniers, 97–98
  deniers, group for, 185–193
  Good Lives Model (GLM), 82, 90
  hope theory applied to, 150–152, 154, 155
  individualized treatment group, 194–199
  motivation to change, 45, 47–48, 151–152
  motivational interviewing, 89
  recidivism and, 155
  treatment readiness, effects on, 43, 45, 47
priorities of treatment refusers, competing, 58
prisons. *See* institutional settings
pro-social modelling
  leadership to promote, 68
  by senior group members, 129
problem analysis, Deniers' Program, 104–105, 107–108
problem identification, 5–7, 13–15, 18
problem-solving skills, 18–20, 147–148
Proeve, M. J., 35–36

R

readiness. *See* treatment readiness
recidivism, sexual, 67, 119, 184
  cognitive-behavioral treatments, effectiveness of, 74
  completion/noncompletion of treatment, effect of, 10, 14, 75–76, 155, 184–186
  comprehensive treatment programming and, 11–12
  denial of offense and, 14, 98–99, 101
  Good Lives Model and, 80, 84, 88, 91
  hope theory and, 152, 153, 154
  lifestyle management and, 15
  meta-analyses of, 13–14, 98–99, 120, 184
  protective factors to avoid, 154
  risk-need-responsivity (RNR) model and, 9, 10
  Rockwell preparatory program and, 135
  treatment efficacy, recidivism statistics to show, 120–121
  victim empathy and, 190–191
recidivism of violent offenders, 43
referrals for treatment, effective, 66
reflections, as interviewing technique, 172–176, 203
refusal of treatment. *See also* obstacles to entering treatment; resistance to treatment
  characteristics of refusers, 56
  choice in, 70
  external motivators for, 151
  reasons for, 56
reintegration into community
  Florida Comprehensive Treatment Program, components of, 23
  treatment coordination and, 14
reintegration into community, treatment during, 14
relapse prevention (RP) treatment model, 7, 77, 84, 91
relatedness, 78–80, 86–87
relationship skills, developing, 22, 103, 109–110
release planning, 105, 111–112
reoffending. *See* recidivism, sexual
resistance to treatment, 186. *See also* denial; refusal of treatment

coercion into treatment, 48
hope theory and, 151, 152
motivational interviewing and, 169, 181–182, 187–189
overcoming, 122–123
preparatory/individualized treatment group, 194–199
Rockwell preparatory program and, 122–123
responsibility, client, 123, 152, 191. *See also* autonomy; choices within treatment, offering
responsivity, 15–16, 24, 64–65, 120. *See also* risk-need-responsivity (RNR) model
conceptual clarity, lack of, 30–31
definition of, 30, 75
hope theory and, 152
individual needs, responding to, 75, 77, 83, 90–91
internal and external, 31
motivational interviewing and, 88
personal characteristics and, 75
shame/guilt and, 36
therapeutic alliance, key to successful, 126
treatment effectiveness and, 74–75
treatment readiness differentiated, 31–32
treatment refuser concerns about, 34–35, 59
righting reflex, 164, 203, 209
risk assessments, 30
denial equated with risk, 99
hope theory, 152, 154
progress in treatment, taking account of, 66–67
Rockwell preparatory program, information provided in, 121
treatment providers, role of, 60
risk factors. *See also* risk management
dynamic, 108–109, 113
offender awareness of, 21

risk management
Deniers' Program, 113
Good Lives Model, 74, 77, 78, 80–87, 89–90
healthy alternative behaviors and, 21–22
lifestyle management for, 15
treatment coordination and, 14
"what works" approach, 30
risk-need-responsivity (RNR) model, 9–11, 24, 29–31
comprehensive treatment programming and, 11–12
critiques of, 9–10, 24, 65, 76, 84
good lives/self regulation integrated model, 77
professional discretion element of, 15
RNR. *See* risk-need-responsivity (RNR) model
Robbers, M. L. P., 61
Rockwood preparatory program for sexual offenders, 16, 118–138
background, 118–120
describing treatment efficacy to clients, 120–121
efficacy of program, 134–135
expressiveness, encouraging, 130–131
future program assignments, experience of, 134–135
group cohesion, building, 128–130
motivation for change, enhancing, 123–125
normalising offending processes, 131
optimism, creating client, 124–125
resistance, overcoming client, 122–123
self-disclosure, enhancing client, 132–134
self-esteem, enhancing client, 125–126

therapeutic alliance, building, 126–127
treatment-related information for clients, providing, 121–122
trust, increasing client, 127–128
Rockwood Psychological Services
Deniers' Program (*See* Deniers' Program)
general approach to sexual offender treatment, 100
preparatory program for sexual offenders (*See* Rockwood preparatory program for sexual offenders)
Rollnick, S., 64, 123. *See also* motivational interviewing (MI)

S

self-actualization, 56–58
self-concept, 7–8, 19
self-control, development of, 22–23
self-disclosure, enhancing client, 132–134. *See also* disclosures of previous deviant behavior or accusations
self-efficacy
  agentic thinking, differentiated from, 141–142
  Good Lives Model, effect of, 92
  hopeful therapeutic intervention, effect of, 149, 155
  motivational interviewing and, 169–170, 189
  treatment readiness and, 16, 38
self-esteem, 7–8, 19
  during and after treatment, 59
  Deniers' Program, 102, 110
  Rockwood preparatory program, enhancing esteem in, 125–126
self-management. *See* self-regulation
self-motivational statements, 123, 129, 130, 176–178
self-regulation, 77, 80, 81, 91, 105, 111

Self-Regulation Model, 77, 81
sexual activity
  Good Lives Model, 78–80, 86–87, 91
  intimacy of, 6
sexual history, 190, 195
sexual interests and arousal, assessment of, 193
sexual recidivism. *See* recidivism, sexual
Sexually Violent Predator Act (Kansas), 17
shame
  as block to effective treatment, 131
  treatment readiness, determination of, 35–36
side effects of treatment, offender concerns about, 58–59, 120, 121
skills development
  Deniers' Program, 103–105
  Good Lives Model, 77, 79–80, 85–86
  hope theory, 152, 153
Snyder, C. R., 140–141, 143–144, 146
specialist forensic interventions, need for, 46
staff
  non-treatment, educating, 67
  treatment (*See* treatment staff)
Stermac, L. E., 147–148, 150
Stewart, C. A., 76
strength-based treatment aims, communicating, 65–66
stretch goals (hope theory), 152, 153
supervision, clinician, 47. *See also* motivational interviewing (MI), supervising clinicians using
support networks, working with, 68
supporting, as supervisory style, 217
supportive environment, leadership to promote, 68

T

therapeutic alliance, 33, 45–47, 76, 126–127

therapeutic engagement, 41–47. *See also* treatment readiness
therapeutic relationship, 33, 46–47, 75
　adverse experiences of offender, effect of, 201
　coercion, perceived, 37
　deniers, treatment of, 100
　enhancing personal relationships between staff and offenders, 64–65
　hostile intent attributed to therapist, 38
　motivations of treatment staff, exploring and monitoring, 70–71
　treatment refusers' distrust of treatment professionals, 59–61, 119
therapist characteristics and behaviors, 75, 100, 124–125, 185
　gender issues, 201–202
　importance of, 10
　righting reflex, 164, 203, 209
Thinking for a Change (T4C), 18–20
treatment, improving context for. *See* context for treatment, improving
treatment completion
　recidivism and, 10, 14, 65, 76, 155, 184–186
　treatment readiness program, completion of, 15–17, 43–45, 155
treatment contract signed by offender, 189–190
treatment graduates
　as mentors, 69–70
　testimonials on program by, 66, 69
treatment interfering factors, 15, 18, 20, 24. *See also* obstacles to entering treatment; resistance to treatment
treatment programs. *See also* comprehensive treatment programming for offenders; denial, treatment for offenders in; Good Lives Model (GLM); hope theory of motivation; motivational interviewing (MI); pre-treatment assessments/interventions
　completion of (*See* treatment completion)
　context for (*See* context for treatment, improving)
　mission statements, 210
　myths associated with, 58, 65, 120, 121
　readiness for (*See* treatment readiness)
　refusal of treatment (*See* refusal of treatment)
treatment readiness, 24–25, 29–54. *See also* denial; obstacles to entering treatment; pre-treatment assessments/interventions; refusal of treatment; Rockwood preparatory program for sexual offenders
　assessment of, 39–45, 47, 49–50
　civil commitment setting, use of programming in, 17–23
　clinical implications of, 45–48
　contextual factors in, 33–34
　definition of, 31–35
　external factors, 31, 49–50
　future directions, 48–50
　internal factors, 31, 49–50
　interventions to promote, measurement of change due to, 43
　interviews as assessment tool, 43, 44
　low readiness of individual or setting, 45–46
　Multifactor Offender Readiness Model (MORM), 33–40, 47
　personal factors in, 33–34, 40
　pre-treatment interventions, effect of, 43, 45, 47
　as predictor of treatment outcome, 33
　problem identification and, 13–15

program participation, effect of, 43–45
readiness ruler, 197
responsivity and motivation differentiated, 31–33
responsivity obstacles and, 34–35
self-report readiness measure, 44
specialist forensic interventions, need for, 46
treatment readiness program, completion of, 15–17
of violent offenders, 41–45
volition and, 33, 34, 40
treatment-related information, provision to offenders of, 66, 121–122
treatment staff. See also therapeutic relationship; therapist characteristics and behaviors
  enhancing personal relationships with offenders, 64–65
  job descriptions reflecting motivational interviewing values, 210–211
  motivations of, exploring and monitoring, 70–71
  preparatory/individualized group, staff team for, 194–196, 199
  supervision of, 47 (See also motivational interviewing (MI), supervising clinicians using)
treatment uptake, strategies for increasing, 56, 63–71

trust. See also distrust
  adverse offender experiences and, 200–201
  increasing client, 127–129, 133
TRY—Treatment Readiness for You, 16–21

V

victim harm, understanding of, 104, 111, 190–191
violence-reduction programs, 42
Violence Treatment Readiness Questionnaire (VTRQ), 41–45, 49, 223–225
violent offenders (generally), treatment readiness of, 41–45, 47–48
vocational programs, 23
volition and treatment readiness, 33, 34, 40
volunteering, by offenders, 23
VTRQ. See Violence Treatment Readiness Questionnaire (VTRQ)

W

Ward, T., 24, 29, 39–41, 58, 65, 76, 216. See also Good Lives Model (GLM)
Webster, S., 119–120
"what works" movement, 29–30. See also risk-need-responsivity (RNR) model
whole persons, treatment of offenders as, 12

READER'S NOTES

READER'S NOTES

Additional Safer Society Press Titles

Knowledge and Practice:
Challenges in the Treatment and Supervision of Sexual Abusers
edited by **David S. Prescott**, LICSW

Addresses the problem of applying knowledge and research to real-world treatment of sexual abusers. The contributors describe personal research applications and suggest how others can learn from and apply this knowledge. Edited to highlight diverse voices, *Knowledge and Practice* brings together leading professionals in the field to produce a "conference-in-a-book." (2007)

978-1-885473-76-9 | 476 pages, paper | $39.95 | Order#: WP133

Supervision of the Sex Offender
Community Management, Risk Assessment, and Treatment
by **Georgia F. Cumming** & **Robert J. Mc Grath**

The authors have drawn upon their combined 50 years of experience in the field to create this easy-to-use, comprehensive guide. The second edition of *Supervision of the Sex Offender* is a title you will continually be pulling from your book shelf for the timely and time-tested methods and techniques you can use for supervising sex offenders in the community. (2005)

978-1-884444-73-9 | 218 pages, paper | $30 | Order#: WP106

Manual for Structured Group Treatment with Adolescent Sex Offenders
by **Jacqueline Page**, PsyD & **William D. Murphy**, PhD

Focuses on treatment of adolescent offenders by building on individual strengths and producing healthy lifelong behavior, while recognizing and correcting problem thoughts and behavior. Activities, games, and exercises are easily adapted to individual or group treatment settings, to meet specific program requirements, and to increase comprehension and response from offenders at differing levels of mental development and progress in treatment. (2007)

978-1-885473-55-4 | 272 pages, paper | $44.95 | Order#: WP130

Engaging Resistance
Creating Partnerships for Change in Sexual Offender Treatment
by **Charles A. Flinton**, PhD & **Robert Scholz**, MA, NCC

The authors believe that any meaningful change in reducing the vast number of sexual offenses will require a multisystem approach that increases client motivation and public awareness, and facilitates changes that hold the offender, society, and the criminal justice/child welfare systems accountable for reducing sexual offending. (2006)

978-1-885473-53-0 | 200 pages, paper | $34.95 | Order#: WP121

Risk Assessment of Youth Who Have Sexually Abused
Theory, Controversy & Emerging Strategies
edited by **Davis S. Prescott**, LICSW

Professionals working with sexually aggressive youth often need to make decisions about these youth. However, there are no empirically validated means by which these professionals can accurately predict who will or won't become abusive in the future. This book summarizes what is known and what is not and offers suggestions for to help clinicians get a foothold for proceding with this difficult, but important task. (2006)

978-1-885473-83-7 | 250 pages, paper| $32.95 | Order #: WP119

The SaferSociety PRESS

Learn how to order. Call 802-247-3132.
Or visit our web site:
www.safersociety.org